CW01023822

Sonya's Report

Sonya's Report

Ruth Werner

Translated by Renate Simpson

Chatto & Windus
LONDON

Published in 1991 by
Chatto & Windus Ltd
20 Vauxhall Bridge Road
London SW1V 2SA

First published as *Sonjas Rapport*, Verlag Neues Leben, Berlin,
1977

A CIP record for this book is available
from the British Library

ISBN 0 7011 3801 7

Phototypeset by Intype, London
Printed in Great Britain by
Butler & Tanner Ltd, Frome, Somerset

Contents

(above) One year old *(right)* Six years old

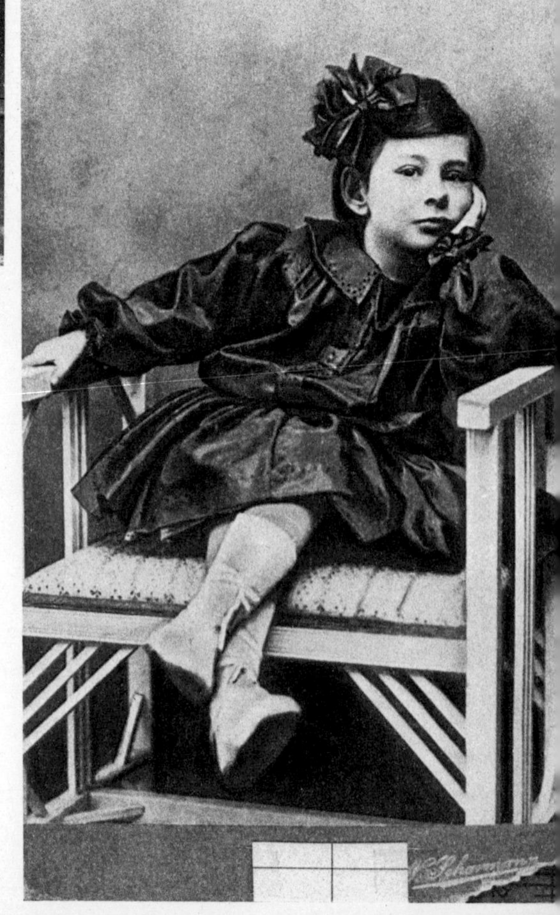

I

Germany, 1918–30

When Mother died in 1947, we six children, long since grown-up, came across carefully preserved letters which we had written home over the years. We each reclaimed our own.

I am holding the earliest of my letters in my hands. It was written in the painstaking script of a ten-year-old, during the First World War, in that hungry year 1918, eight months before the German Revolution. Seriously underweight, I had been sent to acquaintances in the country, who had a daughter my age.

Grossmarzehns, 30th March, 1918
Dear Mother,

I was very pleased to get your card. I don't miss you during the day, only at night when I have gone to bed. Today I talked to Herr Fingerhut; he is Erna's grandfather. He asked me lots of questions. One was 'Is your father very rich?' I said 'Yes!' Then we had supper. First there was a big bowl full of fried potatoes. Then Herr Fingerhut said: 'Erna will eat all those on her own!' so another bowl was put on the table. The potatoes were swimming in fat. They were mixed with four eggs and little pieces of bacon. Then for afters there was jelly and custard. Then I went to bed full up to the top.

Love from your happy daughter

P.S. Would you believe it? All the time I have been here I've only had four slices of bread because there are so many other wonderful things to eat. And that's the truth.

During the summer of that year I was sent to a children's holiday

Liebe Mutter!
Ich habe mich sehr über Deine Karte gefreut. Am Tage habe ich gar keine Sehnsucht nach Euch, bloß wenn ich Abends im Bette liege.

Ten years old – a letter to my mother

centre on the North Sea, which belonged to the Berlin City Council. My six-year-old sister came with me. She had never been away from home before and cried a great deal. I began to call her 'Weepy'.

July 1918
Dear Mummy,

. . . Weepy was pleased to get your letter, but if I was to give her a sweet every time she cried, there soon wouldn't be any left in the whole of Berlin. She doesn't sit next to me at mealtimes any more, but do you think that worries her? She is glad that I don't tell her to eat properly all the time. You see she always nibbles round the bread so that the thick bit of butter in the middle is left to the end. We are eating a terrific lot. You'd better start saving some food for us. The nurse here says there are no potatoes in Berlin. Mostly Weepy is quite good. And every evening she cuddles me till I can't breathe.

August 1918
Dear Mummy,

Just imagine, Weepy has put on three pounds and I have put on four! I must tell you something. A group was supposed to leave here; 600 sandwiches were made and all the suitcases had been packed and put ready downstairs. They were supposed to leave in the morning, but then a telegram came to say that there was a strike on in Hamburg and there wouldn't be any transport. Now they are still here.

I have talked quite a lot with City Councillor Rabnow who is here just now. It's like an exam, he asks me so many tricky questions; Herr Rabnow says that he always thought father was a 'pacimist'. I think that was the word. It means 'for peace'.

Mummy dear, hold tight, now I must confess something. My apron is so badly torn that it can't be mended. Weepy's skirt is almost falling to pieces. And we have only two hair ribbons left between us.

One strange feature of my youth was the contradiction between the large lakeside villa which was our home by Berlin's Schlachtensee, and our relatively simple standard of living. My parents were of Jewish origin, but did not practise any faith. My father, René Robert Kuczynski was an economist, then head of the Statistical Office in Berlin-Schöneberg. Father was more of an academic than an official, as his many publications on unemployment, living conditions and wages prove. His income did not amount to much for such a large family, and the years of inflation made the situation worse. We were perfectly happy, but we lived much more modestly than one might have supposed, in that spacious house which had been the gift of a wealthy grandfather. We children made carefree fun of poor mother's penny-pinching, while she would have much preferred to make time for her painting, which we all loved. Seven decades later one picture still hangs in my room. (Mother's father came from very humble origins and worked his way up to become a banker.)

Our spacious house

Summer 1923. I was sixteen years old, about to leave school, and knew quite well by now what a 'pacimist' was. Inflation had begun. I sent home a postcard from a school trip:

> 11th July, 1923
> . . . Prices here are so hair-raising that I had to borrow 50,000 Marks. Fortunately we were able to get bread on coupons. Whatever you do, don't send me that hat. If you want to send me anything at all, make it sausage. That costs 15,000 Marks a quarter pound here. And if by any chance you do send something, perhaps some sugar? It isn't essential but would be very nice . . .

In August of 1923 our parents were away and I wrote to them from home:

> Dear Father,
> This is the last letter I am sending you and the one I take

Mother

Father

most pleasure in writing, because soon you will be coming home. Everybody is very excited today because the dollar has jumped to three million Marks. We went shopping this morning and this afternoon.

Good news for you. Today's leader in the *Zehlendorfer Anzeiger* begins with the pronouncement: 'Germany's future lies with the statisticians.'

Mummy, we haven't got a single gram of sugar in the house. It's terrible. I don't suppose there will be any for father's birthday either. As for flour – well yes, I did find six coupons, but we used them ages ago. The children eat so much.

By 'children' I meant my brother Jürgen, two-and-a-half years older than I am, and my younger sisters: Brix, born in 1910, 'Weepy', 1913, Binchen, 1919, and Reni, 1923, born when I was sixteen. That baby inevitably became my favourite.

In 1924 I began my apprenticeship with R.L. Prager, Bookshop for Law and Political Sciences, Mittelstrasse, Berlin N.W.

I observed the wealth of small, privileged circles and the poverty in which so many people lived; I saw the unemployed begging on street corners. I pondered over the injustices of this world and how they might be eliminated. And now I also experienced the grim contrast between home life and work: the anxiety of grown-up people trembling at each month's end for fear they might be handed their cards. My friend Marthe was the first victim.

For the past two years I had been reading almost nothing but progressive literature: Jack London's works, Maxim Gorky's short stories, the first book that appeared in German by Lenin, and Rosa Luxemburg's *Letters from Prison* – she was imprisoned because of her revolutionary ideas and her fight for the working class. How strong she was, and how warmhearted, and how she loved nature, just as I did. The photo showed she was not so good-looking – just like me – but of course much more intelligent! All these experiences made me join the Communist Youth League of Germany. The first demonstration in which I took part was on May Day, 1924. The posters we carried read, 'Hands off Soviet Russia . . .', 'Fight Against Unemployment', or 'Fight for the Eight-Hour Working Day'. And then suddenly the police came and charged us with their rubber truncheons, a six-footer handling a slip of a girl seventeen years old. And how it hurt, one couldn't breathe properly. Many left the demonstration in pain and went home, others marched on, new ones joined. I had to take a decision. I went on, continued with the demonstration, not knowing yet that it was a decision for life.

During my apprenticeship I wrote home from a holiday I had been much looking forward to:

August 1925

. . . I feel marvellous here in the mountains, but the beauty of it all doesn't sink in properly as it's beyond comparison

Apprenticeship – across Berlin with the 'book cart'

with the nine-hour working day at Prager's. You simply forget about work and Berlin here. Your card arrived yesterday. Mummy, I beg you – even if it saves money – don't use those postage stamps from the ice age. There are different postmen on duty nowadays and they made me pay a surcharge.

Jürgen might also write me an occasional letter when he can tear himself away from his 'Marx'. Anyhow, I am getting an incredible amount of post. Even the ticket collector at Zehlendorf-West station has sent me a postcard.

Jürgen dear, reading Marx on my own is boring, difficult,

and incomprehensible. Am now reading Wittvogel's *History of Bourgeois Society*. I understand it better.

After he had studied economics and philosophy at several universities in Germany, Jürgen wrote his thesis, published in 1927, *Return to Marx*. His interest in the labour movement was great, but he did not join the party until 1930.

Letter from Schlachtensee to my parents, who were away from home:

9th September, 1925
Dear Parents,

Your news is rather lacking in both quantity and quality, especially as we can only decipher half of what Mummy writes.

Sunday was International Youth Day. 10,000 young people took part – very encouraging. When are you coming home? Stay away as long as you like, we can manage perfectly well without you for a few more weeks.

A young workers' delegation will soon be going to Soviet Russia. Don't be surprised if my next picture postcard comes from there. Actually there is no chance at all of my going, unfortunately.

Tremendous amount to do in the Communist Youth. As soon as I have finished this letter I must prepare a talk for tomorrow on 'Trades Unions and young workers'. 75 per cent of our work has to be for the unions now.

In my second year as an apprentice, I spent my holiday in Ahrenshoop on the Baltic with Aunt Alice, my father's sister. Her husband was a well-known gynaecologist who helped so many babies to an easy birth: shortly before the end of the war she and her husband were gassed in the Teretsin concentration camp.

3rd August, 1926
To all!

It is wonderful here. I am staying with an old fisherman's wife – a room and bed linen, but no meals, 15 Marks a week . . . Another guest is living in the room opposite mine.

To avoid confusion about the one and only front door key, I climb through the window.

Aunt Alice is as nice to me as her dresses are hideous. Her best dress has 24 buttons down the back and I have to do them all up for her.

In the period that followed, father would spend six months of each year in the United States, doing research into various aspects of American finance capital and population questions, at the Brookings Institute, Washington D.C. Several books were published during that period, among them *American Loans to Germany* (1927) and in two volumes, *The Balance of Births and Deaths* (1928). During that time – as mother used to accompany him – a friend took over the household duties and I became 'head' of the family. When my brother Jürgen also went to the States in 1926 to start his postgraduate studies on labour conditions at the Brookings School, many letters crossed the ocean.

Schlachtensee, September 1926
Dear Mummy,

The first letter to America. I trust your maternal feelings will sustain your keen interest in all our little trivia, even if by the time they reach you, they are twelve days old. Actually nothing particular has happened. This should prove to you that the household is functioning normally even without your presence. Reni gets funnier every day. Nobody who sees her can help smiling.

Tell Father and Jürgen that there was a meeting yesterday to protest against compensation for the abdicated Kaiser. 20,000 people in the Sports Palace. Thousands couldn't get in. Ledebour's ringing tones could be heard clearly in the last row. Then Thälmann, Friedländer from the Union of Socialist Doctors, Wilhelm Pieck and some Social Democratic Party delegates to the Soviet Union.[1] Daddy would certainly have spoken too, had he been here. It was tremendously impressive.

Father, who never joined a party, became Chairman of the Committee for the expropriation of the former Kaiser's family and landowning nobility, which in June 1926 had initiated and organised the People's Referendum against the compensation agreements.[2]

Since May I had been a member of the Communist Party. That spring the party worked untiringly for this referendum. After I had stayed out late twenty-four evenings in one month, mother begged father to have a serious word with me. When he reproached me about my constant absence from home, I replied: 'But Daddy, you know it's all for your referendum.' We looked at each other and burst out laughing.

Father was also an active member of the International Workers Aid organisation and represented the left wing of the League for the Rights of Man. As an economist and statistician he calculated a 'minimum subsistence level' each month, which differed from the official bogus statistics and was used by the trades unions in their struggle for higher wages for the working class. These statistics appeared in the *Finanzpolitische Korrespondenz*, a monthly journal published privately by my father. We children regarded it so-to-speak as the sixth daughter in the house and lovingly called it 'Fina'.

September 1926
Dear Mummy,

Reni is the focal point of the house. A mother is always at a disadvantage because she cannot see how charming and totally different her children are when she is not around. Since you left, we haven't heard a whimper or a whine from either Binchen or Reni.

It is so lovely with the little ones that when I am not actually busy on party work I really prefer to stay at home. They are quite attached to me and get upset when I am not there.

We are unanimous in our hope that Mummy will soon stop coming up with more bright ideas on household matters, recommendations on how to cook cabbage, how to clean the house, warnings on the maintenance of good relations with aunts, uncles and cousins and other advice for every imaginable eventuality.

Binchen and Reni, aged seven and three

Schlachtensee, 20th September, 1926
Dear Jürgen,

Terribly busy. Preparing for the Anniversary of the Russian Revolution, 7th November. Choral speaking rehearsals with the Zehlendorf comrades. Sunday a good turn-out for demonstration and meeting to commemorate the twenty-fifth anniversary of the Trades Union International, the Amsterdam one. Enraged by our 'social democratic colleagues' when one of them – a trade union official – insisted that we take down one of the banners we were carrying on the march. Despite everyone's opposition, he grabbed it and tore it to shreds. It read 'Join the trades unions – for the class struggle'. That was too radical for those gentlemen. In other ways, too, they have an unbelievable approach. Whereas with us in the party, if a young comrade says something worthwhile it is valued just as much as if it comes from one of the veterans, in the trades union you are cut short by remarks like: 'We were in the union before you were born. So what are you after?'

Foolish really, to post such little details all the way to America, but then I am so involved in all this, and what else should I write about if not what is on my mind?

To Jürgen, September 1926

Yesterday your friend from the bank was here. He came at 8.30 p.m. and left at midnight, having decided to join the Communist Youth. On 21st September he is coming along with me for the first time . . . When we started talking about the labour movement, I was full of praise for the left-wing 'Friends of Nature' but told him: 'I believe that if you recognise the need for class struggle and revolution, you should join the organisation which is fighting that class struggle in the most direct way, and which takes the straightest path to the revolution.'

I did not paint too rosy a picture of the Communist Youth and tried to bring him down to earth from his idealism. I gave him quite a lot of material to read. I don't know whether he will make any sense of it.

Gerhard Degenhardt became a good comrade. He was later arrested under the Nazis but carried on his activities after his release: during the Second World War he lost his life in the 999 Penal Battalion.

It was also at this time that I met my first real boyfriend. Rolf came from a bourgeois liberal family. He was four years older than I and studied architecture in Berlin. I loved him dearly, but there was one recurring conflict.

To Jürgen, October 1926

. . . your letter came at a good moment – that is, it came at a bad moment and did me good. Rolf came with me as far as Steglitz on the way home. We talked about Russia, the dictatorship of the proletariat etc. When he suggests that the workers are incapable of constructing anything, however small, or in other words when he questions the viability of socialism itself, I get upset and answer back. It is so difficult to discuss with him because his views on communism are purely emotional, without any scientific basis. Besides, for him it is as though we are having a difference of opinion about a book or a work of art, while for me it's about the most vital problems, our whole attitude to life. At times like these he seems like a stranger to me. We didn't even say goodbye when we parted. I was so numbed that I forgot to get out at Zehlendorf; it was midnight and I walked all the way home along the beautiful path around the lake. At least the wonderful night calmed me down. Your letter was waiting for me at home. Afterwards I piled all the Stalin works I had around me on the floor and copied out the simplest and clearest quotations on dictatorship and socialism. They covered pages. I gave them to Rolf today.

29th October, 1926

Dear Jürgen,

We went to the Staatstheater the other night. 'The Robbers', Piscator's production. Something absolutely new. Nothing much left of Schiller. Piscator is a genius. Played in two rooms, one above the other. Rolf also highly enthusiastic.

It seems that the party opposition in Russia, Trotsky etc., has now been finally defeated. On the Kaiser compensation question, our Reichstag deputies acquitted themselves well, but 'the Kuczynski Committee' – apart from one stupid letter – has not lifted a finger. The social democrats really are . . . sorry, but one gets so infuriated.

The 7th November celebration in Zehlendorf should be good this year. Pity you won't be here. Next week will send you *Problems of the Dictatorship of the Proletariat*. All Berlin

The Schlachtensee

party districts, even Zehlendorf, are running courses based on this pamphlet.

5th November, 1926
Dear Mother,

Your letter reached us yesterday. I'd rather you wrote more frequently, briefly and interestingly! But thank you anyhow, since at least we gather that you are both very well. Here everything in best order. If you could see how blooming, strong and healthy the little ones look, you would not worry about them. Don't be surprised, though, if this letter contains so little about them. I am too engrossed in preparations for the 7th November anniversary celebration of the Russian

Revolution; there will be big crowds in the Lindenpark. The houses of Zehlendorf are glowing with red posters. Besides rehearsing the others in the play, I take the roles of 1. Russian peasant woman, 2. Chairwoman of Russian world congress, 3. Narrator for action scenes, 4. Speaker with choir, 5. Crowd scenes extra. Altogether about 40 people are taking part. How is a slip of a girl supposed to keep such a mob in order! Thanks to our enthusiasm it is not too difficult. Everyone completely immersed in their roles.

Schlachtensee, 9th November, Anniversary of the 'Glorious German Revolution'.[3]

November 7th was a complete success. Lindenpark, largest hall in Zehlendorf, packed. Our group performed really well. Afterwards strangers came up to me in the streets of Zehlendorf Mitte to shake me by the hand and tell me how good it had been. Painter F. was also there and presented me with one of his works; the colouring magnificent. Dedicated 'To a courageous girl'.

Something else: Brigitte, Binchen and I need new winter coats. We did make one for Binchen out of the material you had asked us to use; there would not have been enough for Brigitte since it had shrunk so much. And it is such ancient stuff it literally falls to pieces. Please let us know how much money there is for winter clothes. As for my letters to Jürgen, I must insist on sending these directly to him, so as not to hurt his sense of individuality or mine. If you fear economic collapse, I'll try to squeeze the postage out of my pocket money.

I find it hard to visualise Daddy's work in the 'Council'. Does it consist of oyster-eating and working with the magnates of monopoly? If so, I much prefer my German-People's-Referendum father.

15th November, 1926
Dear Jürgen,

... Tomorrow evening is the last session of the party course. I have learnt a lot from it. I had already digested the facts after reading the book, but it was very important to me to learn how to run a course of this kind. I now join in regularly with the Communist Youth in Steglitz. There isn't enough going on in the party branch here.

When my need is greatest, dear brother you are nearest. In other words: your dollar bill came at the right moment. It enabled me to go to the cinema with an unemployed comrade. Russian film *Son of the Mountains*, Russian film *Black Sunday, 1905*, both good but not a patch on *Potemkin*. It also got me into a festival organised by the 'Red Front,' where I danced from eight at night until three in the morning. There wasn't a dance which I sat out. Had a marvellous time. Apart from that I was able to buy Masereel's *Book of Hours* (165 woodcuts), which has at last been published in a cheaper popular edition.

Why have you let Mummy loose on us so soon? I do share your view that she is a wonderful woman and that we would love her even if she were not our mother – but the glorious freedom, staying out with Rolf till half past eleven and happily riding home on the number 20 bus, is over. And in any case, Mummy without Daddy is only half a person.

The other day, a friend of Degenhardt's wrote asking for help. What is Communism? Degenhardt had told him about me, so he came out here one evening. He will buy some of the books I recommended. Pause while I eat three pieces of milk chocolate. Rolf gave me a bar. Not that he bought it for me! We don't hold with that kind of rubbish, but when he gets something like that as a present, he always saves it for me.

Rolf is joining the Rote Hilfe.[4] Of course he would be pleased whenever the party wins anything; he does actually do some work for us and gives financial support. And he is more concerned than many of my comrades – the women and the men – that I should take part in everything. And as for me dropping anything on his account, he is just as opposed to the idea as I am. The fact that I am a communist means something to him – no trouble there. I believe that, if we stay together, it is only a matter of time until he joins the party; but it could well take another two years.

Problems of Leninism by Stalin has now appeared. It is supposed to be absolutely fundamental, but unfortunately costs 4.50 Marks. Shall I send it to you for Christmas? . . . I have read part of it. As I am such a simpleton it took me three hours to read twenty pages, and I left six pieces of paper in it covered in questions.

To Jürgen:

9th December, 1926

A heap of undarned stockings on the floor and on my desk a book by Polgar, *Orchestra from Above*, which I have started to read. Beside it a briefcase full of material for the Luxemburg, Liebknecht and Lenin remembrance day in mid-January, my next task when I have finished this letter. I am now responsible for agitprop in the party's 10th District. I shall be organising another public event, not 7th November style, but an open group evening. That makes it easier to establish rapport with sympathisers who come along.

17th January, 1927

Dear Jürgen,

There's been a lot happening recently. A fancy dress party at the Academy of Arts which I enjoyed enormously. Theme: 'Beyond the Pale'. My costume – bright red scanty shorts and tight-fitting shirt with stiff collar. There are those who say I kissed 20 boys, but without counting Rolf it can't have been more than 19.

Arrived home at half-past six on Sunday morning. Two hours later I was already on my way into Berlin again to attend a party course in the Prussian Council Building. An excellent affair, organised centrally, every other Sunday from nine to four. You see how useful it is for me to be a member of a small district like Zehlendorf. If anything goes on anywhere, I am the one to be sent. Only one person can attend from each district. Steglitz, the next largest district, has over 200 comrades, and I should never be chosen there. Naturally I am learning a great deal on this course. I enclose your Red

Aid contribution card. I am sure you can still stick stamps on in Washington. I see Gerd Degenhardt about once a month.

2nd April, 1927

Well, dear brother, you will know by now that I have landed at Ullsteins, I suppose at present our largest newspaper concern. This is my second day: newspaper and propaganda department archives, Kochstrasse 23, fourth floor. I am looking forward very much to the new kind of party work in the Ullstein branch.

You write that you are going to publish a book which many workers will read. I must say, I found your article hard going, so people who know even less about economics will have even more difficulty. Use plain terms and short sentences. Your ideas need not be any cruder, but if you explain things simply you will avoid people only half understanding them. Using two or three sentences to drive a point home by repeating it in different words often only makes it more complicated.

Don't be taken aback by my fault-finding. Compared with you, I am a humble amateur, and it goes without saying that I admire you as much as ever and regard you as a very special person.

14th May, 1927

Dear Brother,

Many thanks for the birthday present. I hope to use it as you would wish: purchase of a bathing costume – this should please you since you are such a philistine and do not approve of nude bathing. Ticket for the Red Aid rally on Saturday at the Sports Palace. Re-stocking of my letter paper so that I don't have to embezzle Ullstein property (especially during working hours)! And for books, books and more books . . . My evenings are not overloaded with political activities, but fairly busy all the same. I have already written an article on Ullstein published in the *Rote Fahne*[5] a fortnight ago. 1,200 free copies were distributed at the entrance here and made quite an impression. Strange to think that tomorrow I shall be 20 years old.

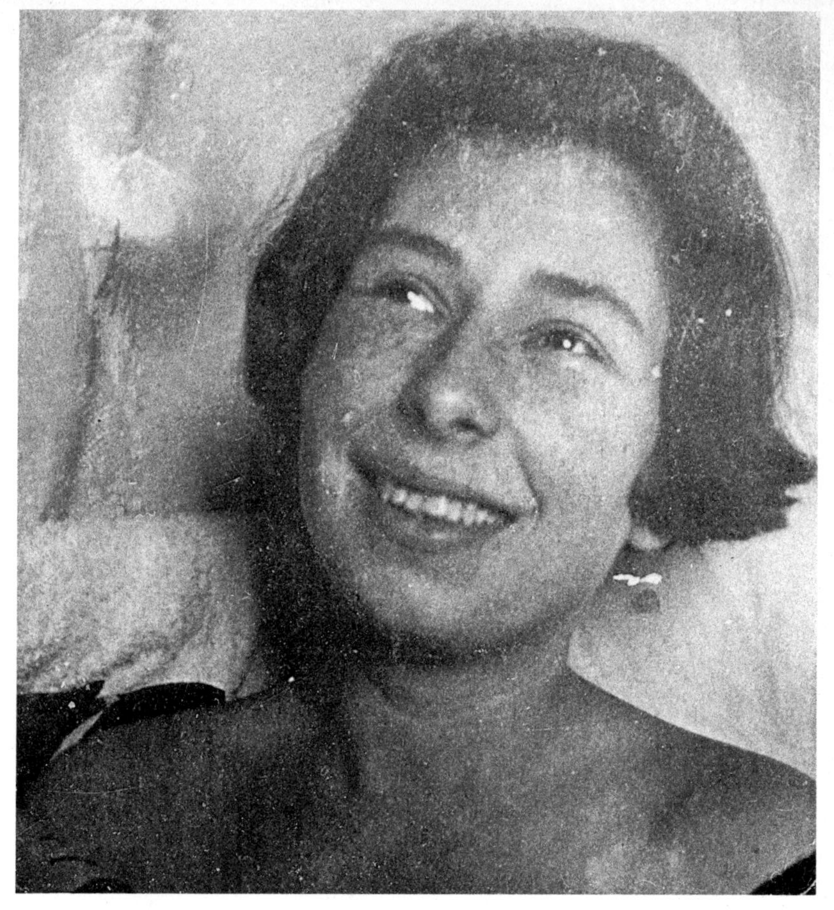

14 May 1927 – 'strange to think that tomorrow I'll be twenty'

To Jürgen:

26th August, 1927

Now to the most exciting event of the last few weeks. Father will already have mentioned to you the library he has bought from Arthur Hollitscher.[6] Marvellous I tell you – almost everything published by Die Schmiede;[7] e.g. the series 'Society's Outsiders'. A lot of things published by Fischer. About five volumes of Wassermann, five of Thomas Mann, Fontane complete in ten volumes, Larissa Reissner,[8] Shaw,

Upton Sinclair, Galsworthy. All the Communist International records, many *Neue Rundschau*[9] which I haven't put into order yet.

The library down below is overflowing. Mother was of course frantic over this squandering of money on books and visualises us all on the point of starvation.

To Jürgen:

September 1927

Yesterday we had the first rehearsal for the 10th anniversary celebrations of Soviet Russia, to take place 7th November in Zehlendorf. These two months of work with the Zehlendorfers will be a joy. Usually I am active in the workplace branch here in Berlin. I spend all my free evenings by the lake. I don't think I shall ever be very fussy about the sort of house I live in, but I do care about landscape. Rather the long daily journey into town and the concrete jungle – the frantic rush, the struggle with bus and tram and the dark lonely road home – as long as at some point I can be out here by the lakeside, if only for half an hour . . .

Father led the delegation to Moscow for the tenth anniversary celebrations of the Russian Revolution on 7th November, 1927. Its members included the poet Johannes R. Becher[10] and our dear friend the painter Käthe Kollwitz.[11]

To Jürgen:

20th November, 1927

Father has returned from Russia. His arrival was wonderful. In the morning, quite early, I went with mother to fetch him from the station. Just to see those two meet! During that second the whole neighbourhood within a radius of ten miles must have sensed how mother and father belong to each other. And yet there was nothing special about it; it's difficult to describe.

For me the most important thing was his first comment: 'Before this I could never understand why England wants war against Russia, but now I do. Seen from England's standpoint, I also find it quite justified. No capitalist state can sit by and watch a non-capitalist, a communist state flourishing and scoring such great successes year after year.' I nearly cried for joy, because if Daddy had not been positive about Russia, it would have been terrible!

During 1928 the Ullstein brothers came to hear of my political activities. I think it was Hermann Ullstein who suggested to me that I should 'resign, since a democratic enterprise can offer no prospects to a communist'. I could think of quite a few anti-Semitic chauvinist colleagues on the other hand, who did have 'prospects' at Ullsteins.

Now I was unemployed. Father suggested that I might spend several months in the USA. I found work in a bookshop in New York, and got to know American literature. Meanwhile Rolf completed his studies as an architect. I returned home and in 1929 we were married.

I could not find a job.

Jürgen had married shortly before. Marguerite came from Alsace-Lorraine and we all had a high regard for her. She was a true scientist, modest, intelligent and cultured.

A letter to Jürgen and Marguerite from Berlin in May 1930 shows that I was still unaware of the fundamental changes which were to affect my life a few weeks later. I congratulated them on the Russian translation of the book they had written together, *The Factory Worker in the American Economy*, and asked them to find out what biographies of Marx the Soviet Union had published. I mentioned that I would shortly be reading Beer's *History of Socialism*.

I never did find time for that . . .

2

China, 1930–33

Rolf and I had often talked about seeing more of the world, and now Germany's economic crisis strengthened our resolve. We asked Walter, a good friend of Rolf's who represented a large German firm in China, to keep an eye open for us.

One day a telegram arrived from Walter; according to a newspaper advertisement the Shanghai Municipal Council was looking for an architect. The SMC was the English administration which controlled a large part of Shanghai. Rolf telegraphed his application. It was accepted – on condition that he must start at once.

What did I know about China when we made our quick decision? The size of the country, its landscape, its art fascinated me. I had read about Sun Yat Sen, the first democratic president after the downfall of the monarchy in 1911, his founding of the people's party, the Guomindang, his good relations with the Soviet Union. Under Chiang Kai-shek, the ruling president, all this changed. The Guomindang degenerated, foreign capital had the upper hand again, and the Communist Party was strictly forbidden. If membership was discovered, it meant the death sentence. In 1927, cells of the Red Army who fought against Chiang Kai-shek had been formed in the countryside. When we went to China there already existed several small Soviet districts under Red Army administration. I reported to the Central Committee of our party my wish to become active in China. The comrades must have found it rather odd that I should bounce in and tell them naïvely what I wanted to do. So far I had not distinguished myself in any way. They spoke to me about the serious position in China, where party work was strictly clandestine and every communist, even by the smallest action exposed to extreme danger.

During the second conversation they agreed that after my arrival at Shanghai someone would contact me. I gave them Walter's address, as we intended to move in with him to begin with.

Since the architect was to be engaged in Shanghai itself – contrary to the customary arrangements for jobs abroad – the cost of our journey was not met by Rolf's new employers. The contract, too, would only be confirmed after a lengthy probationary period. The fares to China took our last penny. If Shanghai turned out to be a failure, we would have no money for the fare home.

We left Germany in July 1930. We travelled to Moscow and took the Trans-Siberian Express to the Soviet Union's eastern border. Unlike other foreigners, we did not travel first class, nor did we eat in the restaurant car. To save money, we secretly used a small spirit burner on the floor of the compartment to brew up soup cubes. We had also packed bread, hard sausage and dripping.

We played a lot of chess. At other times I would lie on my tummy in the upper bunk and watch the landscape rumble by: the Urals, the cities of Sverdlovsk, Omsk, Irkutsk, beautiful Lake Baikal, the Steppes and the endless birch forests. I loved our unscheduled stops. Once we came to a halt by the side of a woodland meadow. It lasted two hours. The carriage steps were too far from the ground to climb down, but everyone was longing to stretch their legs and breathe the fresh air. Men jumped from the compartments and women jumped into their arms. Their lightheartedness was infectious. An accordion sounded and people began to dance. We stood watching and soon hands grasped ours and we danced too, moved by this warm-hearted gaiety.

In Manchuria the East-China Railway began, in Changchun, the Southern Manchuria line. The rail journey to Dalian took a total of fourteen days and from there we travelled a further thousand kilometres by ship to Shanghai.

When we dropped anchor in the harbour, I was appalled by the poverty and exploitation, which was so much greater than anything I had ever seen. Porters, emerging from the bowels of the ship and padding the steep planks to the quay, followed each other so closely that their heavily laden bamboo poles almost touched. Sweat streamed down their bodies; thick veins protruded from neck, temples and legs. A stench of garlic and sweat drifted from this human conveyer belt towards the travellers on deck. Encircling the ship in floating tubs were beggars, moaning cripples with stumps for arms and legs, children with festering wounds, some blind, some with hairless scab-encrusted heads.

On the quayside stood Walter in a light drill suit, a tropical helmet over his blond hair, beside him his elegant wife with a huge bunch of flowers to bid us welcome. At the house a Chinese servant awaited us, pouring iced drinks with white-gloved hands.

We stayed as Walter's guests. Oppressive heat accumulated in our two attic rooms under the roof of the house. Mosquitoes clung to the net strung over the bed. Thus began our first night in a strange land.

Rolf held a respected position; we were frequently invited to parties and had to reciprocate. Various ladies called and expected me to return the visit – an alien world which I hated, a stark contrast to the life I had led until then. I did not protest; I knew that if I was ever to work here illegally as a communist, an outwardly bourgeois life-style would provide vital cover. Weeks and months passed while I waited for some word from the party.

From letters home:

> For a person like me who has always led an active life, Shanghai is boring, unless you work professionally. At home you can't do a thing, because it is all done by the boy, the cook and the coolie. The heat saps all your energy. It is not a dry, searing heat, but hot humidity. You perspire incredibly, not in drops but in rivulets.
>
> Saturdays and Sundays we usually spend at Dr Wilhelm's, a well-known lawyer. Some of his guests play tennis, others lie in deckchairs; tea, whisky and soda, and fruit ices are served. One of Dr Wilhelm's favourite turns-of-phrase is the English expression 'low class people'. For example: 'One can't go there, only low class people do'. You can imagine how much we have in common!

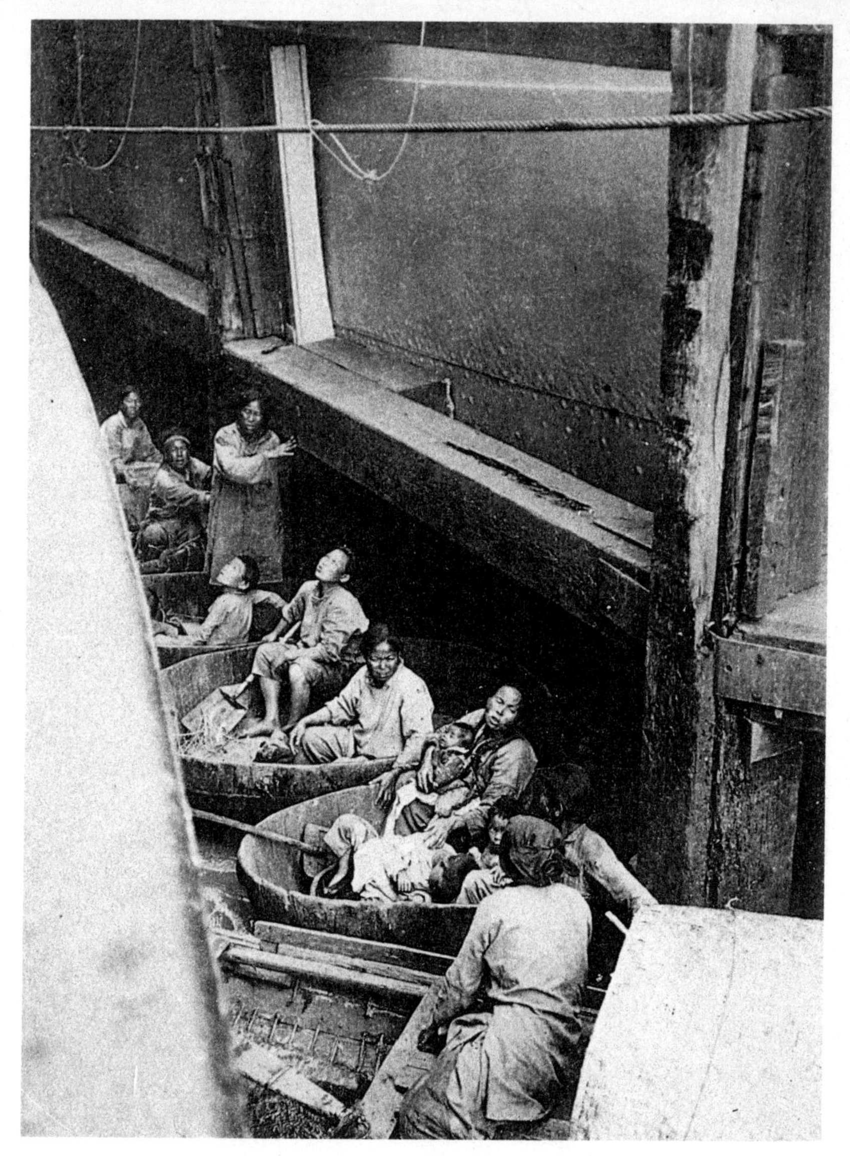

'Beggars in floating tubs encircled our ship'

. . . one more lament about the Europeans. The women are like little lapdogs. They have neither professions nor household duties, nor do they show any interest in scientific or cultural affairs. They don't even bother with their children.

The men are a little better because at least they have a job, and do a little work ... Yesterday, as on several other occasions, I went out to tea ... with Germans, White Russians (émigrés) and Americans. It's always the same. First a bit of gossip over bridge and mah-jong, then yesterday's dog-racing or the latest film. All the cinemas but one are swamped with American talkies, mostly corny musicals which everyone raves about.

... The other day we played miniature golf, very popular in Shanghai; if we now learn to play mah-jong and bridge and shout at the servants, we shall be one hundred per cent Shanghaiers ...

... Bernstein (from Breslau) is a bachelor and a bit eccentric. During the 1914–18 war he enjoyed what he calls his 'finest years', as a civilian prisoner in British India, where he spent his time with friends, eating well and leading a sporting life. When the Armistice came they said: 'Peace has broken out.' The intrinsic good or evil in man is an important problem for him. He cannot understand why some people are more concerned with finding enough bread to eat. Bernstein earns plenty of 'bread' from selling masses of locomotives for Orenstein and Koppel. Most of them out here are just the same.

... Schoolteacher Kuck is a smoothly brilliantined, fair-haired youth with a middle parting; he wears horn-rimmed spectacles over wide, gaping eyes. Originally he wanted to rear cattle, now he rears children (at the German School in Shanghai). Every Sunday morning he goes to the Municipal Orchestra concert and listens intently, chewing figs. Every Sunday afternoon he plays hockey with the Germans against a team of long-bearded thin-legged Sikh policemen.

And then there is a couple named Kann. She is the heart and soul of the local German Theatre Association; he is the heart and soul of the Art Club, a stockbroker by profession. He would have done better to stick to his stocks and shares, because the Art Club is quite dull. A pity, it might have been nice for Rolf.

... Dr. Seebohm is employed by I.G. Farben.[1] Somewhere in Germany he has rich parents with an estate or castle or such like. He has around 300 gramophone records, was film extra in *Miracle of the Snowshoes* and wears a glass eye; he lost the real one in a motor race. He loves Rolf, whose sparing use of words, calmness and stability have made a big impression on his muddled brain.

Professor Stumpf, an engineer at the German Chinese University, has invited us to visit him on Saturday. He has founded a 'Ring of Teutonic weapon bearers'. When he married recently, he received a congratulatory telegram from His Majesty Wilhelm II. If we go there, I fear it will end in disaster.

... The other day at the Ungern-Sternbergs for cocktails.[2] She is the sister of Count Kayserling. Both are highly intelligent and super-sophisticates.

... I have already written about Rolf producing *Hauptmann von Köpenick* by Zuckmayer.[3] All the actors were enthusiastic. Then came a long letter from the Consul General, Rüdt von Collenberg Bödigheim, asking that it should not be performed: 'That detestable play ... The Theatre Association should strive to maintain a higher standard. The dregs of society it portrays do not deserve pity, they only arouse repugnance ...' His letter is unbelievable. Rolf and Walter protested, but the Theatre Association dare not perform it now; neither can anyone hope to change that stupid old duffer's mind.

... Last night we were at Chesterfritz's, an American rolling in money. He owns the largest stockbroking firm here.

... On Saturday we had twelve people to tea; Matsumoto, a good-looking Japanese who lives at Bernstein's and represents Ufa Films here. Weeling and Seebohm of IG Farben, Korf, head of Melcher's, and Dr Vogel, President of the local German Chamber of Commerce. Vogel and Korf are more sensible than the average types out here and we plan to go up river with them on a house-boat. Jimson, head of the Shanghai Municipal Council engineering department, a crazy bachelor who sends us fertilisers for the flowers in our garden because that happens to be his hobby. Mirams, an English colleague of Rolf's who didn't touch our sandwiches because – contrary to English custom – they were served open rather than closed! Tonn and Plaut from the Trans-Ocean News Service and an American called Sauer from the SMC. His wife, a Portuguese born here, told us the following story. One day on a trip into the countryside, she started a conversation with a peasant. He said: 'You speak Chinese but your husband only speaks three words, how long has he been in China?' 'Thirty years.' 'So it takes ten years to learn one word of Chinese,' replied the astonished peasant.

... You are pleased that I am presenting the right society image here. Alas, it's not even howling with the wolves, so much as bleating with the sheep.

My life had undergone a radical change by the time some of these letters were written – but more of that later. To return to those first weeks and months in Shanghai: apart from the heat, the boredom and my problems with adjusting to Shanghai 'society', I was tormented by not making immediate contact with the Chinese people. I found the dirt, the poverty and the cruelty repugnant. My desire for fraternal solidarity and my efforts to like the people came to naught. I asked myself whether I was only a communist in theory, failing where the practice differed from what I knew at home.

My condition was not exactly improved by a constant feeling of nausea. I vomited every day and kept losing weight. The doctors attributed all my irregularities to an unsuitable climate. Not until October did my health begin to improve; at the same time I became aware of a peculiar 'abdominal movement'. The doctor then discovered that the peculiar movement was in fact a child. I was five months pregnant, something none of the doctors had thought to test. 'Fate' had decided contrary to all our plans, but now I was happy that a baby would be arriving in just four months.

As soon as it became a little cooler, I began to explore the streets of Shanghai and at week-ends Rolf and I went on excursions. I

Beggars in Shanghai – 2° below zero

Housing in those days

read for hours, took language lessons and was pleased with my progress. Gradually I became accustomed to the country, recognised the qualities of its people, enjoyed the beauty of the landscape and learnt to savour the culture. But above all I tried to understand political events and to gain a proper insight into their underlying causes.

28/29 October, 1930

Yesterday, Sunday, we went out of town by bus, the only Europeans among a crowd of Chinese. Foreigners have their own motor-car or else they just don't travel. We got out somewhere near a river, to walk, and discovered some beautiful countryside. Now and again we passed a little village, peasant houses, bamboo forests, cotton fields and more cotton fields.

Shanghai has over three million inhabitants. In the so-called foreign quarter live 48,000 foreigners and 1,400,000 Chinese, and in Chapei, the Chinese part of the city, another 1,600,000 Chinese. The foreigners include 6,000 White Russian émigrés, 7,500 British, 1,400 French, 1,800 Americans, 2,000 Indians, 1,300 Portuguese and 1,400 Germans. There are also about 180,000 Japanese, most of whom live in the Hongkew area outside the foreign quarter.

I have been learning all sorts of things about China. The communists here are strongest in the three 'red provinces' – Jiangxi, Hunan and Hubei (see atlas), which together cover an area as large as Germany and have exactly the same population. They have established a soviet government. In the villages there is common ownership of land, free storage of rice crops, no big landowners etc. The red armies in these provinces number 150,000 men altogether, backed up by millions of organised village and town dwellers.

. . . Two months ago, Chiang Kai-shek began a large-scale campaign of 'suppression of the reds', aiming to annihilate them totally by the end of April. A government army of 350,000 has marched on the red provinces for this purpose.

. . . The foreign powers naturally support Chiang Kai-shek. Of the 121 foreign warships here, a large number are

'We got out near a river'

A peasant house

deployed on the Yangzi, fighting alongside the Chinese fleet against the red armies on the banks and on the river.

> ... To understand the situation, you must appreciate that there are many provinces over which the central Nanjing government (Chiang Kai-shek) has no influence at all. A large part of the country is privately administered and taxed by individual generals. Each has his own army and the wars between them are laying waste the land. The Nanjing generals and the 'private' generals have certain points in common – they all exploit the provinces over which they rule and their soldiers all serve under intolerable social conditions.

I still had no contact with the party. I hinted to my brother that apparently the comrades in Germany had not yet moved in the matter. Now I was hoping for news. Although it was not the custom in China for a married European woman to work, I had tried to find an occupation and only gave up when I knew that I was expecting a child. Just at that point an opportunity for employment presented itself.

> 21st October, 1930
>
> Something really nice: I have after all taken on an interesting part-time job. I have already mentioned Plaut to you. He is head of the Trans-Ocean-Kuomin Telegraph Service. To begin with I am going to organise a political archive for him: cuttings from the German and the English press ...
>
> 30th October, 1930
>
> My work is a continual source of interest. Plaut is full of his own self-importance but he really is one of the leading experts on Asia, and on China in particular. I take advantage of this by ruthlessly squeezing everything out of him. He explains things very thoroughly, though of course with his own political bias.

Through Plaut I also got to know a number of journalists – among them the TASS representative. It hurt to socialise with this comrade as a bourgeois woman. For a moment temptation crossed my mind: 'Why not visit him and tell him everything? That I am a comrade and feel totally forsaken here.' But I had sense enough not to do it.

Plaut knew the American writer Agnes Smedley, who lived in Shanghai.[4] In Berlin I had read her book *Daughter of Earth* (published in Germany in 1929) with great enthusiasm. She describes her early life of bitter poverty. Agnes was the daughter of an unskilled labourer who could neither read nor write. By working as a dish-washer and tobacco picker, she managed to earn enough money to study. Later she worked for several years at Berlin University, on Unter den Linden. While living in India, she took part in the revolutionary movement there. I once had a strange experience in connection with her autobiography. In 1929 or 1930, the party organised a big exhibition at Berlin's Potsdamer Platz. John Heartfield, famous as a pioneer of political photomontage, had taken on the interior decoration of the hall, and our agitprop groups performed there every evening. The exhibition was open daily for four weeks, from 2.00 to 10.00 p.m. I was put in charge of the literature sales.

When two Indians came over to my stand, I tried to sell them Agnes Smedley's *Daughter of Earth*. I told them what it was about and described in detail how Agnes had been married to an Indian, a marriage that was later dissolved. Somewhat breathlessly I concluded my sales patter. The older of the two nodded: 'All you say is quite correct, I am the Indian to whom Agnes was married.'

I knew that Agnes was working in China as correspondent of the *Frankfurter Zeitung* but that she herself stood considerably further to the left. I was keen to make her acquaintance but felt inhibited about approaching someone so outstanding in my eyes.

When Plaut heard of this, he simply lifted the telephone receiver and connected me. Agnes and I arranged to meet the following day. I can remember describing myself as 'twenty-three years old, one metre seventy tall, jet black hair and a big nose'. Greatly amused, she countered with 'thirty-four years old, middling height, nondescript'.

The next day was 7th November, the thirteenth anniversary of the Russian Revolution. I had bought red roses for our sitting room to commemorate the day in some way. How wonderful the 7th November celebrations had always been in the Communist Youth.

We had arranged to meet in the centre of town and recognised each other at once. Agnes was holding a bunch of red roses just like the one in our house. She was going to take it to the TASS representative.

We sat, I believe, in the café of the Cathay Hotel. Agnes questioned me closely and since I knew her outlook and found her most congenial, I talked freely about my political views for the first time since arriving in Shanghai. I mentioned that I was unhappy about my isolation but, not knowing whether she was a party member, did not ask her to make contacts for me.

I recounted this meeting to my parents:

> 10th November, 1930
>
> Agnes looks like an intelligent working-class woman. Dressed simply, thinnish brown hair, very lively large grey-green eyes, face in no sense pretty, but well-formed. When she smooths back her hair, you can see the enormous sweep of her brow. Things are not easy for her here. The Europeans have given her the cold shoulder because she offended them deeply soon after she arrived. The exclusive American Club gave a reception to welcome her to Shanghai. Agnes went along and, being so interested in everything Chinese, she asked whether there were any Chinese present. They said: 'No, we don't have any Chinese members.' So she asked: 'But don't you invite them as guests?', to which the reply was: 'Chinese are not permitted to enter the Club.' She got up and left.
>
> The British hate her because of her work for the Indian revolutionary movement.
>
> And the Chinese watch every step she takes, in spite of her irrefuted position as a correspondent of the *Frankfurter Zeitung* out here.

Agnes and I became close friends. There was hardly a day when we did not telephone or see each other.

> 12th November, 1930
>
> On Sunday evening we collected Agnes from her apartment and I made a bee-line for her wonderful collection of German, Indian, Chinese and English books. Then we went out to eat at a Chinese restaurant with her and two Chinese friends. One teaches Chinese literature at a school, the other is Agnes's secretary.

Later the secretary lived for a long time with the writer Ding Ling. I also got to know Ding Ling and grew very fond of her. She had been in the Chinese Red Army for many years. When I met her, she was active in the newly founded left-wing Writers' Union. I had followed Ding Ling's fate and was sure she couldn't have survived her prison term during the black time of the Chinese 'cultural revolution' in the 1960s, which meant defamation of intellectuals, often ending in death. I was overjoyed when I heard Ding Ling was alive, 'rehabilitated and much honoured', in her seventies writing books again. A Chinese professor of literature told me that, when visiting Berlin, in about 1985. I explained to her how I liked Ding Ling and said lightly: 'When you go back, give her my warmest regards, but I don't think she will remember me.' Later I had a wonderful surprise. A parcel arrived with Ding Ling's latest books, published between 1980 and 1983. Each book was signed: to Sonya from Ding Ling. I was so moved, it was a good thing that I was on my own when I looked at a photo of her dating back to when I knew her. Soon after I received her books she died.

Describing our Christmas to the family at home, I wrote:

> At ten in the evening we drove to the Chinese Theatre with Agnes. Mei Lan-fang, the most famous Chinese actor, is on tour in Shanghai and it was quite an experience to see him play women's roles. I just can't express how charming and attractive he looked, though it took a little while to get used to the idea that this was a man acting . . .
>
> As for the Christmas presents – books: Gorky, *How a Man was Born*; Müller *If in 1918*; Ehrenburg, *The Life of the Motorcar*; Seyfullina, *Virinea; Selected Chinese Short Stories*; Erich Kästner, *A Man gives Information*; Pieper's Art Calen-

dar; Cohn Wiener, *Asia*; Stendhal, *Charterhouse of Parma*; Perckhammer, *China*; Hausenstein, *Contemporary Art*; André Maurois, *Byron*; a volume of poems by Rilke; John Dos Passos, *Latitude* 42.

6th January, 1931

Our library has suddenly grown by five volumes from the Malik Publishing House in Berlin: no cause for complaint there! Agnes asked me to review the five books for a journal and I was allowed to keep them in return.

That was all I said in my letter about this journal and its publisher. At that time it was called *Pen Liu* (*The Flood*) and was published by the Chinese poet Lu Xun. It had to change its name frequently and at times could only appear illegally.

Further contributions followed – under a pseudonym of course. I can only recall one of my articles. Its title was 'Pen and Brush in the Hands of the German Workers'. I was reporting on working-class writers and painters in the 1920s.

I visited Lu Xun quite often at his flat, where he lived with a much younger wife and their little son.

Lu Xun, born in 1881, was known as China's Gorky. Like Gorky, he portrayed the ordinary people, their dignity and their suffering. Strangely enough he also looked like Gorky, with his delicate profile and pale, sensitive face. He was suffering from tuberculosis and died in 1936.

He lived modestly. Once when I brought a wooden duck on wheels for his son, who was about three years old, Lu Xun was moved and kept saying what a beautiful present it was.

Lu Xun wanted to publish a volume of Käthe Kollwitz reproductions and I helped him. Afterwards, he gave me a copy in which he had written a dedication of friendship. Since I held Käthe Kollwitz in great regard and much admired Lu Xun, this present was doubly dear to me. It disappeared some years later, in the confusion of war.

14th January, 1931

Yesterday I spent all day translating seven typewritten pages into German for Agnes. It is an article she has written for the *Frankfurter Zeitung* about peasants and the Red Army in China. The translator in Frankfurt had slipped such enormous distortions into her last article that she asked me to help.

During the early days of our friendship, which was so precious to me, I could not understand why a person of Agnes's stature should want to spend her time with me, or why I should have become her confidante.

Agnes was alone; her whole life had been devoted to the revolutionary struggle. I was a communist but had grown up without material worries and was now looking forward to my first child. I lived a sheltered and painless life. I was also much younger than Agnes and quite inexperienced.

Agnes had outstanding qualities. With her books she showed her allegiance to the Chinese people. She made great sacrifices for China's liberation struggle. At the same time she was emotionally unstable. While she was frequently full of fun, infecting everyone with her sense of humour, more often she was depressed and subject to a melancholia which affected her health. Perhaps she needed my equilibrium and optimism. Besides, I was always at her disposal. If she felt lonely, I went to see her. If she felt depressed, she could ring me at three in the morning and I would get up to be with her.

Soon after our friendship began, Agnes told me that she was with us in thought and deed, but would find it too difficult to submit to our party discipline.

Perhaps during those years of illegality she did not wish to admit her membership even to me. But I believe she spoke the truth. I admired Agnes, and there are few people who contributed so much to my development. But when her spontaneous emotional responses coloured her political judgement I could not agree with her. We would argue, and she would leave in anger. A few hours later she would telephone as though nothing had happened and I would be glad that we were friends again.

In her book *Battle Hymn of China*, Agnes states that she always felt sympathetic towards communists and actively supported the movement in China, but never became a party member. The book was published in London by Gollancz in 1944.

Many years later, on re-reading her books, I felt that *Daughter of Earth* showed much more of her embitterment, instability and impulsive reactions than I had been aware of in my youth.

I wrote home:

> 19th March, 1931
>
> ... You ask me what friends we have. Not many really, but an enormous number of acquaintances. As for friends – quite apart, and above all the rest for me – there is of course Agnes.
>
> 4th October, 1931
>
> Agnes is moving into her own two-roomed flat in a large apartment block only two minutes away from us. We are delighted. Rolf is arranging the interior decoration for her, designing the furniture, etc. It is all to be quite modest of course, but his drawings look very promising.
>
> 6th March, 1932
>
> Agnes is ill again. She is to go into hospital next week for injections and radiation treatment for her heart. It is basically a nervous condition. She is completely absorbed in a new book she is going to write on China. Many of our friends play a role in it and we often discuss it, but I must not disclose any more here. I believe it will be quite outstanding. The last two nights I have been sleeping at her flat. She feels better when someone is there at night.

Although I wrote home a lot about Agnes and other acquaintances, I had to keep silent about the one event which was to prove decisive for my future life.

Agnes knew how much I was waiting for my contact with the party and how deeply I yearned to lead an active, useful existence.

Soon after we became friends, she told me that, if I agreed, a communist whom I could trust fully, would come to see me.

The comrade came to our house. It was Richard Sorge.[5] Agnes knew him as, like her, he wrote for the German press, and, given her political views, it was natural that she would have assisted

Dr Sorge in other matters apart from their work as journalists. He did not come with Agnes, but alone. She simply arranged our first meeting. Nor do I believe that she knew the exact nature of Sorge's activities, as a first-rate intelligence officer at the Red Army headquarters, Moscow. I do not need to describe the physical appearance of this remarkable man, who became one of the most successful intelligence officers of the Soviet Union's General Staff when stationed in Tokyo during the Second World War. That has been done by others, many times. He first visited me in November 1930, while we were still living at Walter's. Richard Sorge was thirty-five years old and I found him just as attractive and good-looking as others have portrayed. A slender head, thick wavy hair, his face already deeply furrowed, his intense blue eyes framed by dark lashes, his mouth beautifully formed.

So I am describing Richard's appearance after all, because you cannot think of him without seeing him before you.

When we first met I did not know his name, and it would not have meant anything to me. Richard said that he had heard of my readiness to support the Chinese comrades in their work. He spoke of the struggle against the country's reactionary government, of the responsibilities and dangers involved in even the smallest degree of help for our comrades. Then he asked me to reconsider the matter. At this point I could still refuse without anyone reproaching me.

By now it was obvious that I was expecting a child. Agnes had surely mentioned it to him too.

I felt hurt at being asked whether I was still prepared to take part in this work of international solidarity, under such dangerous conditions. I did not realise then that Richard had to say all this, and that he would not have come personally if he had thought that I was likely to refuse. During the half-hour that Richard remained after my somewhat curt agreement, he talked over the practicalities of using our flat to meet Chinese comrades. I was simply to let them have the room, but not to attend the discussions.

Soon afterwards, meetings took place in our home. For two years, until the end of 1932, Richard Sorge was in charge and after that, as far as I can remember, 'Paul' took his place.

Richard Sorge

Looking back, it seems strange that there was such a short interval between my first meeting with Agnes and Richard's visit. How could he have checked so quickly on my reliability?

I remember Richard suggesting that I should go to a demonstration in the main street, but without actually participating. Laden with purchases in order to explain my presence there as a European, I stood outside the large department store, Wing On, and saw Chinese people being beaten and arrested.

In many cases arrest meant the end. I looked into the faces of young revolutionaries whose death sentence had ben pronounced at that moment, and I knew – if only for their sake – that I would carry out any task asked of me.

Later I heard that Gerhart Eisler, whom I knew fleetingly as a communist journalist and speaker, from Germany, had observed me there and drawn the comrades' attention to the importance of my looking more ladylike on such occasions. In future I should at least wear a hat. I did not even know Gerhart Eisler was living in China, nor did I meet him there after that. I suppose at the time he worked for the Comintern.[6] He knew of the high esteem in which my father was held by the German labour movement.

After I got to know Richard, I learnt that the Comintern had also asked for my co-operation.

Richard wanted me to stay in his group. In keeping with clandestine practice, he thought it would be better if I did not make a change, but he left the decision to me.

I did stay with Richard and his group, but did not give much thought to what its specific tasks might be. Only two years later did I know that it operated under the intelligence department of the Red Army General Staff.

It made no difference to me. I knew that my activities served the comrades of the country in which I lived. If this practical solidarity was an initiative of the Soviet Union – so much the better.

I can no longer remember details of the meetings that took place when I was still living at Walter's house, but my work for the group started after that first conversation with Richard.

I do, however, remember quite clearly Richard congratulating me on the birth of my son in February 1931 and how I – partly embarrassed to be involved in such private matters as having babies, and partly proud of my little son – led him to the baby's crib. I remember how he bent over and gently pulled back the quilt with his hand. For a long time he looked at the infant in silence, and I thought to myself that perhaps he had never seen such a young child.

Walter had helped Rolf to find employment in Shanghai. He had also taken us into his own home. If my illegal activities in his house were discovered, Walter's promising professional career might be destroyed – and much more. Clearly I had to remain silent about our work. Had he known of it, he would have been in even greater danger.

Walter was a successful and ambitious businessman. He was

an intelligent matter-of-fact sort of person who could see through the weaknesses of bourgeois society and poured ironic scorn upon it, while at the same time profiting fully from the material advantages it had to offer. Proud of his rise from a humble background, he had every intention of continuing to climb. Walter showed interest and concern for China. We got on well together and in the course of frequent conversations I was able to influence him. I had known Walter as Rolf's friend since I was eighteen, so my political past was no secret to him, but he suspected nothing of my activities in Shanghai. I believe such a thought never entered his mind, because under the political conditions then prevailing in China, my involvement would have seemed too extravagant an adventure.

Walter's home and his name provided excellent cover for clandestine work. On the other hand I could not organise meetings there regularly, as Walter's wife was at home a good deal. Richard advised me to rent a flat of my own. Rolf and I had intended to move in any case, so now my house-hunting had to take further requirements into account. We found the right sort of place in the French Settlement, the sector of the town which came under French administration. We moved on 1st April, 1931. Our address was 1464 Avenue Joffre; later the number was changed to 1676.

From a letter:

> The whole estate is situated in a kind of small park. A long unkempt garden path runs from the road, to join another which leads to the house. So from all four rooms we have an open view, with no other buildings to block it.

Equally important was the fact that the house had two exits and the whole park was bordered by two or three different streets.

Richard and his associates met at my house once a week in the early afternoon. Sometimes there were longer intervals between meetings. Apart from Richard there were two or three Chinese and occasionally one or two other European comrades present. I never attended the discussions but just saw to it that the comrades were not disturbed. The meetings took place on the first floor. The lower rooms were not safe from visitors.

The rooms or, to be more exact, the concrete cells in which the

Here Richard and his associates met

servants lived, were isolated. They had no windows or any direct access to the house. Cook, amah and boy had to cross the yard and reach the kitchen by the back entrance. In the period between noon and the 'master's' return from work, the servants in most European households were left alone, because 'Missie' would be resting. In any case, servants never came into the rooms unless rung for. I always opened the front door to visitors myself; this followed quite naturally from the way the house had been designed. We had arranged the entrance hall as a living room, and the staircase led from there to the upper storey, so that no one could use it without my knowledge.

Those Chinese comrades who came most frequently became my

The staircase led from the living room

language teachers. This gave them perfectly legitimate reasons for being there, and so their illegal visits went unnoticed.

When there were meetings, the comrades did not all appear at the same time. Nor did they leave together, but departed at short intervals, one after the other. Richard would be the last to go and stayed talking to me for half an hour or more. Our friendly relations could, if necessary, be explained by our mutual friendship with Agnes. From time to time he gave me an article to type which could also serve as an alibi for his visits. In any case, the social life of Europeans in China was such that contacts among them hardly required an explanation. As it happened, no one outside our group got to know of his visits, although in those two years he must have come to our house at least eighty times.

During the first weeks I was reserved when Richard stayed behind and talked to me, because I did not want to appear inquisitive – I really wasn't. Nor was I offended by the fact that I hardly knew what was going on in my own home. I accepted the principles of clandestine work. But the desire not to appear inquisitive made me diffident in talking to Richard. Even when he asked me questions, I answered laconically.

During one of these conversations, after an embarrassing pause, I said curtly: 'It's time you left.' He stood up, fetched his hat and said: 'So I'm being thrown out.' I hung my head and said nothing.

Some friends of Richard believed he had a sadness within him, but others maintained that this was quite incorrect. When I got to know him better, I noticed this sadness from time to time. Perhaps it was the expression of physical suffering. He had been wounded in the First World War, and there were days when – in contrast to his usual vitality, his humour and his irony – he was withdrawn and depressed.

It was early spring – my son must have been about two months old – when Richard surprised me by asking whether I would like to go for a ride on his motorbike. We met near my house on the outskirts of the city. It was my first time on a motorbike, and he had to show me how to hold on and point out that the foot-rests were actually for putting feet on.

Not until six months later, when I visited Richard in hospital with his leg in plaster, did I learn from other comrades that he never kept to the speed limit.

I had been thrilled by his breakneck driving. I urged him to go faster and faster, and he was happy to oblige. When we stopped after a long ride, I was a changed person. Shanghai's detested social life was forgotten, as were the constant pressures to conform to etiquette, the responsibilities of clandestine activities and the unnecessary worries about my tiny son.

I laughed and romped about and talked non-stop. I didn't care what Richard thought. Perhaps he had only arranged this ride to test my physical courage. If, however, he had been wisely seeking a way to establish better contact between us, he had gone about it the right way. After this ride, I no longer felt inhibited and our conversations were more meaningful – proof that human relations really are important and that it may be right, occasionally, to break the strict code of illegality for their sake.

Richard did not give me any theoretical instruction on the rules of conspiratorial work. When the lives of comrades are at stake, other people's experience can certainly be useful, but the knowledge that any thoughtless action might jeopardise the safety of all concerned is a heavy responsibility and, in itself, a most effective teacher. It was obvious that I had to be constantly on the lookout in case anybody was watching the house or, for that matter, me. Before and after meetings with the comrades, I kept a discreet watch on the streets. Nor did I need to be told that it was a good thing to invite as many bourgeois guests to the house as possible so that the 'illegal visitors' would be less conspicuous.

Talking to Richard, I noticed that he was interested in some of my conversations with acquaintances such as Seebohm from IG Farben, Walter, the solicitor Wilhelm, Bernstein, Ungern-Sternberg, Plaut and others, and so I became more purposeful about inviting these people to our house. I liked watching Richard listen to me, and I could tell by his expression whether something was important to him or not.

So, almost unconsciously, I found out what Richard wanted to know from the way he responded to me, and I began to conduct my conversations accordingly. I could see this was useful to him, even though I did not know about the organisation he, or by now I can already say *we*, were working for. I doubt whether I was able to offer him any information of major significance – he himself had far better contacts – but perhaps I was able to fill in the picture a little here and there, and perhaps my judgement of character, of people's behaviour and their views on economic and political problems, was sometimes valuable.

I also soon learnt that facts were not enough for Richard. If I was too brief, he would say, 'and what do you think about that?'

Once he said: 'Good – good, a proper analysis.'

I want to stress once again that neither then nor later was there any sensational moment when I discovered whom I was working for. I always learned just as much as the work required, and as this grew, so I developed a clearer understanding. I believe this speaks for the approach of Richard and his comrades. True, I was not exactly plagued by curiosity in this respect. I was happy to be allowed to work with a group of such marvellous communists. (I shall describe the others in more detail later on.) I learnt from their example without any specific teaching. Clandestine conduct became second nature since the comrades had to be shielded from constant danger. I felt the same intuitive protectiveness towards them as I felt towards my little son. A strange comparison perhaps – but just as my child's smallest sounds would wake me in the middle of the night, so was I on my guard for the slightest incident or irregularity in the vicinity of my comrades.

Looking back on that period today, I have the impression that my letters home were too open. Not, of course, as regards this illegal work, of which there was no hint, but rather in relation to my political views. Perhaps this had something to do with the role I had chosen to play within the bourgeois society of Shanghai. From the very beginning I acted as a bourgeois progressive and never concealed my interest in China. I believe that if you are involved in illegal activities, you should – as far as circumstances permit – find a life-style that matches your character. I did not have to torment myself by adopting the guise of a Nazi. It was out of the question on racial grounds alone. For me, the role of the 'liberal woman with intellectual interests' seemed most appropriate. After 1933, this was the only one possible. Right from the start, I had to bear in mind that some chance event might reveal my past to the foreign community in China. Not that this would have been too catastrophic. In such circles it was not unusual for people to have been communists in their youth, only to 'come to their senses' as they grew older. Because of Rolf's position, we sat squarely in the bourgeois saddle, and none of our acquaintances would in their wildest dreams have imagined that I, as the mother of a small child, would jeopardise my family and everything we had created for ourselves in China by contact with communists.

Our underground conduct was also influenced by the particular circumstances prevailing in China. On the one hand, publications and organisations of a democratic or mildly left hue were not forbidden under Chiang Kai-shek's government, and therefore the comrades could permit themselves more leeway in their clandestine work than would have been possible in a purely fascist state. Europeans in Shanghai lived under British or French administration, and foreigners enjoyed legal privileges which enabled us to do things that would have counted as grave violations or illegal practices under Hitler, or in Japan, or later in the Japanese-occupied areas of China. On the other hand, when it came to rooting out communists, the secret service of the Guomindang (the Chiang Kai-shek government) collaborated actively with their European counterparts, and manifestations of anti-communism were no milder than in a totally fascist country.

Figures which I came across later show that from 1927 to 1935 between 350,000 and 400,000 Chinese communists perished. Only a few returned from the prisons, and most never even reached that far: they were shot, beaten to death, buried alive or beheaded. In provincial cities their heads were impaled on posts near the city gates to intimidate the people.

The problems of underground work cut deeply into my personal life. Repelled by bourgeois society in Shanghai, Rolf moved closer to me politically. He had a good, positive attitude to the Chinese people from the beginning. But when, well before I met Richard, I had told him how I hoped to work with the party, he tried hard to dissuade me. He argued that he was trying to establish himself in a strange and difficult country, and that, because he felt responsible for me and the child I was expecting, he had to advise me not to get involved. He said I was over-estimating myself, that I was not as tough as I thought. If it came to it, I would not be able to bear the cruelty and brutality which communists were subjected to. Nor did I seem to have any idea what the child I was carrying would really mean to me. He had never forbidden me anything, never limited my freedom in any way, but this time he would have to insist.

This disagreement upset me as much as it did him and I decided there and then that if the party contacted me I would not tell Rolf about it. I also thought I should tell Richard this during our first conversation. He was surprised. Agnes had presumably told him nothing but good about Rolf, and quite rightly.

Honesty was one of the ethical principles on which our marriage was based; rather inflict pain and have done with it, than keep secrets or lie. We took it for granted that this was the decent way to behave.

Now everything changed for me. During those three years in Shanghai, Rolf did not know that our house was being used for clandestine meetings, or that suitcases containing secret information, known to Richard but not to me, were hidden in our cupboards for long periods. Some of the comrades became my dearest friends, but Rolf never knew them, or else he met them disguised as harmless businessmen and I had to treat them as such in his presence.

I could not talk to him about the people who were closest to me or the work on which my life was centred.

When I was nineteen years old, I had written to Jürgen about my political differences with Rolf: 'At times like these he seems like a stranger to me. We didn't even say goodbye when we parted.'

Now the shock was even greater and affected our whole life. My reaction is easier to understand in the harsh context of illegal activity in China or against the background of Nazi Germany. I took part in the resistance struggle, yet my most intimate companion warned me against the idea and stood on the sidelines.

Rolf was still as good and considerate as ever and, during the years that followed, he endured the separations and difficult circumstances created by my work, in the hope of saving our marriage.

In Shanghai Rolf was introduced fleetingly to two of our group. Han and Weng. But all he ever knew about them was that they were my language teachers.

Han had a lively face; over and over again he had to sweep his long hair out of his eyes. He was vivacious and very quick on the uptake, which had led to an easy rapport between us. Weng was slow and thorough. I admired his methodical scientific style of work, something which I did not possess. During our lessons I read the Comintern's *International Press Correspondence* (Inprecor) in German with Han and in English with Weng.

About Weng I wrote home:

27th May, 1931

. . . I am delighted with my Chinese teacher. Not that I learn much Chinese, the temptation to speak English is too great as the teacher is so charming. His English is poor; that is why I give him lessons in exchange, but it is good enough to tell that he is a wonderful and intelligent person.

11th November, 1931

. . . This evening my teacher Weng is coming. I talk to him once a week about China. He has just written a book with a lot of statistical material about the requisitions carried out by government soldiers in peasant districts. He gave me a copy in which he had written a nice dedication. Of course I can't read it, but the parts he explained to me are interesting. Apparently this barefaced robbery of the peasants is costing them an enormous amount. A friend is translating it into German – about a hundred pages, rather like a pamphlet . . .

. . . Yesterday was Weng's wedding. We asked beforehand how many guests there would be. He said: 'Quite simple – only family', 130! When we arrived, I was appalled to see my good homely Weng wearing a tailcoat. He had put on 'foreign dress' to avoid the endless Chinese ceremonies, and it really was quite simple. You don't even need an official. The witnesses sign a paper which is kept by the family. Professor Chen Han-sheng was one of the witnesses, he looked splendid in his beautiful Chinese clothes.

There was wonderful Chinese food. Some of Weng's friends took the platform – one sang, another played a mouth-organ. The families had brought along innumerable children; some had to be fed, some had their nappies changed, others chattered away between the performances and they all looking charming.

My teachers worked in a government institute of social sciences, and through them I saw and understood many things which foreigners did not usually come into contact with.

Pasting up matchboxes – 1000 for 30 coppers a day

15th December, 1931

... From half past eight in the morning till half past two in the afternoon a really enjoyable outing. Weng came too. We drove for an hour in bitterly cold weather to reach Ming-on, a Chinese village. To warm ourselves we made straight for a coolies' tea-house, where we drank hot tea and ate nuts. Then we walked to a neighbouring village, where the women spend the winter pasting matchboxes. We watched them – they get 30 coppers, that is 1½d, for 1,000 boxes. If they work 14 hours a day, they can make 1,300.

11th January, 1932

On Saturday morning Han and I took the Nanjing train as far as Wuxi, a town of 150,000 people, well-known for its cotton and silk industry. An overcrowded third-class carriage – unusual transport for foreigners, but all the more interesting ...

Children working, many only ten years old – photo taken by Agnes Smedley

... We had often seen the cotton being picked near Shanghai, in huge fields that look as though they are covered in snow. Now we saw the junks full of cotton bales moored outside the factory ...

I had only half an eye for the cotton production, interesting though it was, as I found the women workers even more interesting.

The Lixin cotton factory employs 2,000 workers, of whom 1,500 are women and a few hundred children. The working day lasts 12 hours with a break of one hour for women and children. The men work without a break and eat at their machines. Most of the women are between 16 and 22 years old and earn eight to twelve shillings a month. The sight of

Workers' housing, five people to a room

all those children, some only ten years old, in that hot hall with its deafening noise, was painful. Children the age of my own young sisters, working twelve hours a day! I saw them standing by the machines eating. Within just two minutes they had to keep putting down their rice bowls to move levers and knot broken threads.

The firm has built two-storeyed terraced houses. One worker showed us his home. Like all the others, it only had one bare room, where there was just about space for two beds. He has a family of five! The room costs 1s. 6d. a month. His children start work when they are ten. For the first six months they are learning and don't receive a penny. If they prove suitable (if not, they are thrown out without any pay) they receive 1½d. to 2d. a day. Depending on how much work there is, this factory allows two or three days off a month, unpaid of course. There are no Sundays.

This letter goes on for many more pages and describes a visit to a silk factory where babies lie on the floor next to the machines, while their mothers lift silk cocoons out of scalding water with their bare hands.

> In the evening we went for a walk through the streets. Wuxi is a walled town with four huge gates which are locked at midnight. A lot of people live outside the town wall in straw tents: peasants from the famine areas, the unemployed. Only four of Wuxi's forty-eight silk factories are operating. Japanese and Italian competition, higher American import duties, the world economic situation in general . . .

And so Han and Weng added to my knowledge of China and its problems by letting me see things for myself. I began to understand and to love the people.

I also felt very close to Professor Chen Han-sheng and his wife. He taught at a University and she was a librarian.

I cannot remember whether Han-sheng ever attended the meetings with Richard, but occasionally they gave me messages for each other. Han-sheng was thin and small, more like a delicate boy than an academic. His intellectual capacities reminded me of my brother Jürgen. And so did his inexhaustible reservoir of quips and anecdotes. He would draw on them for suitable occasions, or else he would invent jokes on the spur of the moment, which amused him as much as they did his audience. He was a dedicated, hard-working scholar and an illegal communist, and perhaps this provided just the diversion and relaxation he needed.

His wife, Gu Shuxing, had an intelligent and beautiful face, tawny skin, dimples and wonderful white teeth. She was politically active and a good organiser.

Rolf got to know them and they became his friends too. Agnes, whose journalistic work benefited from Han-sheng's knowledge and connections, frequently joined us when they were our guests. His status as a respected academic was so high that our relations with him could not be suspect in any way. Socialising with Chinese from 'better circles' was no problem. In the commercial world, private contacts with affluent Chinese business people were considered part of the money-making game. Rolf's municipal building contractor for the British settlement in Shanghai paid us visits and

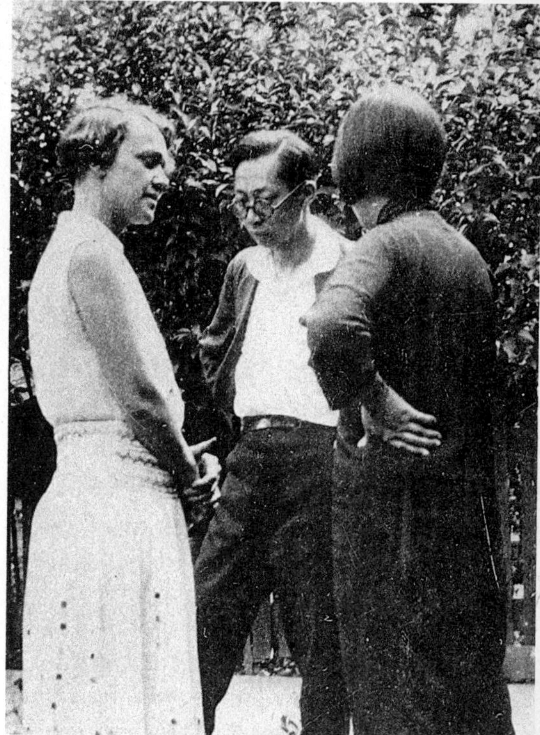

Chen Han-sheng and his wife, with me

With Agnes

overwhelmed me with expensive presents. So as not to appear different from other European wives, I accepted everything. Richard had also advised me to do so.

Among Richard's co-workers was a frail young Chinese girl with short hair, a pale complexion and slightly protruding teeth. She came from an influential family; her father was a high-ranking Guomindang general. He disowned her when she married a man of her own choice, a communist without means. She was intelligent, courageous and modest. I particularly liked this comrade, whom Richard also sometimes met at my house. Her husband had tuberculosis. At Richard's request I rented a bungalow for him in the Mogan Mountains and visited him there several times.

Later, during the Chinese cultural revolution, when I thought of these comrades and all the political discussions we had, and studying 'Inprecor' alongside Han and Weng, I feared for them.

Richard's closest colleagues were the German radio-operator Max Christiansen Clausen, now well known for his exemplary work with Richard in Japan,[7] and Sepp, John and Paul. Sepp was stocky. He had married a White Russian living in Shanghai. It was a painful process settling this young woman into such a different kind of life, and it must have caused Richard considerable worry. Flaxen-haired, rosy-cheeked, good-natured Sepp did not take life too seriously. Whether Richard needed two radio operators, whether they worked shifts, or whether one or the other was being trained to work in another city, I do not know. Perhaps Sepp had some other specialisation of which I was not aware.

Anyway, at that time I did not yet know anything about the job of radio-operator. Sepp, like Max, had been a seaman. There were many seamen among the comrades in the intelligence service; their occupation fitted them for courier work, and if they stood the test, they were given further training.

But I saw much more of John than of Max or Sepp. John was a Pole. We sometimes called him Grisha and, when I noticed that he rather liked it, I never called him anything else. Perhaps it was his real name. Grisha was in his mid-twenties. He had dark wavy hair with a side parting, his forehead shone as if it were polished, his eyes were dark above his bold cheek-bones. Grisha said little about himself; reserved and serious, he had a more complex nature than either Max or Sepp, and I only learnt more of his personal life when we had known each other for some time. I remember that his parents in Poland were not supposed to know that he was in Shanghai. He owned a photographer's shop that provided him with legal cover. He sold cameras and developed films for customers. He was the group's photographer and copied information on to miniature film.

Richard had asked me whether Rolf might design the interior and fittings for the shop, which opened towards the end of 1931 or the beginning of 1932. An acquaintanceship developed on this basis would be a good alibi for Grisha's visits to our house. Grisha also had certain special requirements for his shop which it was easier to discuss with Rolf, without having to tell him exactly what they were for.

I do not remember now by what tricks I brought the two together, but anyhow, I met Grisha officially through Rolf. Grisha thoroughly enjoyed being introduced under these circumstances – kissing my hand and calling me 'madam' – a comedy I found quite painful.

I longed for a good camera, and soon after the shop opened Rolf bought me a Leica there. Enthusiastically I began to take pictures of people and landscapes. Grisha developed my photos.

To my mother:

> 7th June, 1932
>
> The album I have sent you contains photographs taken on excursions and longer journeys. It was not I who ordered the enlargement from the photographer. He liked the picture so much that he enlarged it on his own initiative and presented it to me. Modesty forbids me to keep it in this format and so you shall have it. Walter took it with my camera on the journey to Lanchi.

I can still remember what Grisha said to me about that picture at the time: 'Very well caught – just like you. Could be called "Portrait of a Pirate".' This snapshot, like so many others that Grisha developed and printed for me, is still in my possession, and so is the fifty-eight-year-old Leica from his shop. It still takes perfectly good photographs.

Our son was called Michael (Micha). Rolf knew that I had named him after the American comrade and writer Michael Gold, whom I had met at a holiday camp on the Hudson river during my stay in America in 1928. At that time his *Jews without Money* was one of my favourite books. Later, when he visited Germany again, he came to see my parents, but by then I was already in China. Until his death in 1967 I read his columns in the American party paper the *Daily Worker* (Later *Daily World*) whenever I could. It is a sad loss to the international working-class movement that he was never able to complete his memoirs.

Of course our little son played a great role in my life. Immediately after his birth I wrote to Jürgen and Marguerite:

'Portrait of a pirate'

> I am in heaven over this child and then again appalled how I have succumbed to him. There is nothing left of me right now, either for Rolf, or politics, or books, or you. Only the child, and everything else only in relation to the child. It means a whole new world, with entirely new feelings and thoughts.

When Micha was eleven days old, politics again emerged as a 'rival' and only half the letter I wrote to my mother is devoted to him.

> 23rd February, 1931
>
> I am now weighing him at every meal, that way he gets a little more. If he hasn't gained the minimum weight I feed

Micha, born 12.2.31

him again. Every gram swallowed is important. Rolf often watches his little son. After he has been fed we have to be strict with each other, and put him back into his crib so he can have some peace, instead of kissing him and discussing every feature of his little face.

My constant companions are *Infant Feeding and Care* and *Healthy Children* with *The Volga flows to the Caspian* by Pilnyak for balance. Radek's original and sympathetic foreword is promising.

By the way, very interesting how the European press is suddenly taking the Russian Five Year Plan so seriously. Up to now they have only ever talked about how the workers

> are suffering under the Five Year Plan. I am sure great sacrifices are demanded, but I have the impression that many people are prepared to make these sacrifices in order to achieve their goal. Interesting too, how, now that the capitalists have to concede the plan's success, immediate countermeasures are being discussed: embargo on export of machines to Russia and on the purchase of cheap Russian goods . . .
>
> . . . Am I really not to change Micha's nappies when he wakes up wet at 2.00 a.m.? Surely when he cries I must at least go and look at him, as he's always such a little fidget.

Agnes followed my child's development with love and also sadness. I rang her when Michael smiled for the first time and she saw him take his first steps. He was a bright and happy boy and all the comrades like him. Chen Han-sheng and his wife, who had no children of their own, took a great interest in him. My friend Isa was especially attached to Micha. Isa is mentioned for the first time in my letters home on 24 March, 1931.

> There is a friend I must tell you about. A young girl arrived here one day, without kith or kin but with boxes full of books. She has opened a small shop full of radical German, English and French literature. She was working in a bookshop in Berlin, when a Chinese publisher drew her boss's attention to the potential in Shanghai. Her customers are mostly Chinese students. She is just 23 years old. Plucky, don't you think? Unfortunately she is not very good at selling. I am itching to give her a hand . . .

Isa was even more courageous than I had written in my letter. She too was a comrade, and worked illegally in Shanghai. She had lived with a Chinese comrade in Moscow for a considerable time and had come to China with him. Because of their underground assignments they were not able to live together here and so Isa had left their daughter in Moscow. She longed for the little one, who was not yet two years old, but I knew nothing of all this until later. Isa's husband joined a Trotskyist group; there were political arguments and she left him.

Isa had freckles on her very fair skin, hazy blue eyes and unruly red hair. She was rather clumsy and had no dress sense. By European standards in Shanghai, she was living very modestly. She was a wonderful person and soon she was like a sister to me. Since Rolf also got on well with her, she looked on our house as her second home. We never spoke of our secret work. I did not know whether Isa was in touch with anyone from Richard's group and she learned nothing from me. Her frequent visits were easily explained to outsiders, for it was well-known in Shanghai that I was also a qualified bookseller.

When Isa came to see us, she often asked if she could bath or dress Micha. She did not mention her own child until she received news that the little girl had died of meningitis. Her lack of envy, her straightforward affection for Micha, were typical of her wonderful nature.

We often talked about her bookshop and I helped her organise a Käthe Kollwitz exhibition. Isa was more painstaking than I and less selfish. I was quicker and had more ideas.

I can't recall when I first met Richard's deputy, Paul (Karl Rimm), who sometimes came to see me with Richard. Paul had a round, almost bald head, with small eyes and a sudden friendly smile. His large and heavy frame lumbered slowly into motion. Paul's face did not reveal his intelligence, nor did his quiet good nature lead one to suspect the revolutionary's strength and passion he had so often shown.

Paul came from an Estonian family of agricultural workers. He had been a Red Guard, a Civil War Commissar, elected to a Soviet, trained in the military academy, and later became a Soviet general. I did not know the name which he lived under in Shanghai, nor was I aware that he came from Estonia as did his buxom motherly wife Luise, whom I met on several occasions. I knew that he owned a restaurant in Shanghai as a cover.

I have already mentioned that I did not attend any meetings at our house, but only provided the comrades with a safe venue. I used, however, to bring them a cup of tea during their sessions in the upstairs room. That was unusual among European women, who left every sort of chore to the servants. I therefore also served other guests now and again, so that our servants might regard this as an oddity of mine, rather than special treatment reserved for certain guests.

The suitcase I looked after for the comrades came into use during meetings. It contained printed and hand-written material. Soon Richard brought me a second case. Like the first, I placed it in the built-in cupboard behind the moth-proof chest where we kept our winter clothes during the summer. It was a large trunk, but looked in no way conspicuous; every European household possessed several of them, since no one lived in Shanghai for good.

One day, when I entered the room to serve the comrades their tea, they were handling revolvers; there were also weapons lying in the open trunk and spread out on the carpet. I noticed that neither Richard nor Paul welcomed my presence at this moment, but I was pleased all the same.

Not only bits of paper, but real weapons! So I was of greater use than I had realised. I had thought my work was too trivial and had already lodged a complaint about this.

The weapons may have been types that were of interest either to the Soviet Union (German generals were attached to Chiang Kai-shek's army as advisers) or, for that matter, to the Chinese Red Army itself, which was continuing to fight the government troops with some success. Perhaps the two Chinese comrades who were present on this occasion were learning how to take the weapons apart and reassemble them.

It must have been around this time – Micha was six months old – that the two cases were emptied and Richard advised me to prepare another suitcase – for me and the child. He told me that I might have to leave quite suddenly for the interior and go into hiding there with comrades.

Without asking questions, I packed nappies and Micha's little jackets and filled a bottle with sterilised water. I was glad that I was still breast-feeding, so that there would not be too sudden a change in Micha's diet; he was still underweight. There was no question of milk or milk powder being available outside China's big cities. The Chinese 'amah' who looked after Micha told me that she had breast-fed each of her four children for three years. She said some women were so poor, they sold their milk to rich mothers of infants and raised their own children on rice water. That was a comfort to me because I knew I would be able to get rice for Micha no matter where I had to go into hiding. I told the amah how badly I felt about mothers having to resort to such measures. She answered: 'Me savee, Missie inside much likee Chinese.'

I waited daily for news and did not dare leave the house for fear of missing the prearranged telephone call which might come at any time. I did not tell Rolf that I was worried about anything, besides, my anxiety was only relative, because such things threatened us all the time, and now that Richard knew of a specific danger and an opportunity to escape had been provided, the situation was no more precarious than before.

My departure did not materialise. A fortnight passed, the two cases were filled once again and the comrades resumed meetings. But from now on I held a third suitcase ready packed for Micha and myself.

It may seem imprudent to have stored information and weapons in the same place where illegal meetings were held. But the papers were required during the meetings and I only saw the weapons once. I imagine they did not remain in my house for long; on the other hand, they may have been in my cupboard for the entire two-and-a-half years.

The meetings were interrupted again when Richard asked me to hide a Chinese comrade whose life was in danger. This time I had to take Rolf into my confidence and his reaction was just as I had feared. He objected for the same reasons he had given before Micha was born: the risk for me and for Micha was too great. I told him that his attitude could cause the death of a comrade and for that I should never be able to forgive him. In the end he gave in, but it was clear to me that our marriage could not continue like this for much longer.

Later Rolf became a communist, proving his loyalty to the Soviet Union many times over.

The Chinese Richard had sent to me stayed in our house for about two weeks. He hardly spoke a word of English. When we had guests downstairs he lay on his bed upstairs for fear that his steps might be audible below. I forget what I told our amah and cook about our guest. Once he was actually living with us, Rolf was anxious to make our guest feel at home and was warm and friendly towards him, in so far as this was possible without a common language.

Even after he had left us, our house was closed to the group until his safety was assured. Given the methods of torture employed by the Chinese police, we had to reckon with the possibility that anyone in their custody might divulge an address.

On two occasions Richard gave me a manuscript to type. Once it was some confidential material collected by I.G. Farben about geographical and agrarian conditions in China, market possibilities, etc. The other, about 350 typewritten pages on economic conditions in China, was equally interesting. A German speaking Hungarian, Lajos Magyar, had written it. He was well known as a contributor to 'Inprecor'.

As I mentioned, Agnes had moved near us. On 17th October I wrote home that she was 'delighted with the furniture. The rooms are quite beautiful . . . and once again Rolf has proved himself as a first-rate architect.'

At this time I got to know Hozumi Ozaki, the journalist and writer who worked with Richard Sorge.[8] I saw him several times but cannot remember why and have nothing to add to the portrayal of him in the books about Richard. With him, too, I shared the close contact born of illegality. He had shown me photographs of his little daughter which he always carried on him. It was terrible, years later in 1944, to come across a newspaper picture of him and read of his execution in Japan.

By now I had forged many close links with the country in which I was living, and I suggested to Jürgen that he should visit China.

> Above all, I am convinced that you should get to know Asia. It broadens your horizons incredibly, and its economics and politics are tremendously interesting; I feel it is more relevant and important than America. Scientifically it is almost unexplored territory, with so much material to offer that one could achieve great things here, quite apart from all the human interest . . .
>
> China's street life is exciting: porters, flower sellers,

children, roadside stalls, open-air eating places, impossible to describe, but I am already quite sure that later, in Germany, I will be quite homesick for it. I think if you both came it would be *the* journey of your life.

Of course there were also things which I would never get accustomed to. After I had been in Shanghai for a year I went on holiday to the seaside at Beidaihe.

6th August, 1931

Beidaihe is a wonderful place. Mountain chains and blue sea. It really was time I got out of Shanghai. My weight has gone down to 8½ stone. It is not easy to live in China. I wonder what Marguerite would say if every few nights fat red centipedes, 15 cm long, crawled all over her white walls. Should she have the pleasure of one creeping over her, she would have to put up with a festering burning stripe for months, if not a year. They are almost impossible to kill and always return. They drive me crazy; Rolf crushes them with a hammer. Even the ants are four times the size of ours at home.

The poverty and filth in which the coolies live are as appalling as the self-important and overbearing attitudes of the Europeans. Corruption in China has no equal anywhere in the world. Chicago gangsterism and alcohol smuggling are but a weak reflection of what goes on here . . .

Han-sheng and his wife were planning to open a foreign language school at which I looked forward to teaching German.

To Jürgen:

30th September, 1931

. . . This is what happened: the professor and his wife were the driving force behind the language school, which opened after a great deal of careful preparation. It had been registered with the Education Department of the Chinese city administration. After only three days it was suddenly closed: no personal or political reasons; the administration officials just asked for a thousand dollars. Not an official payment,

> but a barefaced bribe. We don't know yet what we're going to do.
>
> Rolf's building contractor casually mentioned the case of a European detective who was supposed to 'uncover' the forbidden opium dens. There are 36 of them in Shanghai, and on his birthday this detective received a present of 30,000 Shanghai dollars from each of their owners . . .

I describe some of the Christmas gifts we received in 1931:

> A huge iced cake in the shape of a tower, a sixteen-pound ham, two live turkeys, 12 lbs sugar, 4 lbs good quality tea, a choice basket of wines, whiskies and liqueurs. All this as 'a little present' from Rolf's Chinese building contractor at the Shanghai Municipal Council. Another businessman, who has had hardly any contact with Rolf, gave us a cheque for 100 dollars on Shanghai's largest Department Store, Wing On. It is not considered dishonest to accept gifts like this in China or at the SMC: it is taken for granted!

In the same letter I also mentioned the death of my amah's husband. He had been a road sweeper.

> She has a twenty-four-year-old son who is unemployed. Rolf may be able to find him a job with the SMC. Her fifteen-year-old girl works at a shop where she picks wool for ten cents or sometimes up to ten cents five coppers a day . . .

Some of my happiest memories derive from those few occasions when our group did not meet as 'conspirators'. Once in 1932, we gathered in a hotel room: Grisha, Richard, Paul and our dark-eyed, dark-haired host, a vivacious man whom I had not seen before. I called him Fred as the others did. I have forgotten why we met, but I remember what a happy evening it was. Fred's hearty laughter was full of vitality. He had a beautiful voice, knew a great number of songs and was a pleasure to listen to. He was the life and soul of the evening.

Two days later Richard asked me to take some material to Fred. It was a cumbersome cardboard tube. Fred had a long talk with me. For some reason – perhaps because he showed so much interest and yet was a stranger – I began to tell him about my conflicts with Rolf and asked him whether we should separate on account of the work. Fred listened patiently and told me he felt honoured by my confidence. I cannot remember any advice that he may have given me. When I left, after three hours, I wondered whether the cardboard tube was a pretext and Fred was actually probing my suitability for the work.

Many years later I recognised him on a photo with the caption 'The Hero of Madrid'. It was Manfred Stern. Under the name of General Kléber he had won fame as commander, defender and hero of the Madrid battle front in 1936. In Germany he had fought in the March battles of 1921 and the Hamburg uprising of 1923. In China, in 1932, he was chief military adviser to the Central Committee of the Communist Party of China. He went to Spain as a high-ranking officer of the Red Army.

Then there was an excursion across the Huangpu river with Richard, Paul, Grisha, Sepp and Max. I wrote home about it:

27th October, 1932

The other day we went to Pudong, a factory quarter on the other side of the Huangpu river, opposite Shanghai. We visited the experimental settlement of the Chinese YMCA. They run a school there and have built about 30 houses for factory workers. The rent is four Marks a month (then about 4s). I asked how they chose their tenants. Of course they must be Christian and they must also earn between 40 and 60 Shanghai dollars (in 1932, about £3 or £4) a month. That is a high wage, so clearly only the worker aristocracy are admitted . . .

We also visited the clay huts of beggars, coolies and the unemployed. Huts is a euphemism for these holes. Some are made out of old tin cans. They have no windows or floors, a little stove for cooking food stands outside in the open air. I cannot describe what the people look like. Grown-ups walk around almost naked, in just a few rags. There are thousands of such hovels. Some families are lucky: their children find work in the nearby factory where they earn six dollars a

Human dwellings (above)

Huts is a euphemism for these holes (below)

> month. The huts belong to those who live in them, but two dollars a year 'ground rent' must be paid to the owner of the land, for the privilege of putting their 'houses' there. The incredible thing is that people stay alive at all. Right next-door there is a villa with a beautiful garden. Its Chinese owner was previously a supervisor of factory coolies who had carefully saved his pennies. Next to the big house is a smaller one where he used to live a few years ago. And now the big house is no longer good enough and he owns an even larger one in Shanghai. He has just married his fourth wife – a further sign of wealth.

It may have been unusual for comrades who worked illegally to meet for such a sight-seeing excursion like this, but it was not irresponsible. I have already explained that most Europeans knew each other.

On this excursion we went into the countryside and I can remember playing in a meadow. Paul played 'see-saws' with me; we stood back to back with our arms linked and tried to lift each other up. How I managed to heave our hefty Paul on to my back I cannot imagine. Richard's photo exists to this day, but unfortunately it only shows me being lifted by Paul. All that can be seen of him is part of an arm.

One of the nicest of these excursions with the comrades was with Agnes, and Arthur Ewert's wife Elise, known as Sabo. I was glad that Richard, after some hesitation, allowed me to join this unforgettable three-day houseboat trip with communists who also must have been illegal. None of us mentioned work. I remember Sabo especially well. Her experience as a comrade, her common sense and dry humour impressed me. I also met Arthur and Sabo once or twice in Shanghai. I admired Arthur's ardent character and his intelligence – but he lost his temper easily. When he got too worked up, Sabo would bring him down to earth again. They were one of those couples who belonged together, inseparably, for life. Both came from the working class and were communists from the days of their youth. I had heard Arthur's speeches as a member of the Reichstag and had read his articles in the press. Thirty years after our meeting in Shanghai, I learned that he had

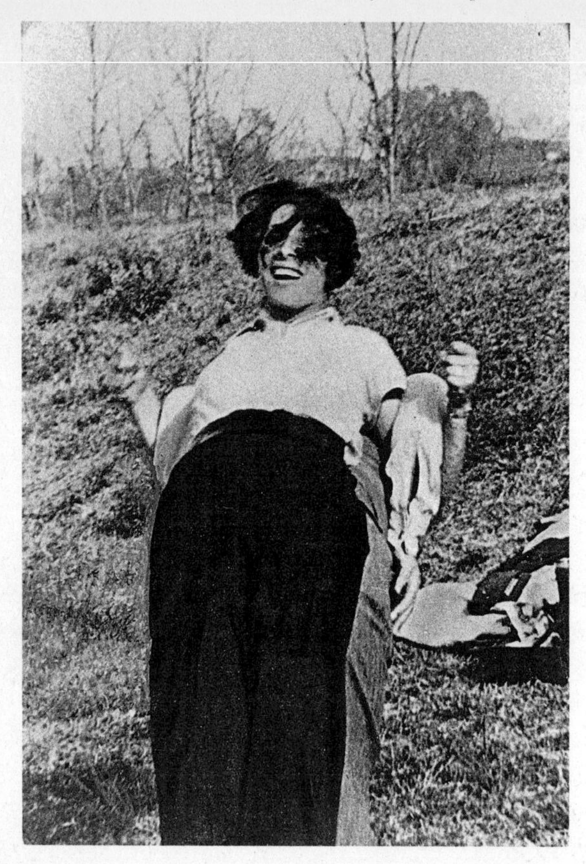

'See-saws'

been arrested for illegal work in Brazil and tortured to insanity. Sabo was, as always, with him in Brazil. She was deported to Nazi Germany where she was put into the Ravensbrück concentration camp and died while there. I wrote about Sabo's death and Arthur's fate in my book *Olga Benario*.[9]

Apart from our evening with General Kléber, the excursion across the Huangpu and the houseboat journey, I never met any comrades outside the course of our work unless they also frequented our house socially. I have vivid memories of our cheerful mood, but I forget what we talked about. I suppose it is not very important to recall how ably Sabo cooked for us all in the houseboat kitchen and how Agnes told us jokes, how General Kléber sang in a hotel bedroom or how I ran races round the meadow with Richard and Paul until we all collapsed into the grass from too much running and laughing.

I speak of great personalities and only report trivial details. But in my situation, these few hours of relaxation had a great effect on me; they were something quite rare and precious.

In September 1931, Japan attacked Chinese Manchuria. The terminology the Japanese employed to justify their aggression is only too familiar to us all: 'Japan is overpopulated and needs living space', and later on, 'Hitler's Germany must be protected against the common enemy – communism – and its breeding-ground, the USSR.'

From letters home:

> German newspapers seem to be saying very little about the political situation here, therefore a short report. The conflict between Japan and China dominates everything. You will have heard in outline that the Japanese army has occupied part of Manchuria, with Mukden as their capital . . . For the present it is a question of Japan's interest in Southern Manchuria. Soon Northern Manchuria will follow and that concerns the Soviet Union, co-owner of the East China railway. Whatever happens, Russia will want to avoid a war before completion of the Five Year Plan. She doesn't want war at all, but the Japanese advance towards her frontiers spells danger . . .
>
> . . . As for Southern Manchuria, Japan's ownership of the railway gave her strongholds there. The Chinese were quick to react. They built a parallel railway line which threatens to decrease their rival's income; they had success with the soya beans planted by millions of Chinese peasants who emigrated to Manchuria in recent years. The peasants are just as poor as when they arrived – a hoe, a clay hovel and clad in rags – while the Chinese government bought up their soya beans dirt cheap and made huge profits. Manchuria also possesses large reserves of iron ore and a considerable industry; in all, a richer country than you might think if you saw the parched earth and wretched clay huts. The Japanese invasion was

well-timed. The Chinese troops, money and generals had all been thrown against the communists and partly against the separatist Canton government.

... Anti-Japanese feeling is strong with all the Chinese. In Shanghai there is a total boycott of Japanese goods. The workers have all left the Japanese factories, Japanese building sites and Japanese shops. The Chinese government gives no support to the anti-Japanese movement. On the other hand, Chinese students are very active ...

... The eminently respectable Anti-Japan Committee summons people to meetings. Some tame speaker is to hold forth. Around 50,000 students and workers turn up, make impassioned demands for immediate action and shout down the speaker. Someone mounts the platform and makes a fiery speech which sounds suspiciously like the 'red bandits'. The Committee is horrified. Thousands of students occupy whole trains and travel to Nanjing where they challenge Chiang Kai-shek to put his cards on the table: they beat up Wang, the Foreign Minister, for not taking any action against Japan and they put forward strong radical demands ... Chiang Kai-shek responds with brutal counter-measures.

In Beidaihe, Mrs Bau, who is married to a Chinese Professor at Peking University, told me: 'My husband has so many difficulties teaching: half his students are in prison and only half of those are ever seen again; many of his pupils are beheaded. Serves them right too, I have heard that the communists drive nails through the hands of children from rich families to fasten them to their desks, and they pull wires through their ears' ...

... It can be assumed that Manchuria will go the way of Korea, i.e. that the Japanese will appoint a Manchurian as 'ruler' and then declare the country 'independent'. Translated into Japanese, this means it will be turned into a Japanese colony.

This prophesy came true. My other forecast, that Japan would intervene in Northern Manchuria, did not. The Western powers, who welcomed every step against the Soviet Union and communism, merely voiced a mild protest against Japan's aggression. The Soviet Union stood alone in delivering her sharp warning to Japan. She was fully aware of Japan's dream: to occupy Northern Manchuria and create trouble on the border with the USSR. The Soviet Union reinforced her troops and fortifications in the Far East, forcing Japan to alter her plans. At the end of January, Japanese forces attacked Shanghai. The soldiers of the 19th Chinese Route Army, who kept up their courageous struggle for weeks, were the only ones to fight actively against the Japanese. Chiang Kai-shek betrayed them and signed a truce granting major concessions to Japan.

The war in Shanghai overshadowed all other events for those who lived through it.

Outwardly, the Europeans lived in relative security and were not directly threatened by any military action. But this attack was such a clear and brutal lesson in the methods of capitalism that in many cases it acted as a catalyst. All those who were in any way touched by the maelstrom of the war came out of it as different people. I believe that this period contributed fundamentally to Rolf becoming a communist; it had a decisive influence on Walter as well. And again I shall quote from a letter – this time one from Rolf to his parents, which was quite unlike his previous reports home.

> 22nd February, 1932
>
> . . . Inwardly everyone is profoundly affected by what has happened. It is an outrageous and shocking thing to invade a weak country, and to plunder and burn the last possessions of its poorest people. What we are witnessing here is a military aggression conducted solely for economic interests, just as we used to read about in history books.
>
> . . . There are constant arguments, which often run high because the attitude of the foreigners is so detestable.
>
> This society, which will always support the side from which it hopes to derive the greatest profit, and betrays those on whose backs it has ridden to its affluence, deserves the worst.

One day, I believe, we shall arrive at a point where history will pass judgement on the world.

On 29th January, 1932, I wrote home:

> There is unrest in the Chinese parts of Shanghai . . . We can hear continual shooting, and barricades of timber and barbed wire have been erected at the end of every street. The Japanese are behaving atrociously and the 'neutral' Settlement too. The Council's International Volunteer Corps has actually designated a Japanese unit to guard the European Settlement at a particularly sensitive point. Needless to say these soldiers have been shooting into the Chinese city from there, while the Chinese dare not risk returning fire into the Settlement . . .
>
> Yesterday we climbed on to a roof and watched Chapei, the Chinese city, burning. Whole streets were engulfed in huge flames. The North Station has been burnt down, as has the Commercial Press, the largest printing works in China and one of the largest in the world. What is most vicious about the Japanese attack is that they began the fighting two hours after the Mayor of Shanghai had fully complied with the conditions of their ultimatum.
>
> 2nd February, 1932
>
> This letter is still here. There was no point in posting it since nothing can leave the city. The Settlement is in a state of siege. After 10 o'clock at night no one is allowed on the streets. Our house is full of lodgers. The cook has brought his daughter and his wife's sister; then Amah turned up with three of her children, and all of them are sleeping here. People are still fleeing the Chinese city. They come in their thousands, on foot, on carts, in rickshaws, in cars – women and children, bundles and blankets. Many sit helplessly in the streets. Empty houses are overflowing with refugees.

During this period seven relations of Amah and Cook were living with us. We had a letter from the English company that owned our house which was absolutely typical. It warned us that our

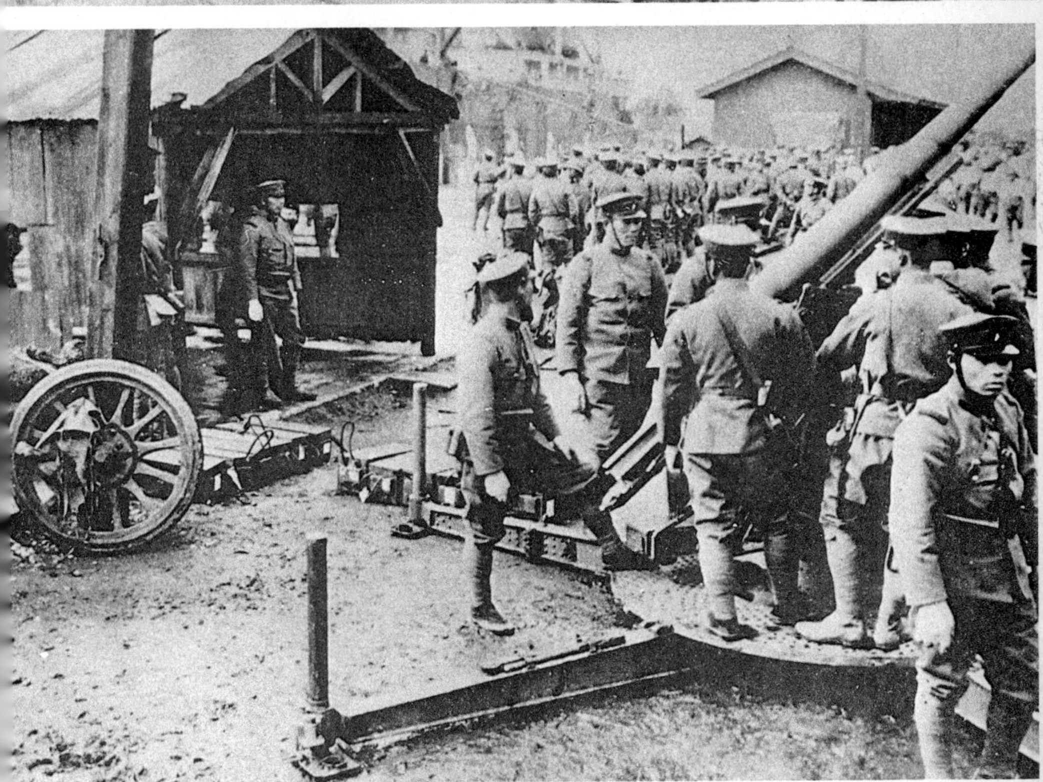

Shanghai's 'Chinatown', Chapei, bombed by the Japanese (above)

Japanese soldiers in Chapei (below)

contract forbade letting the premises to Chinese; they had received a complaint that we had infringed the agreement.

The comrades' meetings at our house were not interrupted. During the day, the Chinese were all in the back yard. Nevertheless, Richard criticised me – I believe for the first time. My readiness to help the servants contrasted too starkly with the behaviour of other foreigners and was therefore conspicuous.

Our group was very busy during these weeks. Apart from all the military questions relating to Japan, Richard was interested in the Chinese part of Shanghai and in Honkew, the Japanese quarter. He wanted to know the mood of the Chinese population, the views of the Europeans, the morale of the 19th Route Army, its composition, its attitude to the Japanese, and to the Chinese Red Army against whom they had previously fought.

My letters reflect the impressions I gained at the time.

2nd February, 1932

... We received word that a Chinese friend of ours who lived in the Japanese quarter had been arrested, and went to search for him. This part of the town looks ghastly. Whole streets are empty except for a few corpses and the only sound to be heard in the deathly hush is the rumbling of heavily armoured Japanese military vehicles. Most of the windows are smashed and doors have been broken down.

Fortunately Isa and I had a Japanese visiting card as a credential. All the guards let us through. Our friend lived with his brother-in-law, a dentist, whom we found at the house, but he could not give us much hope. Chinese who came from areas where there was sniping, were shot out of hand. He told us that when he heard soldiers in his house he had hidden in a large basket upstairs, together with his nine-year-old son. Apparently our friend had thought that if anyone tried to hide, they would be still more suspicious. This friend, an intelligent young man who had studied in America and was well-read, probably owned books on Russia. When the dentist finally ventured downstairs, the desk had been ransacked and our friend was gone.

I had visited the Japanese quarter at Richard's request. The visiting card mentioned in the letter to my mother belonged to Hozumi Ozaki, whom Isa also knew. And Lao, our missing friend, had been a regular customer at her bookshop. Richard agreed that we should go together on this not undangerous mission, which was best undertaken by women.

8th February, 1932

We've got so accustomed to the shooting that we hardly notice it. Two of our Chinese friends are missing. Yesterday when searching for them, I went to see 117 prisoners whom the Japanese had handed over to the British. They are the only Chinese still alive after passing through Japanese hands. The British discovered this group and rescued them. Their condition is terrible. Most of them were arrested in their houses or picked up from the streets – harmless civilians, workers, coolies and students. Their hands were tied behind their backs, for several days without break, while they were in custody. They have wounds from beatings and bayonet stabs. One of them was kept awake forcibly throughout four days and nights. Enough of war. The Japanese are probably not even particularly cruel; the Chinese treat their communists in exactly the same way. And as for the 1914–18 War – oh well, I'd better stop.

Rolf, through the Shanghai Municipal Council, had managed to get me the permit to visit the police station and refugee camp.

13th February, 1932

Yesterday was Micha's birthday. Amah and Cook had got together and bought the one-year-old a little suit and a pair of shoes. Blouse and trousers of bright orange silk with a pink tie. He looked terribly funny in it. I hoped he would wet himself before the guests arrived, so that we could change him into his normal blue outfit. But for fear of this Amah put the poor child on the potty every fifteen minutes.

Micha is now 71cm long and knocks the ends of his crib with his head and feet. I haven't bought him a bed yet because the refugees have the one spare room and so I still have Micha with me (secretly I am pleased about this delay).

In the evening there was so much gunfire that we could not sleep . . .

20th February, 1932

The fighting continues. The Chinese 19th Army is surprisingly stubborn and courageous. It fights with almost no support from the government which could have won the battle against the Japanese long ago. Unfortunately it doesn't want to, and especially not Chiang Kai-shek. One positive result is that for the first time the Chinese masses are united, and united against Chiang Kai-shek. Even the simplest of them have now grasped what this man really stands for. I won't write too much about all this since the German reporters here – Bosshardt for Ullstein and Dr Vogel for the Munich, Hamburg and Cologne papers, whom I met the other day – seem to send home detailed reports.

And all this is officially still called a 'truce'. The Japanese methods can be judged by the following: Chinese soldiers, about two to four thousand dead. Chinese civilians, around ten thousand dead. Refugees from the Chinese part of the city, over 600,000. The factories in the Chinese quarter, Chapei, are of course at a standstill. In addition, the closure of the Japanese factories in Shanghai resulted in 300,000 Chinese workers losing their jobs in just one day. There is no support for them of any kind. The mass poverty is terrible. And what is being done about it? The European Volunteer Corps has been withdrawn from the Settlement borders and replaced by regular troops because the volunteers are now to protect the interior of the foreign Settlement from possible troublemaking by the Chinese refugees and workers. The refugees who lived with us left for their homes a few days ago, but all seven have returned. Japanese soldiers are prowling everywhere. I do not really want to describe how they go about their killing, and much else that I have heard from reliable sources.

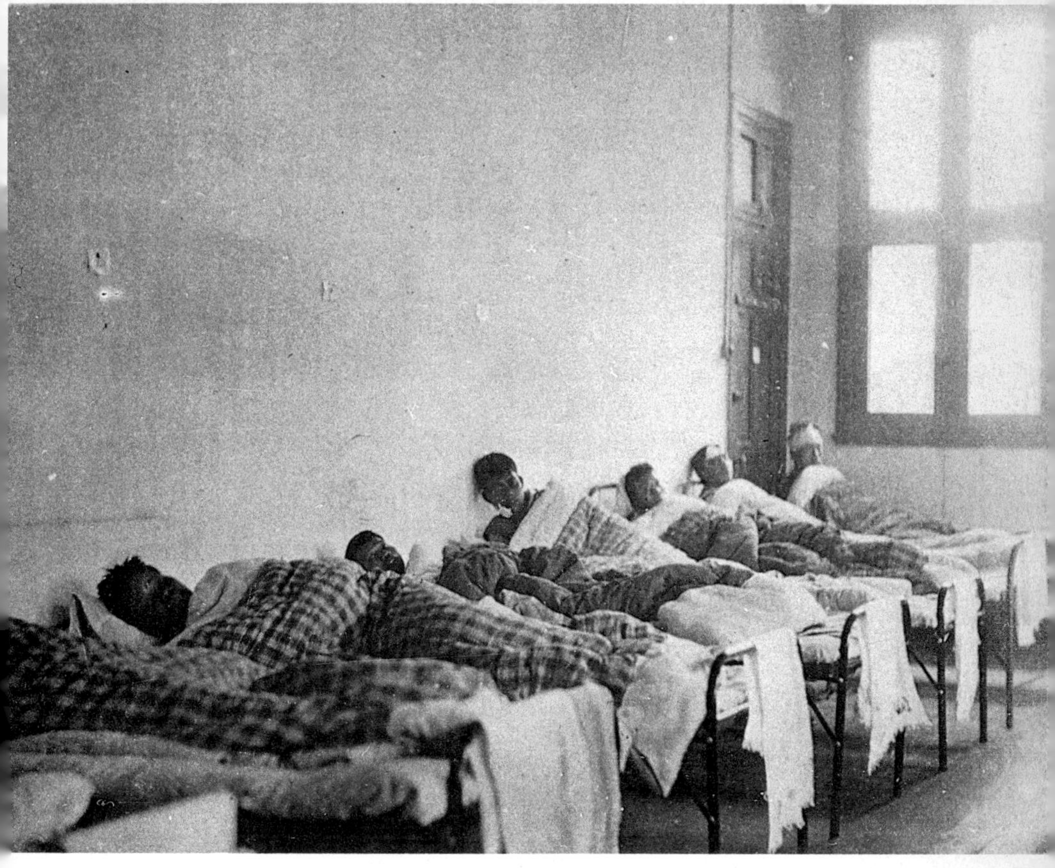

Wounded Chinese soldiers, 1932

Soon an opportunity arose to make contact with the Chinese 19th Army. In the name of charity, it was possible to visit wounded soldiers in the hospitals. Han came along as my interpreter.

Our mission held no great risks, but it was difficult to gauge how far I could go in my questions without our warm and rapid contact with the soldiers being noticed by the nurses and the Chinese welfare ladies. After two visits, Richard thought it best for us to stop going to the hospital.

My questions concerned the mood of the soldiers, their social background, their reasons for joining the army, their impressions of the Red Army and of the Japanese army in Shanghai, and what motivated them personally to fight so bravely. I spoke at length with seven or eight of the less badly wounded. Richard was amazed that I managed to have such open conversations. Normally it was not easy to gain access to the army. China did not offer anything like the same facilities for collecting information as a European country: there was 96 per cent illiteracy and little published material.

I was also able to give Richard an accurate picture of the mood among the Europeans, for the invasion had become the chief topic of conversation. Walter now played a considerable role in my reports to Richard. I was pleased that in the course of our long discussions, Walter was agreeing with me more and more. The political events which radically affected so many people's ideas left their biggest mark on him.

Walter was one of the leading European businessmen in Shanghai, and had connections with Chinese business people and the Nanjing government; he travelled a great deal to different parts of China. I was aware of the importance his co-operation could have for us. The day came when I told Richard that I should like to win Walter to work for us. Of course I could not predict his reaction, but if he said no, I would only have risked his discovering that I was politically active. He would keep this to himself and not respect me the less for it, of that I was sure. Richard agreed.

Inwardly tense, I spoke to Walter, tacking cautiously around the subject before coming to the point. And then I told him only that it was a question of support for Chinese communists; all the rest was left to Richard.

Walter agreed to co-operate. I arranged the first meeting with Richard, who told me afterwards that the conversation had been constructive and very interesting. From that point on I no longer had any part in their association. I believe that Walter was very useful to Richard; they kept in contact for many years. My impression was that Richard's personality fascinated Walter and riveted him to our work. Later he broke connections, without turning against us or harming anyone. The last time I saw him was in May 1936. He died a few years ago.

The situation in China gradually calmed down. I wrote to my brother on 11th April, 1932: 'At the moment Japan is keeping quiet, but we expect things to flare up again. Nobody thinks the peace can last. Next time it will probably be outside Shanghai.'

The assessment proved true. In fact, Japan's belligerent incursion into Chinese territory continued more or less unpunished for six years until, in 1937, the Chinese finally succeeded in creating a united anti-Japanese front. It included everyone from the communists to Chiang Kai-shek; even he had to give way in the end to the will of the entire people. The united resistance brought Japan's offensive to a halt.

In Shanghai, conditions for foreigners returned to normal in April 1932. The indigenous poor were left with their gutted houses, millions of unemployed and – their dead.

From a letter to my parents:

> . . . we both find these awful conditions extremely harrowing. The dirt, poverty and misery defy your imagination. And it is not something you can ever get used to. The other day I found a dead baby in the street. Its nappies were still wet . . .

Our trips inland were still an important part of my life in China, and the best way to relax. We could not get very far on Rolf's rare free days, but 'inland' began quite near Shanghai.

Letter to my parents:

> Easter was wonderful. We spent it, appropriately enough, in a religious atmosphere – a buddhist monastery. We left Shanghai on Thursday afternoon by steamer for Mingpu (see map of China). Arrived there eight o'clock Friday morning. South of Mingpu is a temple called 'Son of Heaven', which you can get to in a small motorboat. The two-and-a-half-hour trip is great fun, especially the mode of transport – a little tug-boat. First class is the motor boat itself, where we lay on the roof throughout the journey. Second class is relegated to five rowing boats with dome-shaped bamboo roofs, which are towed along behind, all full of lively Chinese . . . In one of these boats there was a singer with drum and gong, who escorted us on our journey with long ballads. Near

where he was sitting everyone listened without a murmur and showered him with copper coins.

The temple is situated in glorious surroundings. Behind the first temple is a carp pond, behind that two goldfish ponds. Rice is spread out to dry on the wide stone courtyards and the monks turn it with bamboo rakes. We slept in Chinese beds and ate Chinese food. The beds are very wide, with four poles at the corners to hold up mosquito nets, and straw mats for mattresses. The food is buddhist. The monks keep asking why I speak Chinese but not Rolf. They simply cannot understand how a woman can be better at something than a man. But suddenly Rolf rises in their esteem by sketching the temple and two of the monks, to the wonder of all concerned.

At Whitsun I went on a longer excursion with Walter and Erich Landauer. Rolf, generous and good-hearted as always, was pleased for me whenever I had a chance to get out of Shanghai, even if he could not come himself.

Erich Landauer, a young chemist and nephew of Gustav Landauer, had come to China. His uncle had been a member of the short-lived revolutionary government of Bavaria in 1919, and was murdered on 2nd May of that year. I wrote home about Erich: 'He is the sort of person you miss so much out here: stimulating, intelligent, witty and a scientist.' Erich had left-wing views and I hoped to win him for our work, but he married a petty bourgeois Chinese and was greatly influenced by her, so I did not try.

19th May, 1932

The trip was delightful. Left Saturday noon – six hours by train to Nangchinchia, a small station beyond Hangzhou. We stayed at a nice Chinese Hotel . . .

The next day was my birthday. First thing in the morning, the hotel boy brought me a whole sheaf of telegrams, which I soon recognised as Walter's forgeries. Later we took a ferry to the other side of the river. From there the train goes to Lanchi, a ten-hour journey through beautiful countryside. Our good friend Bernstein (of Orenstein and Koppel) built this narrow-gauge railway for the Chinese and it is his pride and joy. Most of the time we sat on the open platform

Terraced rice fields

outside the carriage, dangling our legs. We decided not to run alongside lest the little train 'lose face'. The line runs through terraced rice fields. Here and there you see skittle-shaped gravemounds and beautiful old trees planted to honour the dead. These trees have a practical use as well. When the winter barley has been harvested, there is no room to dry it out on the flooded ricefields. It is tied together in small bundles and hung from the trees, which look as if they are wearing yellow coats. Green mountains tower beyond the rice fields . . .

Lanchi lies on the river Tentang . . . Bernstein had given us a letter of introduction to the Mayor of Lanchi, whom we visited on the evening of our arrival. The next day we were to begin our boat trip down river, and the Mayor could not be dissuaded from assigning two of his policemen to accompany us for protection. And sure enough, later at night,

Winter barley hung from trees to dry

when we were already in our beds, the police chief of Lanchi appeared with two of his men and it took us considerable effort to get rid of them. Next morning we hired a junk and set out in excellent spirits on our river journey, the most beautiful I have experienced in China to date. With the current in their favour, the oars of the three-man crew moved us swiftly forward. These boats have curved bamboo roofs in three separate sections, so that you can make them bigger or smaller, as required. During the morning we stopped to swim; heaven for me to be in the water again at long last. In the afternoon we stopped in the wilderness to climb a bewitching mountain. This southern area is fertile. We soon lost our way, or rather there was no way to follow, and we battled on against boulders, thorns and sharp grasses. After

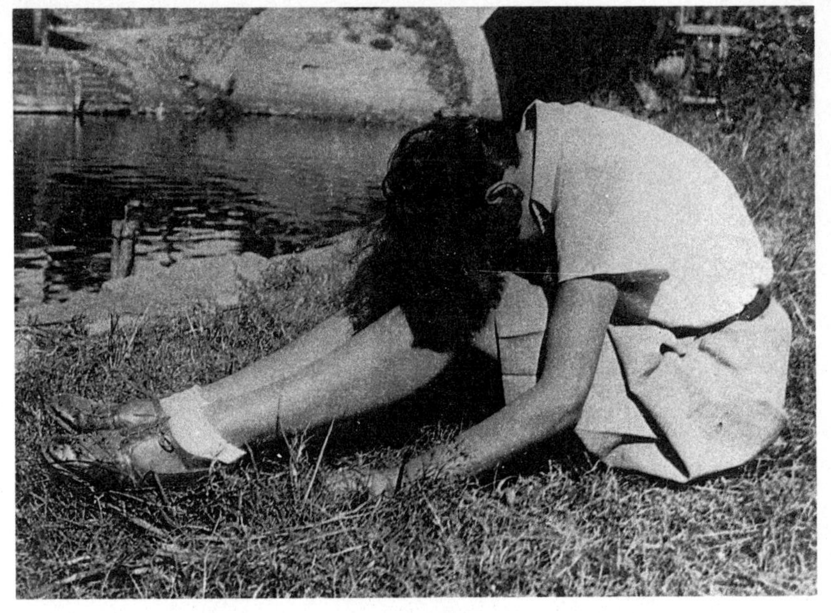

After the hike

two hours we had to give up. We were still a long way from the top, but we came to a spot where we were rewarded by a glorious view of the river and the surrounding mountains. Erich, who has a special feeling for animals, plants and rocks, was enraptured by beautiful black and yellow striped centipedes (I less so!), by butterflies and tropical flora. We made our way down again, scratched and bruised, knowing we had been the first Europeans on this mountain. It was the sort of endurance test I love.

The crew cooked our evening meal. We had decided to go to bed straight away, that is to spread our blankets on the bare boards under the bamboo roof . . . The moon came out, the oarsmen were singing softly, the mountains grew higher and higher. Sleep was forgotten, it was too beautiful . . .

In the same letter I had written: 'Last Sunday, like the week before, Kisch and Agnes came to see us.' Egon Erwin Kisch was known as a Czech-German journalist. His first book, *Der rasende Reporter* ('Reporter on the Rampage') was already famous for its

Our boat, at dusk on the Tentang river

biting social comment and quick-wittedness. Reports from many countries of the world followed.

I had already mentioned in an earlier letter that Egon Erwin Kisch had come to supper and stayed until two in the morning. I also intimated that we had quarrelled and I had told him he was conceited. We did not hear from each other for three weeks, but then we made our peace and I wrote home to say how interesting and stimulating I found him.

4th May, 1932

. . . We are on good terms now. He phones: 'Yes, my child, this is your good old Uncle Kisch. I'd like to come and see you on Sunday.' Last time he visited us, Kisch was tired and went to sleep on a bamboo camp-bed, tie-less and with rolled-up sleeves. We took a snapshot; I hope it comes out well. We shall then send it to him with the caption 'Reporter on the rampage'. He is leaving Shanghai in the morning for Peking.

Kisch was very enthusiastic about the F. article 'In Japanese Hands', but doesn't know who wrote it.

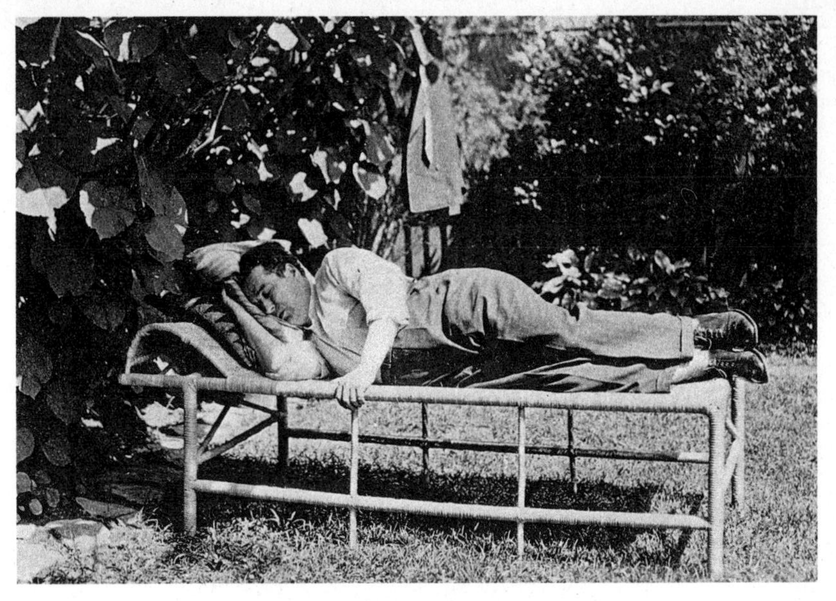

'Reporter not *on the rampage'*

It was an article I had written for the *Red Flag* under a pseudonym in April 1932.

I had a high regard for Kisch as a writer. The reason I had reservations was that I knew he was only going to stay for three months, and then write a book on China. Agnes and I were annoyed at what seemed to us a superficial approach. How could anyone imagine he would even begin to know this country in such a short time. We were quite unaware of the amazing way Kisch worked. He prepared himself thoroughly, possessed a talent for grasping essentials quickly and never left anything unchecked.

In the summer of 1932, Agnes and I planned to spend the hottest period in Kuling, 1,200 metres above sea-level in Jiangxi Province. Agnes went ahead and rented a bungalow for us. Originally Soong Ching-Ling wanted to come too. I had known her for some while by then. She was the widow of the progressive Chinese President, Sun Yat Sen. After his death she had moved even further to the left politically. At that time Soong Ching-Ling recognised the importance of co-operating with the Soviet Union. Sometimes I

Feuilleton der Roten Fahne

Nummer 88 3. Beilage
Sonntag, 24. April 1932

In japanischen Händen / Bericht aus Schanghai von A. Z.

Den Kampf zwischen den imperialistischen Ländern Japan und China, den die Japaner mit Unterstützung der fremden Mächte in Schanghai begonnen haben, müssen chinesische Arbeiter und Kulis, chinesische Frauen und ihre kleinen Kinder mit ihrem Blute bezahlen.

Die Grausamkeit der Japaner richtet sich hauptsächlich gegen unschuldige chinesische Zivilbevölkerung. Da die Nankingregierung den Kampf gegen Japans Einfall nur schwach führte, half das chinesische Volk sich selbst. Viele in Schanghai schossen aus ihren Häusern zurück auf die angreifenden japanischen Truppen. Dies veranlaßte die Japaner ein Blutbad anzurichten; für jeden, der geschossen hatte, wurden hunderte Unschuldige hingerichtet. Ganze Stadtteile mit dichter Arbeiterbevölkerung zündeten die japanischen Fliegerbomben an. Kulis und ihre Frauen und Kinder verbrannten, wurden gefangengenommen und hingerichtet, Hunderttausenden gelang es zu fliehen. Chinesische Studenten, die zum großen Teil Revolutionäre sind, wurden von den Japanern unter der Parole „Kommunist" in ihren eigenen Häusern erschlagen.

Wir standen auf einem hohen Dach — gegenüber der brennenden Chinesenstadt — und blickten hinunter auf den endlosen Strom der Flüchtlinge aus dieser Gegend. Da kam Chang außer sich vor Erregung, die Treppe heraufgestürzt. Chang ist ein kleines braves Männchen, ein Doktor für Augen, Nase und Ohren und ein Christ. Sein Bruder Ju-sen ist unser Freund. Ju-sen ist groß und so unglaublich schlank, wie man es nur bei Chinesen findet. Er hat in Amerika studiert, er war lange in Moskau — er übersetzt jetzt revolutionäre Bücher aus dem Englischen ins Chinesische. Viel Geld hat er nicht und von dem Geld, das er hat, kauft er sich Bücher. Das letzte, was er mir gezeigt hat, war ein Buch über die roten Dörfer Rußlands, für dessen Erwerb er lange gespart hatte.

Ju-sen ist von den Japanern erschossen worden!

Chang erzählt. Zuerst hat man ihn selbst verhaftet. In der Straße, wo er mit Ju-sen zusammen wohnt, hat ein Chinese auf die Japaner geschossen, und Chang, der sich auf der Straße befand, wurde sofort mit seinem neunjährigen Söhnchen zusammen verhaftet. Man führte ihn mit vielen anderen zusammen ab, man zog ihn völlig aus und durchsuchte ihn nach Waffen. Natürlich hatte er keine bei sich, aber plötzlich entdeckte ein findiger Japaner eine Nummer auf der Innenseite von Changs Hut. Nun war alles klar. „Eine kommunistische Geheimnummer — jetzt bist du des Todes", waren die Begleitworte des japanischen Entdeckers. Chang in höchster Not flehte um Gnade — in dieser Minute erschien ein japanischer Nachbar Changs, der ihn als gutbürgerlichen Doktor kannte, und man ließ ihn frei. Die Hutnummer war die Hausnummer Changs, die ein Hutreinigungsgeschäft mal eingeschrieben hatte.

Chang eilte nach Hause und beschwor Ju-sen, alle roten Bücher zu verbrennen. Ju-sen überlegte. Er hat das Buch noch nicht einmal gelesen, er hat lange dafür gespart, es zu kaufen — er nimmt das Buch in die Hand, da hört er Schritte, japanische Soldaten erbrechen die Tür mit Kolben und betreten das Zimmer. Chang ist auf den Boden gelaufen und hat sich in einem Wäschekorb versteckt. Ju-sen bleibt aufrecht mitten im Zimmer stehen — er haßt die Japaner, diese imperialistischen Räuber, aber er hat nicht auf sie geschossen.

Diese Soldaten sind auch nur Kulis ihrer Regierung, viele darunter sind Arbeiter — er sieht sie ruhig an — das ist das letzte, was wir über Ju-sen hören.

Die Soldaten verließen das Haus, Chang kroch aus seinem Korb und lief herunter. Ju-sen war verschwunden und sein Schreibtisch mit den Büchern durchwühlt.

Das hat sich alles erst gestern abgespielt, vielleicht lebt er noch, vielleicht ist er nur gefangen. Er spricht fließend englisch, er ist flink und intelligent, bei einem Verhör wird er geschickt zu reden verstehen, aber er ist stolz und wird nie verleugnen, daß er ein Revolutionär ist.

Wir müssen versuchen ihn zu retten. Vielleicht kann ein japanischer Freund uns helfen. Wir durchqueren das gestrige Kampfgebiet. Es ist heller Sonnenschein — die Straßen wirken unheimlich geisterhaft, sie sind völlig tot. Niemand, außer den schwerbewaffneten japanischen Soldaten, an allen Straßenecken, lebt hier; was nicht gefangengenommen und getötet wurde, ist geflohen. Jedes Haus hat Wunden: Schüsse in die Fensterscheiben, Glassplitter — aufgebrochene Türen. Immer wieder werden wir von Japanern durchsucht und argwöhnisch betrachtet — die einzigen Menschen in den toten Straßen. Wir finden unseren Freund mit der Binde der japanischen Bürgerwehr am Arm als Wachposten an einer Ecke. Er spricht leise zu uns, und der Hoffnungsschimmer erlischt. Jeder Schuß Gefangener wird sofort erschossen. — Nein — nicht sofort. Erst werden sie ein paar Stunden gequält und gefoltert. Untersuchungen und Nachforschungen werden überhaupt nicht angestellt.

Jeder Tag bringt neue Notizen in den Zeitungen. „160 chinesische Kulis und Studenten verhaftet, 120 verhaftet — 60 verhaftet."

Heute eine Nachricht, daß in einem japanischen Klub 117 chinesische Gefangene entdeckt wurden, die nach längeren Verhandlungen an die europäische Settlement-Polizei ausgeliefert wurden. Diese Gefangenen sind die einzigen, die lebend aus der Gewalt der Japaner entkommen sind. Da sie ausnahmsweise nicht von der weißen Polizei geschlagen wurden, gab man ihnen auf Tage Asylrecht, um zu zeigen, wie die Opfer der gelben Imperialisten zugerichtet sind.

In der Hoffnung, daß Ju-sen unter ihnen sei, ging ich zur Polizeistation. Ich fand ihn nicht, es waren alles Kulis und Arbeiter. Ich sah die Gefangenen 24 Stunden nach ihrer Einlieferung. Da waren sie noch im Zustand äußerster Erschöpfung. Ein Teil wurde gleich mit schweren Wunden ins Krankenhaus geschafft. Man sah also nur die „leichteren Fälle". Rechts lagen

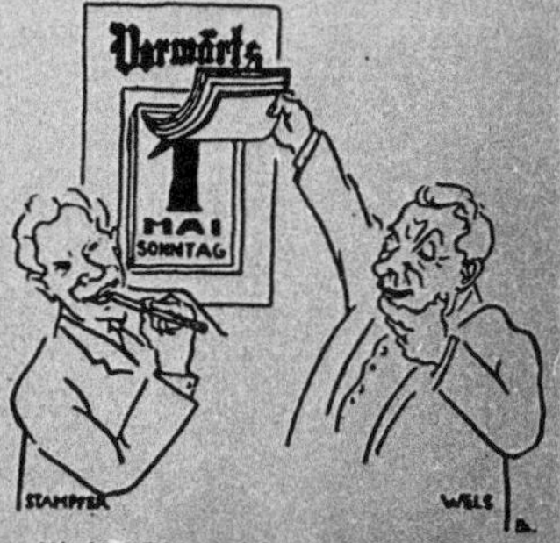

Wels: Dieses Jahr könnten wir eigentlich wieder mal die Parole „Arbeitsruhe" ausgeben.

auf dem Steinfußboden, in graue Decken gehüllt, die mit den Kopfwunden. Der erste in der Reihe war völlig blauschwarz im Gesicht. Man hatte ihn so geschlagen, daß die eine Gesichtshälfte unförmig aufgequollen war; die Augen konnte er nicht öffnen, die Lider waren schwärzliche geschwollene Deckel. Neben ihm lag einer mit verbundenem Gesicht. Die meisten schliefen unruhig stöhnend. Einer lag wie tot in der Ecke, er war während der Einlieferung zusammengesunken und noch nicht wieder aufgewacht. Das einzige, was er hervorgebracht hatte, war, daß die Japaner ihn vier Tage und vier Nächte lang gewaltsam wach gehalten hatten. Die meisten waren vier Tage in Haft gewesen. Während dieser Zeit erhielten sie nichts zu essen, und niemand löste ihnen die auf dem Rücken gefesselten Hände. Bei der Einlieferung in die europäische Polizeistation hatten alle geschwollene Gelenke. Von 117 Mann waren 97 nicht fähig, ihre Teetassen in den Händen zu halten.

Der Ausdruck der Gesichter war vollkommen verstört. Vor ein paar Tagen waren sie noch zu Hause gewesen. Einer reinigte seine Stube, ein anderer kochte in der Herdecke, das Mehl noch an den Händen riß man ihm fort und band ihn zusammen mit anderen entsetzten Kulis. Die Japaner sprachen unverständliches Zeug. Einer konnte es ihnen übersetzen — sie sollten von Dächern auf die Japaner geschossen haben — sie wurden geschlagen, gequält und mußten hungern. Als die Europäer sie abtransportierten, seufzten sie erleichtert auf, endlich wurden sie nicht mehr gequält, nun würden sie wohl erschossen werden. Auf Rettung hoffte niemand.

Ein Junge war dabei, auch ihn hatte man gefoltert, aber von den fremden Weißen, von denen er viel Böses wußte, wollte er sich nicht erschießen lassen, er riß sich los und sprang in den eisigen Fluß. Man rettete ihn — er liegt abseits im Saal in graue Fetzen gehüllt und blickt fiebernd um sich. Unter den Schwerverletzten im Hospital ist einer bereits an seinen Wunden gestorben. Ein junger Diener eines europäischen Hotels. Man mißhandelte ihn besonders schlimm, weil er eine Uniform trug — die Uniform seines Hotels!

Beim Betreten des Saales folgte uns ein großer dicker Polizist mit einem grauen Lappen und einem Eimer Wasser. Das Zimmer sollte wohl aufgewaschen werden. — Ich drehte mich um, und da saß in der Ecke auf dem Fußboden gegen die weiße Wand gelehnt ein winziges Chinesenkind. Es hatte feingebürstete schwarze Haare und kugelrunde dunkle Augen. Es lutschte am Daumen und war ängstlich und blaß. Ein 18 Monate altes Baby, dessen Vater von Japanern erschossen worden war. Als er mit dem Kind auf dem Arm durch die Straßen floh, traf ihn ein Bauchschuß tödlich und verletzte das Söhnchen am Fuß. Die chinesischen Polizisten der Station adoptierten den Kleinen. Als ich auf ihn zutrat, kniete der Polizist mit dem Aufwascheimer vor dem winzigen Menschlein und wusch ihm mit dem grauen Tuche die Ohren.

Vor der Eingangstür begegnet mir eine chinesische Frau. Ihr Gesicht ist unbeweglich. Sie fragt, ob sie die Gefangenen sehen darf, sie vermißt ihre drei Söhne, 13, 15 und 22 Jahre alt. In ihrem Wohnviertel brach plötzlich eine Panik aus. Sie rannte mit ihrer Familie die Straße entlang: Schießen, japanische Soldaten kommen, Menschen fallen um — sie findet ihre Söhne nicht mehr. Aber tot sind sie nicht. Das darf sie gar nicht denken, dann würde sie selbst sofort umfallen — seit acht Tagen geht sie ununterbrochen durch alle Flüchtlingslager der Stadt, ihre Söhne zu suchen, treppauf treppab läuft sie und sieht vielen tausend Vertriebenen ins Gesicht. Die Schlafenden dreht sie um, in dunkle Ecken leuchtet sie mit Streichhölzern. Sie lernt bei jeder neuen Suche etwas zu über die Grausamkeit der Japaner, die, ohne von den weißen Räubern gehindert zu werden, gekommen sind, weil ihr Land schwach ist, die von ihrem Land ein großes Stück wegfressen wollen und die viel, viel Blut schlucken. Das Blut des arbeitenden chinesischen Volkes.

Frauen am Hakenkreuz

Die nationalsozialistische Bewegung gräbt ihr Frauenideal aus den modrigen Grüften der preußischen Wilhelminen. Sie ist sich mit dem Dulder von Doorn darin einig, daß für die „deutschbewußte" Frau die drei Ks. zu gelten haben; Kirche, Küche, Kinder.

Fügen wir dazu den Gretchenzopf und den Strickstrumpf, so hat der SA.-Ehemann alles, was sein Herz begehrt.

Goebbels, der es wissen muß, hat dieser Tage wieder in einer Versammlung bestätigt, daß die oberste Tugend der arischen Frau die Bedürfnislosigkeit ist.

„Jammert nicht: Es geht uns schlecht! Die alten germanischen Frauen haben auch von Gerstenkaffee und Schwarzbrot gelebt, das könnt ihr nachlesen in den alten Familienchroniken."

Eine bemerkenswerte Geschichtsfälschung. In welcher alten Familienchronik hat Herr Goebbels das Bild einer alten germanischen Frau gesehen, die eine Kaffeemühle zwischen Knien hält und gebrannte Gerste mahlt?

Tacitus, der uns die Gebräuche der alten Germanen ausführlich geschildert hat, sagt nichts darüber, daß sich die Brunhilden an einem Schälchen Heeßen zu erquicken pflegten.

Nach dieser neckischen Bemerkung über das Kaffeestündchen auf dem Bärenfell wird das Programm der „nationalsozialistischen Frauenschaft" weiter entwickelt.

„Die Nationalsozialistinnen beabsichtigen keineswegs, die Frauen aus der politischen Tätigkeit auszuschließen, ihre Arbeit soll sich lediglich auf den naturgegebenen Anteil beschränken."

Welches dieser „naturgegebene Anteil" ist, wird gleich erläutert:

„Der Einfluß der Frau auf die Politik besteht in der Schaffung der rechten Atmosphäre des Hauses, richtet sich auf das Familienleben."

(„Männe, soll ich dir was verbinden? — Josephadolf hat seine Schularbeiten immer noch nicht gemacht!")

Der arische Vater streicht sich den Hängebart. Er greift langsam zum Stock, denn

„der Mann muß wieder Würde im Amt als Familienvater empfinden."

Der Bart ist wichtig. Er hat ihn sich zugelegt, weil — nach dem Programm —

„die Unterschiede zwischen den Geschlechtern vertieft werden sollen"

und weil,

„die NSDAP. die Gattenwahl nach dem Gesetz der Kraft und Schönheit im Sinne deutschvölkischer Merkmale"

fordert.

Dann werden die Tagesfragen besprochen. Die völkische Frau legt ihr Haushaltsbüchlein vor, denn

„wenn Frauen nicht zur Sparsamkeit erzogen werden, ziehen Not und Schulden bald in die Familien ein."

Und die Basis, auf der dieses kleinbürgerliche Ideal der Frau als Koch und Gebärmaschine ruht? —

„die Grundlage für all dies ist das Christentum Adolf Hitlers."

Unter heftigem Stricknadelklappern der versammelten Luisen sagte Joseph zum Schluß:

„Glauben Sie, Verstand allein macht nur wenig."

Warum so bescheiden, Herr Goebbels? Sie haben sich bei ihren politischen Geschäften bisher nicht vom Gefühl leiten lassen.

Die klassenbewußten Arbeiterfrauen bedanken sich für dieses Programm.

Sie haben keine Lust, als Dienstmädchen in der Sudelküche des Braunen Hauses angestellt zu werden.

Slang

Der Weltkrieg

hat begonnen! Wer schweigt, ist mitschuldig. Schriftsteller, macht mobil gegen den Krieg der Imperialisten!

Dokumente und Kurzberichte zum jetzigen Krieg

Internationaler Abend des Bundes proletarisch-revolutionärer Schriftsteller Deutschlands am Dienstag, dem 26. April, 20 Uhr, im Nationalhof, Bülowstraße 37.

Wahlresultate

werden am Sonntag im „Klub des graphischen Block, Enckestraße 4, verlängerte Charlottenstraße, bekanntgegeben.

My article in the Rote Fahne

called at her home with Agnes, but I also visited her on my own. She was a dainty, graceful woman. Her life was not easy. One of her sisters was married to Chiang Kai-shek, the other to his Minister of Finance. Her influential family had disowned her because of her political views. She once gave me a Chinese dress which I continued to wear for many years. Richard thought it would be unwise for me to be seen with her in public, and she did not come to Kuling after all.

I wrote to my parents about the journey and our stay in Kuling:

> July 1932
> The day before yesterday I arrived safely in Kuling, warmly welcomed by Agnes. The five-day journey up the Yangzi takes you through beautiful countryside, but it is depressing, because wherever you stop beggars paddle alongside in wash-tubs – refugees from last year's floods, and the Yangzi is already rising again this year. Houses are half under water and a lot of land has been swallowed up. The journey by road after the steamer trip was rather difficult. In pouring rain along sodden bumpy paths in an open rickshaw, followed by an hour in an ancient bone-shaking bus to the foot of the mountain. From there another three hours up steep paths in a swaying sedan chair. You begin by purchasing a ticket. After five minutes the coolies put down the chair complaining that the customer is too heavy, and demand a tip. You comply, otherwise you won't reach Kuling before dark. When it gets very steep they suddenly say that you have to walk, although there is a notice which expressly states that they must carry the passenger all the way. I get out and, with Micha in my arms, climb up part of the steep stony track to the top. The coolies follow, grinning.
>
> Things like this make many people complain about the Chinese. I get furious too, at times, but what can you expect from underpaid, over-worked coolies?
>
> On the boat I had occasion to meet missionaries of every type. Well, not exactly, since for the most part there is only one type – frightful! And their wives are even worse – particularly the Americans. Sweetly smiling dried-out scarecrows.

Some are better of course. One elderly woman went to Kuling for the first time in 1907. Her little girl could not take the heat of Hankou and the doctor said that only a cooler climate would help. She took the child into the mountains and, with the assistance of the Chinese there, built a house of stone and clay in three weeks. After a few days her child was running around healthy and cheerful. Said child is now accompanying her mother again, looking about 39 years old, very bony, wearing an impossible hat and a knitting bag over her arm.

To the parents:

5th July, 1932, Kuling

Agnes and I go for long walks every afternoon, with beautiful views down the Yangzi valley and towards the Hubei mountain ranges, where the reds are. Up here you can understand their tactics, because these mountains are also covered with dense jungle, and where mountains have no paths, enemy troops cannot get through. Only the local reds, i.e. the Red Army with help from local peasants, can find their way.

Unfortunately there are no forests here, only scrub-jungle. The Chinese peasant is too poor to wait for a tree to grow. He gathers the scrub, uproots the little trees and turns them into charcoal or brooms to sell. Only bamboo, which matures in six weeks, can survive in China.

27th July, 1932

Agnes, who came here five weeks ahead of me, has gone back to Shanghai. I sometimes go for walks with Dr Vogel from the German Chamber of Commerce, now staying here. Last week an excursion with him and Professor Othmer, who is *the* Chinese language specialist. We visited a temple, where he read and translated fluently all the inscriptions, including those in ancient script which even the Chinese cannot decipher. He is considered to be the leading foreign expert in Chinese dialects. Apart from that he is not exactly my cup of tea.

My letters home never betrayed that I was sometimes troubled too. Mother, with her six children, had enough problems to cope with, nor was it in my nature to pour out my heart to her. The last two weeks of my stay in Kuling I felt deeply depressed. Some time before, two European comrades, a married couple from Switzerland called Noulens-Ruegg, had been arrested. I did not know them personally but their fate disturbed us all. They were to be sentenced to death by the Chinese courts. Richard organised the money with which their death sentences were to be commuted into imprisonment.

The Noulens had a five-year-old son whom Agnes showered with presents after the arrest of his parents. I did not think it right to spoil him like some little prince and told her so. The question arose as to whether I could look after the boy, and I was eager to do so. I would try to give him the maternal affection he needed and Micha would have a big brother. But Richard would not agree. It meant giving up my illegal work and neither he nor I wanted that.

In Kuling we heard that the Noulens-Ruegg couple had begun a hunger strike. When we sat down to lunch that day, Agnes suddenly said that she couldn't eat. I told her – probably somewhat coolly – that this would not help the Noulens. Agnes got up and left the table. In the afternoon I went for a walk on my own. When I returned, I found a letter from her: she could not stay under these circumstances but would return to Shanghai; I was too preoccupied with my own personal happiness and my family; private matters played too great a role in my life; I did not after all have what it takes to make a real revolutionary.

I sat with this letter in my hands and could not grasp its meaning. There were two things that with the best will in the world I was unable to understand. Agnes surely knew me well enough to realise that I was ready to take any risk at all if there was a chance of helping the imprisoned parents. This was as certain as the fact that I might have to share their fate myself one day.

Did Agnes need me to tell her how much my thoughts went out to them and particularly to the mother of the five-year-old boy? Must I exhibit my emotions in order to prove them?

What shattered me was that such a close friendship could be

damaged like this. I brooded over it, trying to work out where Agnes had got those ideas about me. Perhaps she was right in some ways? I enjoyed life and could take enormous pleasure in the most everyday things. Did I perhaps attach too much importance to them? Every breath my son took was like magic to me, and I was determined to have more children, although I did not think my marriage would survive its present conflicts.

Agnes had once remarked sadly: 'I sacrificed my children to the struggle.'

True, I would not face prison as calmly as Agnes because of my bond with Micha, but was I therefore more likely to betray anyone?

I was constantly aware of the possibility that I might be arrested, and so I hardened myself physically to improve my resistance. I didn't smoke, or drink alcohol. That way I would not suffer if I were suddenly deprived of them.

This sudden break in a friendship which had played such a significant role in my life and, as I had believed, in Agnes's too, was a heavy blow.

Later, in Shanghai, we met again from time to time, she probably came to our house as well, but the old relationship was gone. I felt that Agnes had not altered her opinion of me and, uncompromising as she was, she acted accordingly.

Now the conversations with Richard became even more important to me. I looked forward to his visits and always had something to tell him. Only once did I mention the estrangement from Agnes. Richard seemed to regard it as a quarrel about some matter of special concern to women, and showed no desire to get involved. This meant a lot to me. If I had lost Richard's trust too, I do not know what would have become of me. People I valued could easily shake my self-confidence.

Isa and I still saw each other frequently.

Among our bourgeois guests we preferred Fritz Kuck, the teacher, because of his understanding for the Chinese people. After 1933, Kuck was one of the first to become a Nazi. In his case we found this particularly hard to understand. He had travelled widely, he read a great deal, and his horizon was broader than that of the average European in Shanghai. For a long time he was in love with a Chinese girl who was engaged to someone else.

One morning in mid-December of 1932, Grisha phoned: I was to come to his apartment that afternoon. Richard wanted to meet me there. I had hardly ever been to Grisha's home and, as I understood it, I was only to come if he phoned again. Later he told me we had agreed that he would only phone if the arrangement was changed. Anyway, there was a misunderstanding and I did not go – a misunderstanding which I could not overcome for a long time.

That evening we had guests, the sons of Professor Richard Wilhelm, a former missionary in China and later Director of the China Institute in Frankfurt am Main.

Professor Wilhelm died in 1930. One of his two sons was a sinologist like his father and lived for some time in Peking; the other, an architect, had an introduction to Rolf.

I wrote to my parents about this particular evening:

> 17th December, 1932
>
> . . . The Wilhelms were disappointing. The Peking Wilhelm is bearable; he is more lively, but a pure academic. A sinophile in the old style, he prefers the China of 3,000 years ago, and is not very interested in the China of today . . . He spoke at the East Asia Society about the China Institute. Then Kuck showed slides of his journeys to Shanxi and Gansu. I had invited them all to our house for supper, but they were tongue-tied and boring, except for Kuck, and it was something of a fiasco. The architect and his wife hardly opened their mouths, although since they had come from Germany so recently we were all burning with questions . . .

During dinner the telephone rang. The party was sitting at table in our hall where the stairs led up to the first floor. It was separated from the living room by a bamboo-patterned curtain. I went into the living-room. The telephone stood on the desk which fitted into an alcove. Next to the telephone stood a framed photograph of the Schlachtensee, its shores covered in hoarfrost.

I see it all as though it was yesterday – even the way the guests were seated around the table in the adjoining room.

I could not take it in, that Richard had gone

I lifted the receiver and Richard Sorge spoke: that afternoon he had waited two hours for me and phoned repeatedly but nobody had answered. He had wanted to say goodbye. I groped for the chair in front of the desk and sat down. Richard asked me whether I was still there. He wanted to thank me for always looking after him and the others so well. But this was only a beginning and much more lay ahead of me. I was to keep a stiff upper lip – I must promise him that. But now – all the best, the very best, and goodbye.

In the room next door the guests were waiting for me to come back. I looked at the chair in the corner and could not grasp that Richard had simply gone. Never again would he sit in this chair to talk to me, to listen to me, to advise me, to laugh with me.

What had I been thinking of? Had I only just realised how much he meant to me? If only I could have had ten minutes to pull myself together. But the stiff upper lip was already being called for. I went back. None of the guests noticed anything amiss.

In later years I would meet the other comrades again – Isa, Grisha, Max, Sepp – but not Richard.

For a long time I had planned to visit my family in Berlin in the spring of 1933, almost three years after leaving Germany. I looked forward to seeing my parents, my brother and sisters – and the familiar landscape around the lake where I had grown up. Moreover I was particularly keen to take Micha out of the damp climate of Shanghai; the doctor had advised a change of air for him.

But spring brought those terrible developments in Germany: on 30th January, 1933 Hitler came to power and the reign of terror began.

Having left in 1930, it was impossible for me to understand how the German working class could permit the fascists to take power. Anxiety about the fate of Germany and of my family weighed heavily upon us, but little of this was expressed in letters home.

> ... We are aghast at the developments in Germany ... The papers carry little about it but what they say is quite enough to banish everything else from our minds. Knowing that only some of what is happening finds its way into the press here, we were particularly glad to receive your telegram. A heavy heart robs one of words but we beg you to write as much as you feel able ...
>
> News of Germany is of course the first thing we look for when we open the papers. The swastika is fluttering over the Consulate here, alongside the 'black white and red'. We are lucky that Rolf's employers are English. Unemployed Germans of every profession arrive daily in Shanghai. By now Rolf must have had ten architects asking him for a job. Here too, the situation is getting more difficult all the time.

It soon became obvious that my projected journey would have to be 'postponed'.

In China there were political problems too.

19th February, 1933

The China-Japan conflict continues. It is expected that Japan will soon take the province of Jehol without resistance from the Chinese. The Chinese government is still not willing to deploy troops against Japan. They are continuing to use their soldiers to fight against the Red Armies, especially in Jiangxi. For the present, Japan will not advance against Tianjin or Peking. When and whether she will attempt war against Russia is difficult to say.

Whereas nine months ago Chiang Kai-shek and the Nanjing government were standing on shaky ground, they are now stabilised again. Chiang Kai-shek has had some success in his fight against the Reds which compensated for the credit he lost during the Japanese aggression against Shanghai. T. V. Soong, who is a gifted man, has not exactly straightened out the government finances, but at least he has saved them from total collapse. The leaders of the renegade southern powers and the Canton government have been weakened and some have fled abroad. The Nanjing government has made serious efforts to secure the Yangzi regions against floods by building dams, and this has won it an influence in this area that it did not enjoy before. Although I should not talk of the Nanjing government as if it were independent, as it takes its orders and its money from America . . .

21st May, 1933

There is no sign of an end to the war in the north . . . The Chinese southern cliques are drawing together and it is said they plan to march on Nanjing with Canton at their head, to overthrow the government. We have heard this kind of talk before. Whether it will really happen this time remains to be seen. The political cauldron is always on the boil here . . .

That apart, I am spending my time enjoying China. I get out of Shanghai as much as possible. There are such wonderful villages and gravemounds and temples; and the streets and the people! I think if I stayed here another few years I would be so completely absorbed that I would never want to

> leave. Especially at a time like this, it is a consolation to be in a country where you can feel at home. I wish I could bring you all here!

That was the last letter from Shanghai to be preserved, and my last letter home to Berlin-Schlachtensee, Terrassenstrasse 17.

3
Moscow and Manchuria, 1933–35

Richard must have reported fully to the Red Army Intelligence branch – 'Centre', we called it – when he went back to the Soviet Union. Anyhow, Paul and Grisha spoke to me about my future. They asked whether I would be prepared to go to Moscow for a training course of at least six months; my return to Shanghai might not necessarily follow.

The condition was that I must leave my two-year-old son somewhere else. I could not risk taking him to the Soviet Union with me as he was bound to learn Russian there.

This proposal came as a complete surprise and meant a decisive change in my life.

I accepted.

The thought of giving up my work and living 'normally' again would never have occurred to me, and a course of instruction would help me to do my work better. Every day I was witnessing Japan's acts of aggression; comrades from my homeland kept warning that Hitler meant war, and it was clear to me which country both these aggressors were likely to attack eventually. In the light of all these factors, my decision was quickly made.

These days it might seem improbable, or perhaps Utopian, that international events should have determined my private life in such a manner.

Let me answer with a question. Why, only three years later, did thousands of comrades go to Spain to fight fascism and war? And in the 1970s, how many young citizens of the GDR would willingly have set off for Vietnam, had the opportunity arisen?

To me, the work that I did – in whatever country – was my Spain, Vietnam, Chile.

I knew how painful I would find the separation from Micha, and where could he go for such a long time? My parents were unable to take him. As they were Jews and father had been active in left-wing organisations, his life was now in danger. Our home had been repeatedly searched by the Nazis. Mother was making preparations for the family to emigrate to England, and father had already secretly fled to London in the summer of 1933. Rolf's parents owned a weekend chalet on the Czech side of the Riesengebirge, the mountain range then forming the border between Czechoslovakia and German Silesia. They had helped father to cross the frontier, and from there he proceeded to London. They were also willing to take Micha, although they did not know my reasons for asking. I only needed to say that the change of climate would be good for him and that Rolf approved it as well for the sake of the child's health. It was quite usual for foreigners in China to send their wives and children on prolonged home leave to Europe, so it was a normal goodbye to Rolf.

Taking leave of my comrades in Shanghai was difficult: they were staying behind to face constant danger. However, I did not have to say goodbye to the large trunk that had lived behind the camphor chest in our bedroom for so long. It was to be filled with dispatches and accompany me on my journey. Paul or Grisha had arranged that a Norwegian freighter which did not usually carry passengers would take me to Vladivostok. This sea-route was linked to the East China Railway, which belonged partly to Russia and partly to China. Grisha took me down to the harbour where a petty police snooper known to us as Bernard, was idling around. We decided that I should go ahead, while Grisha would wait a while and then bring the dispatch trunk to the ship, which was lying off the quay.

With Micha and my other luggage I took a junk to the freighter and waited on deck in the dark for a long time; at last I heard a soft call from Grisha. We dragged the trunk up the ship's ladder and said goodbye to each other. I looked into his face once more; then he was gone and the only sounds were the junk's oars on the water.

Often we watched a canary

I was not exactly welcomed aboard the steamer. The First Officer had been detailed to give up his cabin for me. When Micha was asleep and I turned on the light, a dozen or so mosquitoes had settled on his face. Someone had opened our porthole. The crew wanted nothing to do with me. I had my meals served separately and lived in isolation. This did not worry me; I was happy to concentrate on Micha, who was delighted with all the free time I had at my disposal. Every day I invented three or four stories for him: my reward was his rapt expression. Micha was two years and four months old. He loved his rhymed picture book and knew the three dozen verses by heart. We often watched a canary together that lived in a cage on deck. The weather was beautiful and the timber that the freighter was carrying filled the air with a wonderful fragrance.

New situations can evoke an exhilarating sense of adventure. An uncharted and very different future lay ahead of me. How would it all turn out? Only the impending separation from my child dampened my spirits. I would miss at least half a year of his development at an age when every day brought something new. The thought of the parting knotted my stomach. At least Micha would be in his grandmother's loving care, and the mountain climate would be ideal for him.

Grisha had told me that I was to be met on arrival in Vladivostok. The ship approached the quayside; the harbour looked like something out of a picture book with its perfectly curved bay.

Nobody was there to meet me. My luggage was unloaded and the meticulous Soviet customs wanted to open everything. I could not allow this to happen, even within the Soviet Union, because of the dispatches I had with me and explained that I was only in transit, whereupon my cases were sealed.

Left at the quayside with my belongings strewn around me, unable to speak a word of Russian, I refused to move or have my luggage transported to a hotel or railway station. But without an address in Vladivostok or in Moscow there was nowhere else I could aim for. Shaking their heads, the officials left me sitting on a trunk. There was no one else left on the quayside. It was hot, the granite paving stones burnt to the touch. An hour passed; no one came. My child grew thirstier, and waiting had never been my strong point.

A pilot – a large man with a red beard – must have been watching me. He spoke a little English. I repeated that I was to be met. He noticed my impatience and laid his hand on my shoulder. 'Look into the sky,' he said, 'how far away is the sun, and at night the stars. Then a few hours waiting will seem no more than seconds.'

It all seemed so strange. In other circumstances I might have considered the pilot's remarks banal, but now a wise man had spoken and I felt calm.

He was proved right. A naval officer with gold stripes on his sleeves appeared and took us to the home of another seaman, whose daughter was a little younger than Micha. There we stayed for a few days.

The comrades took good care of us. They showed me the city, which I thought was beautiful, and took me on an excursion into the countryside. I have good memories of that first comradely togetherness with Soviet citizens in their homeland.

They took me to the station, promising that someone would

meet my train in Moscow and take care of my luggage. I was to continue straight on to Prague and thence to Grenzbauden. The train journey to Moscow took about nine days. On the first day Micha looked out of the window in amazement, but in the evening he did not want to lie down. The loud noise of the wheels close to his ear frightened him. So I lay down beside him on the bunk until he went to sleep in my arms, and I realised once again how difficult it would be to part from my son.

During this journey I discovered how much Russian men love children. They all adopted Micha and spoilt him. Between meals his tummy absorbed astounding quantities of pickled cucumbers and sweets. The upper bunk was occupied by the director of a fish-processing factory. When he developed a cold, a conference was summoned in a neighbouring compartment, where it was decided that the boy must not risk infection. A Red Army soldier with a clean bill of health changed places with the sick man.

Many a time my thoughts went back to that journey in the opposite direction of three years before. How much had happened since then.

When we arrived in Moscow, no one was there to meet me. On the train I had met a German comrade whose husband worked in Siberia. She had given me the address of her friend, a communist from Hamburg who lived with her husband in the Sokolniki district of Moscow. After waiting for a long time in vain, I took a cab, drove there, fabricated a story to explain my presence, and almost without question she took my luggage for safe-keeping. Comrades helped comrades, that was only natural.

We continued the journey to the mountain chalet in Czechoslovakia. I told Rolf's parents that we were considering a move to the Soviet Union, since Germany was now out of the question and the Soviet Union needed architects. I would learn Russian and teach English for which I had a contract at a school.

In view of the Japanese attack on China and political developments in Germany, Rolf had already considered such a possibility. His parents were not too happy about the plan but they remained friendly and, as always, ready to help. My mother also came to the chalet to meet us. How I longed for this reunion; how eager I was to show my mother her first grandchild; but living in

Nazi Germany, she could not enjoy anything any more. She was separated from father, was continually abused, and had to give up the lovely house where her six children had grown up and the country where she was born. Later she succeeded in leaving with the children to join father in England.

The parting from Micha affected me even more than I had foreseen, especially as I did not know how long the separation would last. The worst was that, although I made a great effort to control myself, Micha seemed to sense something. He began to cry bitterly and kept repeating: 'Mummy stay with Micha, please Mummy stay with Micha.'

On my return to Moscow I was met by an officer who took me to the Hotel Novaya Moskovskaya by the river Moskva. My luggage was collected from the family in Sokolniki. The couple from Hamburg became my friends. When the Soviet Union needed skilled workers and specialists, Lisa and her husband decided to follow their political convictions and came to Moscow. I believe Lisa's husband worked in fur processing. They lived on an old estate opposite Sokolniki Park. The log houses were in poor repair and the paths unpaved. When it rained or the snow melted, water lapped around the house, but inside it was cosy. Lisa had two children, a boy of Micha's age and an older girl. They offered me something that I had lost for the time being – family life. I enjoyed visiting them, and although I had no way of letting them know beforehand there was always a plate of soup for me as well. When Lisa's husband became factory director, nothing changed in the way they lived.

Soon after my arrival in Moscow I was collected from the hotel and driven to the Arbat where our Centre was then situated. Two officers spoke with me, asking after my health and my personal wishes. They called me Sonya and I gathered that Richard had chosen this cover name. Perhaps that is why I liked it. Whatever the reason, I immediately felt at home with my new name.

The officers proposed that I should have a break before beginning my studies. They asked whether I would like to spend four weeks in a rest home on the Black Sea near Odessa.

Four weeks of holiday would postpone my reunion with Micha but they meant well and I did not like to refuse.

The train journey to Odessa took three or four days. I enjoyed the sea, and the dry heat that was so different from China, and above all the contact with Russian people. There were no other Germans at the rest home until, to my amazement and joy, Max and Sepp turned up. They had come to Moscow with their partners. Sepp's wife had been very frightened of travelling to the Soviet Union but quickly settled down. Neither of the women came to Odessa.

I often went for walks with a Bulgarian who had been on Dimitrov's staff and was now attached to the Red Army. We looked at the sights of the city together, especially the steps made famous by the Potemkin film. I also visited the Bulgarian settlement in Odessa with him.

There was a Soviet officer whom I admired greatly. He wore the Order of the Red Banner on his tunic. At the time it was the highest military honour anyone could receive. I was longing to find out why he had been decorated, but dared not ask.

After my return to the Moscow hotel someone in the lift touched my shoulder. It was Agnes Smedley.

Neither of us had known that the other was in the Soviet Union. Overjoyed, we fell into each other's arms and all past shadows vanished. During the months that I stayed in Moscow we saw each other often and, as before, her presence greatly enriched my life.

Agnes had come to Moscow to publish a book against the Guomindang. The Soviet Union, however, had been actively supporting the formation of a united front of all anti-Japanese forces, and felt it would be imprudent at that point in time to publish a book on Chiang Kai-shek and his party as scathing as the one Agnes had written; I don't think it was ever published.

My school was located in a large red brick building. A sentry stood outside the gate. Soviet military personnel worked and, I believe, also lived there. There was a Russian village nearby, but I do not remember its name; the bus to Moscow drove past the Lenin Hills and Gorky Park. Today the village is no more, having long since been swallowed by the city. The foreign group, seven or eight of us training as radio-operators, was accommodated in one wing of the house. I remember Gerda, my German roommate, and Kate, a charming, intelligent French girl who became my friend. I don't think she was more than eighteen years old. I remember the German seaman Lutz and Czech Marek and the Greek Niko. Later another French woman, Jeanne, joined us. We were in our early to mid-twenties, only Marek was older. Our tutor was a German with whom we found it difficult to establish a personal relationship. Sepp, whom I already knew from Shanghai, was his assistant. We were all on good terms with Karlosh, an older comrade who had been a communist since his youth. He came from Latvia but had lived in the Soviet Union for a long time. Karlosh was responsible for all organisational matters concerning the trainees, but he was not so good at organising his own affairs. On a dozen occasions he was supposed to move into a flat of his own, but time and again he had withdrawn in favour of others and remained in his 'kitchen-bedsit'.

I settled in quickly; building the apparatus was fun, and I held my own in Morse, but I did not get on at all well with the theory, where I must have been a willing but untalented pupil. I built transmitters, receivers, rectifiers and frequency meters, learned to speak Russian and found the political lectures stimulating.

After Shanghai, it was a welcome change to be among comrades all the time and not to have any responsibilities for once. The days passed according to the timetable and with no other duties; all we had to do was learn.

I blossomed: my cheeks grew rounder and rosier and for the first time in my life I weighed over 10 stone. Karlosh suggested making a poster of me as propaganda for the Soviet Union. If I had not been longing so desperately for Micha I would have been happy. Once a month I was allowed to write to Rolf's parents and once a month I received mail at a cover address which Rolf's parents believed to be my real one.

Gerda shared a room with me. The food did not agree with her and she suffered from the cold. She was very pretty and well-groomed but her face was pale and she never seemed to be entirely well.

Due, perhaps, to the sectarian views I had developed in the Communist Youth, I did not understand how anyone could possibly be a good communist who put such store by elegant clothes, lipstick and perfume. I found Gerda superficial, but she was not unfriendly. We got on, without being particularly close. A Russian sergeant fell in love with her and gave her a present, a tiny revolver decorated with mother-of-pearl. Karlosh, the old Bolshevik, was so taken with her that I told him – in my direct and not always tactful manner – that he must try to preserve an objective judgement, however pretty the woman was. Crestfallen, he came to me later and said I was right.

Kate, the French girl, was in a completely different category. She was a woman of great intelligence and feeling, deeply class-conscious, and she may well have been the most valuable comrade among us. Her black hair shone as though lacquered, she had dark, bright eyes with beautiful brows, a round face and a small plump figure. Kate spoke fluent German; she tackled Russian with great zeal and made faster progress than any of us.

Lutz was a good-looking German seaman and not short of admirers. We all made a fuss of the Greek Niko because he could not communicate with anyone – he only spoke Greek. Marek, a worker from Czechoslovakia, was older than us. Learning did not come easily to him, and as a result he did everything more thoroughly. Marek was a reliable friend who won everyone's confidence. He liked me and I used to tease him. If he wanted to go on working after I had finished, I would dance around him singing 'Teacher's pet, teacher's pet!' It was the first German phrase he learnt. I spoke hardly any Russian and certainly no Czech and I don't know how we conversed, but converse we did. If I came back late from Moscow, he would still be awake.

Before long, Agnes took over a flat belonging to some journalists who were on their travels, and I used to go and see her almost every Saturday after school. She would have supper ready for us. We would go out somewhere together or, if she was tired, just sit and talk at home. On Sunday mornings we regularly made our way to Mikhail Borodin's for breakfast.[1]

During the twenties, Borodin had been adviser to Sun Yat Sen, the bourgeois revolutionary president of China who had worked for co-operation with the Soviet Union. Borodin led the political mission while General Blücher was military adviser.

Mikhail Borodin

In *China in the Twenties*, the Russian author Marc Kasanin writes:

> The two outstanding figures were Blücher and Borodin . . . His [Borodin's] appearance was as effective as it was unforgettable. He was tall and broad-shouldered, and endowed with a very pleasant low-pitched speaking voice . . . His unusual gifts as an orator, his almost magical faculty for charming his listeners and influencing them, ensured him great success and unquestionable authority . . . Each word had weight and thought behind it, each gesture was full of significance and force.

When I met Borodin he was chief editor of the English-language weekly *Moscow News*. He enjoyed seeing Agnes, the American journalist who knew so much about China. These breakfast conversations, which often lasted for hours, were extremely interesting for me. Borodin was not very forthcoming about his own time in China, but because he loved the country as we did, and because Agnes had so many questions, the conversation regularly reverted to the same themes: China and the possibility of a united front; the role of the working class in relation to the peasants; the dangers of an inadequate knowledge of Marxism coupled with decisions being taken in isolation. Borodin's wise reflections had a calming effect on Agnes.

Sometimes sons, daughters-in-law or other guests came to breakfast. Mrs Borodin was an excellent cook and her table was adorned with all manner of delicious food. On those days we needed no lunch. Borodin and his wife spoke English well, which made conversation easier for Agnes and me. Mikhail Borodin was particularly nice to me; perhaps he was touched by my first-time-in-the-Soviet-Union brand of enthusiasm. He would organise boat trips or sightseeing, and when he could not come along himself, he always asked me to recount my discoveries. When Agnes was given a ticket for the Red Square tribune on 7th November, he saw to it that I received one as well.

Agnes introduced me to the Hungarian Lajos Magyar who worked for 'Inprecor', and we were able to give him a copy of his interesting manuscript on China which I had once typed for Richard. At the time Richard had allowed me to make a copy for Agnes, too. The Hungarian was delighted with this gift, as he did not possess a copy of his own. Agnes met many journalists and through her I also got to know the brilliant *Pravda* correspondent Mikhail Kolzov. He was a witty and vivacious person; his book *The Red Battle*, which appeared years later, is considered by many to be the best book ever written about the Civil War in Spain. And Agnes's ex-husband Chatto, the man to whom I had tried to sell *Daughter of Earth* at the Berlin exhibition, also came over to Leningrad, where he was working at the Academy of Sciences.

Agnes and I visited the Chinese comrade Liao. He was married to Dora, a young worker from an industrial town in southern Germany. They had a charming son of about six, whose name, translated into English, was 'Young Falcon'. They lived in a ground-floor flat consisting of just one living room and a tiny bedroom. An amazing number of people used to congregate there, and Dora showed remarkable resourcefulness in looking after them all and making them feel at home.

What I found most interesting at Liao's were the visits of Wang Ming, then one of the leading members of the Communist Party of China and their representative in the Comintern. He made a great impression on me, but unfortunately I cannot remember details of our conversations. It is easier to remember how much we like or dislike somebody than what they say to us. By the mid-1950s he no longer agreed with Maoism. He died in Moscow in 1974. In December 1990, the wonderful photographer Eva Siao – of German origin and married to the Chinese poet Emi Siao – told me that she had been a good friend of Liao and Dora in Beijing. They died years ago, but Minjiu, the 'young falcon', now over sixty years old, had kept up the friendship with Eva Siao, who had been close to Dora during her slow and painful death from cancer. Minjiu, who speaks Chinese, Russian and German, had become a talented engineer. Eva loves his intelligence and his character. He has a wife and three children.

The publishing house of the MOPR (International Organisation for Revolutionary Fighters' Aid) had asked Agnes to write something about children in the Red Provinces. Since she was very busy, she asked me to take over this assignment from her and arranged for me to meet an officer of the Chinese Red Army who had just come from there. The publishers liked my manuscript and it soon appeared in print, illustrated by photographs that Agnes and I had taken in China. I sent a copy to Michael Gold, who worked for the journal *New Masses* in the USA. He had it translated, and it was serialised, I believe, in a progressive children's paper. Neither the American nor the Russian edition seem to have survived, but I still have the German manuscript of *Pioneers in Soviet China* and the photos that went with it.

It was unusual for students at our school to meet so many people outside the collective. My superiors knew exactly whom I saw; I never did anything behind their backs. I was allowed to see Agnes, they knew of my visits to Borodin and that I was writing a pamphlet for MOPR. I was grateful for their tolerance. This period in the Soviet Union, and the people I met there, contributed so much to my development.

Quite apart from our demanding school work, we also had political tasks. Among other things I was responsible for the wall newspaper. The one I prepared on 'Fascism in Germany' received special recognition during an exhibition at the House on the Arbat where our department of the Red Army General Staff had its headquarters. I only mention this to show what a full life I was leading. True, it was sometimes hard never having time to myself, being with other people day and night. Then I would go for a long walk and come back feeling relaxed again. I loved the cold of the Moscow winter.

In February 1934 I was called to the Arbat. A major talked to me. He did not know any foreign languages; I had to tell him my life story in Russian, which I managed. I had, after all, been learning the language for six months. He said I was to work even more intensely during the coming weeks because I was to be sent away quite soon – to Mukden in Manchuria.

Later I learned that my colleagues regarded Mukden (called Shenyang after the liberation in 1949) as a sort of punitive station, an exile to the end of nowhere, and I was told it had been considered to my credit that I agreed to go without excuses or reservations. I believe only people who did not know China could think like this. Mukden was, admittedly, a backwater, but the political situation in Manchuria was very interesting, and Mukden was a focal point.

Back at school I started cramming without rest as though I had an examination to face.

During our second conversation, the major told me I would be going to Mukden with a German, preferably as his wife; the appropriate passport would be provided. This man would also be my immediate superior. Somewhat taken aback, I tried to convince the major that this was out of the question. Rolf and I were known everywhere in Shanghai, Shanghaiers travelled to Mukden and I had met several Mukden families. After officially taking home leave in Europe, I could not suddenly turn up with a false passport as somebody else's wife, especially as I had been registered as Rolf's wife by the German consulate in Shanghai. The plan was unrealistic unless I got a divorce from Rolf and that would take time. The major asked me for the names of my acquaintances in Mukden. I could not think of any and sensed that he neither believed me, nor accepted the explanation I had given, until I remembered Walter Fuchs, a sinologist from Mukden whom we had met by the Yellow Sea during a holiday in Beidaihe.

Soon after this visit to the major I was called to Centre for a third meeting. This time I related at once to the officer I spoke to. 'Andrei', an Armenian with a long slender face, dark curly hair and dark eyes, was to be my superior for a number of years. I soon realised that I was dealing with an intelligent person, an expert in his field, who had trust in me. He understood my position and his tone was comradely, although he maintained the authority of his military rank. He liked to draw on the experiences of those who had been abroad. Later I met his family, and on one or two occasions, during my visits to Moscow, I stayed with them for several days.

Andrei told me that they had reconsidered their proposal. I was to live in Mukden on my old passport, as I had suggested. The marriage idea had been abandoned, 'regrettable as this might be for the comrade concerned'. Andrei's laughter was so infectious that I had to join in.

It was through Andrei that I came to know Natasha, who worked at the house on the Arbat. I liked her very much. She was clever and warm-hearted and her wonderful large black eyes expressed a firm honesty which no one could evade. Her severe face had a beauty all of its own. I felt sorry, and I believe she did too, that we could not see more of each other. We made up for the loss much later.

Andrei and I discussed the options for my legal cover in Mukden. I was sure I would find something suitable, but asked above all for permission to visit Rolf in Shanghai.

What worried me much more was my prospective superior in Mukden. We were to be bound together for a long time in clandestine isolation. What if, with the best will in the world, we were not suited to each other? Our work and life together could become a torment. Andrei told me that Ernst, as he was known in the organisation, was a sailor from a working-class background. That at least was a comforting thought because usually I got on well with seamen. They were hardy and tough, had seen something of the world and soon found their feet in unusual circumstances. Besides, they loved the sea.

Ernst had completed the same kind of course. I hoped that he understood more about building transmitters, because my knowledge was still shaky. Naturally I told none of my fellow pupils what was planned for me.

My last question to Andrei was whether Ernst knew about my son. No one had given it a thought! Andrei proposed that I should tell Ernst myself.

This was the last straw. To travel with a total stranger into an uncertain future without even knowing whether he would accept my child!

Sepp and I were driven to Ernst's school. I hung up my coat in the passage and was shown into a room where I waited in the icy cold. Perhaps it was not all that cold and it was only nervousness which made my teeth chatter. The door opened; Sepp came in, followed by a comrade some inches taller.

'This is Ernst, this is Sonya, get to know each other.' Sepp vanished.

I had already resolved to keep quiet and let Ernst start the conversation. After all, he was my superior; Ernst had very fair hair, narrow blue eyes, a large nose and thin lips. He was broad-shouldered, slim and muscular.

'You are shivering,' he said, 'would you like my coat?' Without waiting for an answer he took it off and put it over my shoulders. The coat was long and heavy but I suddenly felt much lighter.

Then I remembered that I still had to settle the most important point: 'I have a small child I can't leave behind.'

'You have what?'

'A boy, a three-year-old boy. He goes where I go.'

I had long since decided about Micha. I would not allow us to be split up unless I were involved in a revolution or the armed struggle of the partisans. If Ernst refused to accept the boy, I would not go.

Ernst was silent and I thought: He'll get his coat back in a minute and I shall go and see Andrei.

'Why should I object to a child? We need a new generation.'

Sepp and I drove back. A few days later I was asked to pack my things and spend the last fortnight learning with Ernst. His school consisted of a few log cabins near a village in the forest.

There was little time left for finishing the course, but enough to see that Ernst had far more technical know-how than I did and that he was a tenacious and thorough scholar. Sepp was a practical expert with not so much of a head for theory, but Ernst bombarded him with questions and did not rest until he understood whatever was bothering him, completely. He never watched the clock, ignored most of the breaks and went on working after supper. I felt quite a weakling by comparison and willingly adopted his methods. I was quicker at Morse and it consoled me to think that there was at least one thing I could do better.

During the fortnight we spent together, I managed to create a comradely atmosphere, as I usually did in my friendships with the men I worked with, giving Ernst no cause to assume or expect more.

He was pleased with my hard work. He did not know that without his example I might have been less industrious. He also seemed visibly relieved that I was neither spoilt nor capricious, and I tried to project a hardened and tough image. I wanted him to feel that we were going to make a real team that could face any dangers together.

Before our departure General Davidov of Intelligence bade me farewell. I also paid my German party dues. I had asked the comrades in Shanghai whether this was possible, and Richard had arranged it for me.

Agnes I never saw again. There would have been an opportunity in 1948 or 1949, when she was in Oxford and I was living in a village nearby. But my position was critical at the time and an irresponsible visit from me might have jeopardised her politically. In any case, I did not know how she might have changed over the years. How should I approach her? All I had heard was that she had grown bitter and aloof. Her books were very well received

In accordance with her wishes, Agnes Smedley's ashes were taken to the Cemetery for Revolutionaries in Peking, in May 1951

in those days. She died after an operation in March 1950, and my heart was heavy.

Ernst and I travelled to Prague separately and took rooms in different hotels. My own passport, which I only used from Prague onwards, suggested that I had been in Europe all the time. We booked second class on the boat, an Italian steamer called the *Conte Rosso* – or was it *Conte Verdi*? – sailing from Trieste. Contrary to normal practice in our service, I had refused to travel first class.

Now at last I could collect Micha from the chalet in the Czech mountains where he was living with his grandparents. After that we were to travel from Prague to Trieste.

I had been separated from Micha for seven months and seeing him again was all I could think about. After so much yearning I was hungry for children. I followed them on the streets just to watch them, and I looked into every pram.

In Prague I only saw Ernst when necessary, but on the eve of my journey to the mountains, he suggested going to the cinema. That was not in the schedule, but he was the boss, and so I agreed to the diversion. We saw *Maternelle*, a beautiful French film with the leading roles played by children. It had a disastrous effect on me. I was so moved that after ten minutes the tears were streaming down my face.

Ernst could not have much use for a colleague who began to howl at the mere sight of a film. At first I hoped he would not notice. I just let the tears flow without wiping them away and tried my hardest to suppress the fresh ones. In vain. They gushed as though from a newly opened spring. I felt very ashamed, and in the end I said: 'I'm not usually like this.'

Ernst put his arm around my shoulders: 'I'm glad you are like that.'

After the film I did not want to go to the café with my eyes red from crying, but Ernst insisted. That evening he talked about himself for the first time, about his father, a fisherman in Hamburg whose money went on drink; about his mother who worked and went hungry for her four children to give them a decent upbringing; about how he fought his father for ill-treating his mother, and how he left home and went to sea. It was as a sailor that he joined the party, but again, he did it the hard way. There probably never was an easy way for Ernst. When his new philosophy took hold of him, he studied its theory. While his mates played cards, went ashore, or relaxed in the 'tween-watch hours, he read and struggled with the foreign words and long complicated sentences he did not understand. He did not let up until he could say in all truth: I am a Marxist.

Ernst talked for a long time.

The next day I went to the mountains. There are many things which I have forgotten, but I still remember that train journey because I was so happy. Every minute brought me nearer to my son. I tried to moderate my excitement; the boy would not run joyfully into my arms, perhaps he would not even recognise me.

The last hour to the little house (see arrow) was the longest

Rolf's mother met me at the station. I was bitterly disappointed that she had not brought Micha along. The last hour – towards the little house on the edge of the wood – was the longest. I could not settle to any conversation, and I had not eaten since early morning. We went indoors. A small boy, a stranger, ran to his grandmother and hid behind her skirts. My son did not even want to greet me. For three days he rejected me, was naughty, obstinate and withdrawn. On the third day I had to drag him away against his will. It took some time before we both recovered our balance.

From Prague to Trieste Ernst travelled in one compartment and I in another with my son. Later we would meet officially, as passengers aboard the ship.

The liner was already in harbour. Our journey was to take us via the Suez Canal and India, with stops in Cairo, Bombay, Singapore and Hong Kong.

After we left Trieste, Micha developed whooping cough. He could not play with the other children and I had to spend a lot of time nursing him and worrying about my puny sparrow. Ernst quickly grew fond of Micha; he was kind and patient with him, and thought I was a good mother.

We had left the Soviet Union in snow. On the ship I went around in a sleeveless white dress and swam with Ernst in the swimming pool on deck. The long voyage with its warm days and clear nights, the sun and the stardusted sky created an irresistible atmosphere. Ernst and I had ample time to talk and discover more about each other. I was twenty-six and Ernst twenty-seven. At night, when we stood leaning over the ship's rail looking down into the water, whispering or silent, I was no longer quite so sure about wanting our relationship to continue on a purely 'comradely' basis. Ernst sensed this and I knew that he himself had never really held with the idea. But I did not want to give in – I did not want to commit myself on this dream-boat, for the workaday future might be very different. If our feelings changed, we would still be shackled by our work, so it was better not to plunge straight into anything.

There were other barriers between us on the journey too. I had been right to refuse a first-class cabin. I have always expressed my disapproval of uprooting German workers – who have, after all, been selected for intelligence work because of their courage and loyalty as communists – and planting them in that sort of environment. Every first-class passenger would be able to tell from their behaviour that something did not add up. Besides, if you are abroad it is better to start modestly and learn stage by stage how to move in bourgeois circles. I was also against giving personnel large sums of money. There were cases, although rare, of comrades who had always lived simply or maybe on the verge of starvation, succumbing to drink, womanising, losing their moral fibre or even going completely to pieces.

Not that Ernst drank. If he had, I should never have accepted him as my superior.

Later, in Mukden, his cover work was as a representative of Rhein-Metall typewriters. How he contrived to find this position I do not recall. He travelled as a 'businessman with a small private income'. Ernst's German was not grammatically perfect, his tastes were garish, his manners not those of a businessman. He might well stick a half-smoked cigarette behind his ear for later use. I tried to talk to him about this, but whichever way I put it, he took offence, became aggressive, called me snobbish, narrow-minded or intellectual.

Once he showed me a picture postcard he intended to send to his mother. It was of a castle with little spires and turrets bathed in a pink sunset.

I didn't say anything. He sensed my hesitation and asked: 'So you don't think that's beautiful?'

Not wanting to lie, I said: 'I think it's unnatural, a little bit gaudy.'

'I see; well, I'm only a worker and I don't understand these things.'

Ernst knew full well that I considered his to be a stronger personality. I respected the ardour and sensitivity of his communist values, I admired his zeal, his enormous willpower and his greater experience. He had worked as a courier for a long time and had already finished two training courses in the Soviet Union. If I worried about 'correct' behaviour, that was not a value judgement on my part, it was merely an essential aspect of his legal cover. His authority as my superior was never in question as far as I was concerned, but even though I did not like to quarrel, I had to express my honest opinion about books, art and people. Yet he seemed to be annoyed by any advantage I might have acquired in life; my education, my fluent English, my greater confidence in handling people.

We arrived in Shanghai in the first week of April 1934. The journey had taken three weeks.

Rolf welcomed his son and me with great happiness. There had been no opportunity to warn him that we were only coming for a visit, and it was not easy to tell him this on our arrival. When I finally did, he was very depressed but, as always, calm. On no account did he want to accept the separation as permanent. Rolf possessed a special kind of persistence which nobody would suspect beneath such a gentle exterior. He did not reproach me in any way or make any difficulties; he even accepted that I might not be living alone in Mukden. He only insisted that under no circumstances would he give up Micha or me for good.

I felt that the situation was hard enough for Rolf, and he certainly had a right to his son. If this was how he wanted it,

MANCHOUKUO BOOK-AGENCY

EDUCATIONAL, MEDICAL, SCIENTIFIC BOOKS.

専門書籍販賣
滿洲國支部
ユー・ハンブルガー
奉天郵政管理局
投遞箱第三〇號

My legal cover

then this was how it would be. In any case, by now he was no longer just a sympathiser holding back from commitment, but a communist who was ready to work with us. The Japanese war in Shanghai and fascism in Germany had achieved that. But for me it made the separation even more complicated.

If we were not going to divorce officially, I would have to find a sound legal reason for my stay in Mukden. I visited various bookshops in Shanghai and succeeded in being appointed representative of Evans & Co., an American bookshop in Shanghai. I bought a small range of books at wholesale prices, took along catalogues and obtained what mattered most to me – a written confirmation that I represented the firm in Manchuria. Potential customers were to be the Japanese administration, hospitals, students and Japanese industrialists. I had visiting cards and letterheads printed: Manchoukuo Book Agency, Educational, Medical, Scientific Books, Manch. P.O. Box 30, Mukden. (Manchoukuo is the Japanese name for Manchuria) I still have a sheet of that stationery in my possession.

As the representative of a commercial firm I would also be able to justify the journeys within Manchuria that would frequently be required for our work.

Grisha – perhaps through Walter – had found out that I was in Shanghai and we arranged to see each other. I did not regard this as a serious breach of cover since we were generally known to have social contact. It was a warm reunion and I was able to give him news of his brother, whom I had visited in Moscow.

Before we left Shanghai, Ernst and I bought parts for our

transmitter which we could not expect to track down in Mukden, and stowed them away in our luggage.

We knew from a comrade who made the journey from Manchuria to Shanghai, carrying $20,000 in cash to help our comrades, the Noulens-Ruegg, how White Russian and Japanese informers were constantly watching the passengers.

Ernst and I made this journey in the opposite direction; Micha came too, of course. Not for one single moment during the whole of that 1,800 kilometre journey did we dare lose sight of our luggage. On the Manchurian border all our cases were opened. Our transmitter parts consisted, in addition to smaller pieces, of two valves which in those days were still the size of a milk bottle. Border searches like this one were part of our way of life.

We had hoped to obtain the transformer, which we needed to build the rectifier, when we arrived in Mukden. This transformer was like a heavy iron block measuring approximately eight inches square. But contrary to our expectations there were no parts at all to be had in Mukden, and so Ernst had to travel all the way back to Shanghai to find one. We might have been able to buy a transformer in Tianjin which would have been much nearer, but its concealment required careful preparation which would be easier in Shanghai. Ernst asked Rolf for his help; it was given willingly. A heavy armchair was bought and delivered to our Shanghai house. Rolf and Ernst carefully removed the filling below the seat and suspended the transformer between the springs by tying it in with wire. Both Rolf and Ernst were thorough and conscientious people. At the last moment they decided to secure it doubly with strong string. The filling was then pushed back and the fabric nailed on. The chair was sent to Ernst's address (or it may have been to mine). I imagine it must have been to mine, because it would have been quite natural for me to have furniture sent on to Mukden. The chair arrived but the wire binding the transformer had broken. Held only by the string, it was now hanging so low down that the fabric had almost worn through. A little more movement on the journey, and the sharp iron edges would have torn right through, causing the transformer to fall out. With the Japanese spying mania in Manchuria, suspicion and detection would have been certain to follow. A salutary reminder to take not twice, but three times the normal precautionary measures.

In May 1934 we arrived in Mukden and booked in at the Yamato Hotel. The Rhein-Metall typewriter and a letter of recommendation that Ernst had acquired, as well as my letter from the Evans Bookshop, were left lying around in our rooms, to make the task of the inevitable snoopers easier. In the hotel we never spoke a single word about our activities.

Our tasks in Mukden were determined by the specific situation in Manchuria. From the first day of the Japanese attack, the most progressive forces in China had decided on active resistance. Groups of partisans were formed in the mountains and in the small towns and villages. Their members were workers, peasants, students and soldiers. Many were led by communists. Manchuria, through its industry, had a strong working class.

The partisan movement was nothing new in China. The VIth Congress of the Communist Party of China, six years before, had decided to build up partisan sections which later became the nucleus of the Chinese Red Army. Representatives of the Communist International attending the congress applauded this decision. Even before that, the Executive Committee of the Communist International, the Comintern's highest body, had pledged all their parties to support the Chinese comrades in every possible way. Naturally the Soviet Union played the major part in providing this international aid, and it is hardly surprising that the comrades in Japanese-occupied Manchuria expected and received their help. Chinese comrades learnt the art and craft of partisan activity in the Soviet Union, and those who were chosen were very proud.

We knew the cover names and meeting places of some partisans who were to set up their own groups, train them and lead them into action. The groups formed in this way did not, in my time, fight against Japanese troops. Their campaign involved disruption of communications, operations in industrial areas and attacks on Japanese commando posts.

Our transmitter was to establish contact between the partisans and the Soviet Union, pass on questions and reports from the groups and – in so far as Ernst, who had gone through the same training, could not answer their questions himself – pass back to them the advice of the Soviet Union.

Ernst and I were to work with three partisan leaders. As is so often the case with apparently important missions, ours too was reduced to all kinds of minor tasks woven into our daily lives and bearing their own little successes or failures. Unfortunately we began with a failure.

One of our first tasks was to take up the prearranged contacts. We also had to find accommodation suitable for building and operating a transmitter.

Every evening since my departure from Moscow, I had gone over in my mind the dates and places fixed for these contacts as well as my transmission code. It was one of our principles that the comrade with higher rank and responsibility should be protected, and so we had already agreed in Moscow that I would be the one to meet the partisans and also see to the transmitting. It would be quite wrong for anybody to infer from this that Ernst might be avoiding danger. He was courageous and rather inclined to take too much upon himself.

The meeting with Li, in Harbin, was to take place a few days after our arrival in Mukden. After the long journey from Shanghai to Mukden, I did not want to subject Micha to another journey of twice 600 km. His whooping cough had weakened him, and I was doing all I could to build his strength up. Ernst offered to look after him and was given a list of instructions, which included all the tricks which, with any luck, might induce Micha to imbibe his cod-liver-oil.

Of all the cities that I have known in my life, the Harbin of those days was the most sinister. Apart from Chinese and Japanese, it was full of Russian émigrés. They had never accepted the October Revolution and, bearing their past as a mark of Cain, they were now completely demoralised. Many stood at street corners, in ragged clothes, begging, a sight that made an even worse impression in a Chinese city than it would have done in Europe. Beggars, pickpockets and prostitutes dominated the scene. People were frightened to walk the streets alone after dark.

Someone had hit upon the bright idea that I meet Li late at

night by the entrance to an isolated cemetery. Having made my way to this district, which was deserted but for the occasional drunk staggering along, I was frightened – not of the dead but of the living. I waited ten minutes. My fear grew. Twice abuse was hurled at me by passing men. I waited twenty-five minutes. Li did not come.

Now I was obliged to stay in Harbin for the next appointment at the cemetery on the following evening. This time I waited for twenty minutes. Li did not appear. Feeling very low I returned to Mukden.

Ernst and my son were sitting in the hotel dining-room having their supper. Ernst was carefully steering a spoonful of pudding into Micha's mouth. I was moved, and Ernst was glad to see me. The delay had worried him. When he heard more, his face darkened and he went so far as to ask whether I had really been at the meeting place, whether I had waited long enough. He could not abide failures in our work.

Now we were forced to wait – I believe it was a fortnight – for the reserve date.

So far we had also drawn a blank with our house-hunting. The inflated apparatus of Japanese officialdom requisitioned all empty properties for its own use and all that remained were a few luxury villas, abandoned by fleeing Chinese generals. Chiang Kai-shek never did have any influence in Manchuria. Before the Japanese invasion, Zhang Xue-liang ruled the country and before that his father, General Zhang Zuo-lin.

At last Ernst found a room with a German couple in financial difficulties, who were forever quarrelling; many European business people suffered from the Japanese competition.

I needed self-contained accommodation to operate the transmitter station. I went to view yet another luxury villa. This one belonged to a relation of General Zhang Xue-liang. His former servant showed us around the house, but it was much too big for us. As we were leaving the estate, I discovered a small garden house built of stone. The servant smiled. That was where the owner, a general, had kept his mistress; an underground passage led to the villa. I asked if I could see the little house. The servant took a long time to find the key. I climbed the stone steps and on entering the front door discovered three small wood-panelled rooms. In the basement there was a kitchen, servant's room and the exit to the underground passage. There was no heating, bath or toilet, but the house seemed suitable for my work, although the roof was rather too low for my aerial. The servant shook his head – he would have to write to the general in Peking. The answer was prompt. For the equivalent of thirty shillings a month I could have the little house and choose some suitable furniture from the villa. A couch – perhaps it had served for the general's visits to his mistress – was already installed; this now became my bed. For Micha I bought wicker-work children's furniture. We acquired a primitive iron stove and on the teak writing table stood, as always, the picture of my childhood lake in Germany.

Having the servant's quarters below my own was convenient. If I locked the door, no one could intrude. It was also an advantage that my rooms, though on the ground floor, were high above the basement, so that no one could look in. Besides, the windows had solid shutters which could be locked for the night from inside. We used the lavatory built for the former servants of the big house, which was about 50 metres away in the courtyard: a wooden construction, country-style, with no flush. The only thing missing was the heart-shaped hole in the door! Micha and I used to 'bath' in a wash-tub which, in winter, we would set up in front of the coal-stove in my room. Two mythical animals carved in stone sat either side of our front door and protected me – I hoped – during my lonely work at night. A brick wall separated our estate from the German Club. The tall poplars behind the wall nodded in towards us.

Before we began looking for accommodation I had a disagreement with Ernst. For him it had been a foregone conclusion that we would move in together. He felt hurt and could not understand that I would not agree to such an arrangement, even though I was as fond of him as he was of me. We got on very well, but he was the sort of person who always had to have his way. As far as our work was concerned I accepted this, although he was ruthless with himself, overtaxed others, and insisted on a greater contribution from me than I was physically able to sustain. I also adjusted many aspects of my personal life to suit him, but I had

The house in Mukden with the two bamboos holding the aerial

an independent character, and could not live in an atmosphere entirely determined by my partner. Ernst needed a good and simple wife who gave in to him in every respect and lived *his* life. To change him would have demanded a great deal of effort. It was not a challenge which I wanted to face in our situation.

Until my transmitter was in service, I had regular meetings with a comrade attached to the Soviet service. He was small and deformed, with short-cropped hair. I gave him coded messages and received coded answers. He was the comrade whom Centre had asked, before I left Moscow, whether there was a sinologist called Fuchs living in Mukden.

Now I had to inform the Soviet comrade in 'Report number one' of our failure to contact Li. Centre's reply was definitely cool. In their eyes, this was our first independent task, and we had not carried it out.

As soon as I had moved and the chair with the transformer

My dual-purpose Chinese ruler

arrived, we built the transmitter, that is mainly Ernst built it, since he was much better at that side of things. We used the same type of transmitter Max described in the book *Dr Sorge signals from Tokyo* by Julius Mader.[2] Our transmitter could be constructed from receiver parts, though even these were not readily available. If I remember rightly, it was called a Hartley transmitter with a three point system. We did not however – as Max did three years later – omit the rectifier, with its component transformer that caused us so many headaches.

Our equipment in Mukden was still of massive proportions. There was no question of being able to dismantle the apparatus every time. Apart from the heavy rectifier and the large valves, we used coils made from heavy copper tubing that we shaped by winding them round a beer bottle. The coils alone took up more space than a whole transmitter did a decade later. For a Morse key, I used two rulers. The lower one was of brass, covered with Chinese characters, (for me it was a ruler, the Chinese used it as a paperweight), the upper one was of wood with a cotton reel attached to it as the grip. As I moved the wooden cotton reel, a bolt through its centre would tap the metal ruler below. One wire led to the bolt, the second wire I jammed under the brass ruler. The key was dismantled each time and took only two or three minutes to assemble. The Chinese adage engraved on my ruler read: 'Whoever achieves the wisdom of "spirit" and "life" in all its profundity, will live to be five hundred years old.'

The heaviest piece of furniture that I had collected from the villa was a large desk. I had brought the 'camphor chest' with me from Shanghai and it just fitted under the desk. We lowered the transmitter and rectifier into the chest, covered them with a made-to-measure board loaded with our moth-balled winter clothes or, according to season, our entire summer wear. The chest itself was heavy and so the additional weight was hardly noticeable; it had metal fittings and a secure old-fashioned lock. In my little house this was a sensible place for the camphor chest, which was an essential part of any foreigner's household. A thorough house search would have revealed the transmitter, but we hoped we had done enough to fool the type of police snoopers who always went poking around European households in Mukden. Considering the weight and size of our equipment there was no better hiding place available. Gradually we learned to use smaller parts and about a year later Ernst succeeded in fitting the transmitter, except for the rectifier, into a portable gramophone from which the motor had been removed. During our time in Mukden, however, the transmitter remained in its camphor chest. Ernst was untiring. In Shanghai we had bought an American textbook for radio mechanics and amateurs which he studied day and night. There were 250 pages of small print, and as Ernst knew no English, I had to interpret. There were a lot of technical terms which I could neither translate nor explain. That made him angry. When, at last, he had ploughed through the whole book, he knew most of it by heart.

In Mukden I transmitted twice a week from my house. I did not always have news to send but had to report to Centre in case they had a message for us. If there was interference, if either we or they could not be heard, I tried again the following night.

Although I subsequently did build transmitters on my own, I never became such an expert as Ernst. But I was good at Morse. Later I learnt that my transmitting was quicker and more accurate than the average. I could also take down the fastest incoming signals without making any mistakes. On a night when everything went smoothly, work was a joy. But with our weak transmitter that was a rare occurrence.

How often I had to interrupt my news transmission to ask: 'Are you receiving me O.K.?' How often the reply was negative and I had to repeat everything. The Vladivostok end was also frequently jammed by other stations and unintelligible on our ordinary receiver. Even when our messages were not very long, this could stretch the work over several hours of the night and make listening even more a torture than transmitting, because it required the utmost concentration. It was an odd situation where harmless listening turned out to be more nerve-racking than dangerous transmitting. I admire Max Christiansen-Clausen, Richard's radio operator in Tokyo, who was apparently sending 500 groups per hour across an even greater distance. With me, 500 groups might take half the night because I had to repeat things so often. Sometimes it would be two strenuous nights until I held the message in my hands at last, and then the deciphering would begin around three or four in the morning; the notes had to be destroyed as quickly as possible. The new day began by seven o'clock at the latest: that was when my Micha came to wake me.

The text which we transmitted or received contained between 60 and 500 groups, each group having five figures. On rare occasions it might be more. We signalled at different times but always at night. We could only select one of two frequencies because with our length of receiver aerial the transmitter only worked on a specific wavelength. It was called a Fuchs aerial. With repetitions, the transmitter had to be in operation three or even four times a week, thereby making triangulated detection easy for our opponents. It is amazing that the station was never discovered.

I could not get wrought up every time about the danger I had to face: the shortcomings I have described played far more on my nerves. If all went well I felt good. My house with its closed shutters was like a fortress. I covered the light so that only a faint glimmer – just enough for reading and writing – fell on the desk. Everything else lay in darkness. Micha was fast asleep in the next room. The town slept. Only I was awake sending news of the partisans into the ether – and in Vladivostok a Red Army man was sitting and listening.

But there were often nights when I cursed the alarm clock and the coldness of the room. The coal fire in the stove went out overnight. I sat at the Morse key in my tracksuit, wrapped in blankets, with fingerless gloves on my hands. Aeroplanes circled over the house. One day they were bound to catch me. For a moment I would hope that my partner would not give his call sign. I wanted so much to climb back into my warm bed. But then I would only have to get up again the following night.

I went to the second rendezvous with Li, and again I waited in vain. The third time, I believe, Ernst went instead of me, but to no avail. Later Centre heard, or perhaps we did, from one of the partisans, that Li had taken fright at the task assigned to him. Since he was supposed to take charge of an already existing group, we lost the whole group. It could have been worse: he had left me in the lurch, but he had not given anybody away. How would he have reacted under arrest?

Centre had recommended Li to us as a particularly promising worker. No doubt they had good reason to hold him in such esteem.

In work of this kind it is difficult to judge a person with absolute accuracy, especially when they are new to it. Only when danger threatens can you test a person's reliability, and even after years of good work, a reliable comrade might change. It would certainly be wrong to mistrust your colleagues; you cannot work like that. You should not only try to know them as well as possible, but constantly look at them in a new light. Regular contact should be maintained wherever feasible, and preferably also a personal relationship which shows regard for the individual. Moral support from Centre is important for comrades in dangerous isolated work – however hardened they may be. Respect for their work, acknowledgement of their achievements, and an understanding for personal problems must under no circumstances be neglected.

A further reflection: how much superfluous information did Li have about the comrades with whom he had undergone his training? Their correct names, the provinces from which they came, whether they had families, where they were to work in the future? The surest safeguard against betrayal is to permit absolute minimum knowledge to anyone. A banal statement certainly, but a fundamental principle which is best driven home by concrete examples.

Our partisans were to concentrate their activities on the Japanese-owned railway line that ran through Manchuria. They were successful and disrupted communications by destroying the network in a number of places. Above all, they concentrated on derailing military trains. The groups grew, took in new members and so increased their striking power. The degree of alarm that their activities raised among the Japanese was evident from the press and a harsh upturn in counter-measures.

We informed Centre of the groups' plans and achievements, reported on the political and military climate and developments, and passed on information about new members.

Our partisan groups did not form close-knit units. Their members led normal lives as workers, peasants or clerks. They came together for a few hours or days at a time, either to train or to take part in some organised action against the Japanese. And even then this would not always involve the whole group, whose strength would only be known to its leader. At that time this type of partisan work was quite common.

Apart from giving guidance to the groups, one of our most important tasks was to get hold of the explosive materials they needed. Ernst and I visited chemists and general stores in Mukden and other towns. We bought chemicals which, while not dangerous in themselves, would produce explosives in combination. I especially remember one occasion when we bought some ammonium nitrate (ammonium saltpetre). Ernst did not speak Chinese so I went with him, and Micha came along to make it all look as harmless as possible. We found a shop where they had ammonium nitrate in stock. I wondered whether to take two pounds or more; after all, it was used in large quantities in agriculture. I asked for ten pounds. The shopkeeper misunderstood and brought out a hundredweight. Overwhelmed but happy, we took a horse-cab to transport the purchase to my home.

If I remember correctly, a kilo of ammonium nitrate mixed with about 20 per cent sugar or aluminium powder or permanganate was enough to cause an effective explosion if it was packed against a rail. Then again, maybe this was what we mixed with the potassium chlorate, another basic ingredient that we were able to buy quite easily. We may have used something else to ignite the ammonium nitrate. We also bought sulphur, hydrochloric acid and other chemicals whose names I have forgotten, but we left it to the groups to mix them and pack them into shells.

Care had to be taken when transferring the materials to our partisans and they faced even greater problems in finding ways to transport it.

The partisan I liked best was called Feng, and he played the most important role in our work. He was tall and strong like many northern Chinese. Feng radiated calm and dignity. Although still young, he bore the same quiet, friendly, serious manner at all our brief meetings. He combined this seriousness with warmth and respect.

I met Feng in Mukden or in Andong, a fairly big town near the Korean border where he lived with his wife and two small children. He always dressed in the Chinese fashion. I do not think he owned a single item of European clothing, apart from a hat.

The greatest difficulty for me was that Feng, like the other Chinese with whom we were in contact, spoke only Chinese. I had neglected my Chinese lessons during the latter period in Shanghai and already forgotten a great deal. My reading and writing were poor, nor was I yet able to use a Chinese dictionary. And we were supposed to give guidance to the partisans and pass on their reports! I had to broaden my vocabulary as fast as possible. To communicate with my Chinese comrades, I gave them an exercise book containing the words I knew, and told them to limit their reports to words chosen from this. Similarly, instructions from Centre or Ernst could only be passed on by me to them with my restricted vocabulary. Needless to say, that was a pressing incentive to learn the language as quickly as I could. Every time I met the comrades, I handed them a piece of paper with the new words I had absorbed.

To my parents:

28th September, 1934

I have Chinese lessons every day now and compete with my 'boy' in learning to write. A nice intelligent lad who goes to school every afternoon; I am pleased to give him the few coppers and time off. In return he cooks wonderful meals. The more you learn, the more pleasure you get from it. I can

> now write and read 600 characters, and speak many more. People who know over 2,000 are considered to be sinologists and usually end up a bit crazy. My fellow-citizens already fear for me.

My language teacher in Mukden, like most Chinese, hated the Japanese conquerors. When he knew me better, he confessed that only the material plight of his family had driven him into giving me lessons, for my firm's stationery included the word 'Manchoukuo'. This was the name that the Japanese had given to his country and all Chinese hated it. He sensed that I had great interest and sympathy towards China and its people, but with such a letterhead I would never win a friend among the Chinese.

I told him I also needed the money badly and that this had driven me to use the name Manchoukuo, since the customers for my books were Japanese.

When I left China in the autumn of 1935, I could read and write around 1,000 words and speak still more. Micha, with his many Chinese friends, used the vocabulary of any four-year-old Chinese child.

The Chinese language is not based on an alphabet but on characters. What makes it even more difficult, and for a foreigner almost impossible, to learn is that different characters can be pronounced exactly alike, except for a variation in pitch.

So we were forced to violate the rules of illegality and exchange written messages to avoid any misunderstanding. The Chinese were frequently searched by the occupying Japanese police, but no alternative was open to us.

I was always relieved to see Feng appear at our meetings. We would only stay together for a very short time in some street. I could not talk much with him or any of the others, and we knew almost nothing about each other. How could an outsider understand what bound us together? We were working under a common threat for a common cause. But the danger for the Chinese was even greater than for us. Once, after I had met Feng, occupation police suddenly swarmed all around us. The street was sealed off and the Chinese had to stand still with their arms above their heads. Our eyes met and, quite apart from the danger,

Micha with his Chinese friends

it was shamefulness of this maltreatment that seized me. But even with his arms in the air Feng preserved his dignity.

The police did not find the scrap of paper – they were looking for weapons. It would also have been obvious that the handwriting was not that of a Chinese.

Feng had removed the hundredweight of ammonium nitrate from my house. He therefore knew my address.

A meeting had been arranged with another group leader in Jilin, 500 kilometres from Mukden. That place must surely have been suggested by the Chinese partisans. All I can say is that the detested cemetery in Harbin seemed an ideal choice compared with this locality. The trains did stop at Jilin, but there were hardly any people about. I was the only foreigner who got off. I followed a Chinese comrade who was waiting for me as agreed. No words were exchanged. He took a rickshaw and so did I. The two rickshaws must have jogged along for a good forty minutes over pot-holes and sandy paths. Clouds of dust enveloped us, unfortunately without disguising us altogether. It was obvious that no Westerners, let alone a European woman, had set foot here in years. All heads turned towards us. If the aim had been to make me and my partisan stick out a mile, we could not have done better. At last we stopped in front of a shabby little hut, and before we had a chance to step inside a crowd gathered around us and looked me over in amazement. Tea was brought in and served by the partisan's wife. Under these circumstances I had to perform a veritable conjuring trick to hand over the explosives. The partisan was fearless and worked hard, but had no idea how to conduct an illegal meeting.

In Mukden as in Shanghai, I took part in the everyday life of bourgeois society. In the spring of 1934, fascism was only beginning to penetrate the German community, although the first refugees from racial persecution had arrived.

In the eyes of the Japanese, those who had relations with the German consulate and its community were far less suspect. I therefore took care to maintain my contacts. I was still invited to the German Consul's receptions and could visit the German Club. For my closer acquaintances I chose people who were in no hurry to become Nazis and showed an interest in China.

Of course my social status as the girlfriend of a typewriter salesman was fairly low in comparison to my position in Shanghai as the wife of a respected architect with the British City Administration.

To my parents:

Spring 1934:

Everyone is very friendly here in the German Club, etc . . . I spend quite a bit of time with Dr Fuchs, someone we met and liked three years ago in Beidaihe. He teaches at the Japanese school here and goes on some marvellous trips during his holidays. He is in his early thirties and speaks twelve languages – a calm and balanced person who has always something good and stimulating to talk about . . .

. . . I also see a Belgian architect who has recently turned up in Mukden. He is from Ghent, lived in Paris for a long time and spent eight years in London as well. He shares our style of life and our way of thinking and his company is a real joy compared with anything else on offer here. Then there is a nice handsome Japanese called Matsumoto, a friend of Bernstein, whom I know from Shanghai and who now works here. Finally there is the new doctor. Have I already mentioned him to you? Elderly German Jewish emigrant. I play tennis and go dancing with the architect. I eat Chinese food and go on excursions with Fuchs. I go to the cinema with Matsumoto. The doctor couple visit me. What they all like best is coming to my place because I have such a funny little house and such wonderful gramophone records and the boy cooks so well. Happily I only have the pleasure of the women's company as a group, at the Club or a tea party, where I have to cultivate a modest but resolute smile for the obligatory two hours.

I could have done without the wives of my acquaintances. But I missed Isa and Agnes.

I have forgotten the name of the Belgian architect. I called him 'Schlips' (neck-tie) and concerned myself with him largely because I had the impression that he was politically close to us. I should have liked to win him for our work, even if only in a fringe capacity. But his past, and his months in Mukden where he was not earning a living, were too much of an unknown quantity.

In Shanghai, we had already had our doubts about trusting Bernstein's boyfriend, Matsumoto. In Mukden I was almost certain that he was doing more than just selling Ufa Films and here he was much more dangerous for me. When he visited me once without warning, I was wearing the Chinese dress which Madame Sun Yat Sen had given me. He said it suited me so well – could he take a picture. Bernstein already had some snapshots of Rolf and me, but in any case it would not have been difficult for Matsumoto to take photos of me without my knowledge.

I welcomed him in a friendly manner – any reserve or evasion on my part would have aroused his suspicion. I regarded it as useful training to be on my guard in his presence without alerting him. I had already developed a reliable instinct for this sort of behaviour.

Of course, my letters home were much more cautious than those sent from Shanghai. Once I wrote: 'I have my hands full at present making out invoices and collecting the money.' That was not true. I did not sell many books, but to keep my parents from worrying too much about my separation from Rolf, I stressed the importance of my work.

I wrote to father about the situation in Manchuria:

> 20th July, 1934
>
> This country is extraordinarily interesting. The Japanese are carrying out large-scale development programmes. In Mukden they are building whole new urban districts. Huge new government buildings are going up in the capital Xinjing. Air routes and newly laid railroads stretch across the whole of Manchoukuo. Japanese goods swamp towns and villages. They are fast squeezing out all the European firms. During the last two years, 60 per cent of the European merchants in Mukden have gone bankrupt. At the same time half of Manchoukuo is flooded and the other half suffers from drought. The result is serious famine. Last month bandits and anti-Japanese groups carried out 650 attacks in the Fengtien province of Manchoukuo alone.

There had always been groups of bandits in the mountains of Manchuria, who used to raid the richer villages. With the growth of partisan groups, whom the Japanese also called bandits, it was difficult to obtain accurate figures for the partisans as such.

Of course I also explored the surrounding countryside:

> Over the week-end went on a wonderful excursion with the Consul's niece and Dr Fuchs. There are some unbelievably beautiful places about two-and-a-half hours' train ride away, and the people in Mukden have absolutely no idea that they exist. A mountain landscape with a deep blue river, sheer rocks and green mountains, unexpected gorges, ancient trees, neat little villages, quite enchanting. Ate, slept, bathed Japanese style . . .

Poverty outside the walls of Mukden

In another letter I complained of the 'silly people, the work load and Mukden's small-town atmosphere'.

Never once did I mention the existence of Ernst, although I was with him every day.

With my assortment of books, I also travelled two or three times to Fushun, the industrial centre of Manchuria, rich in coal and oil. I had a look around, photographed the landscape and people and visited the managers of industrial concerns, who bought a few books.

I never really tried to take advantage of the important people who counted among my potential customers in Mukden, or elsewhere in Manchuria. Occasionally I visited the odd civil servant, army officer or industrialist. We had not been asked to establish contact with the Japanese, and neither Ernst nor I made any such suggestions to Centre. Nevertheless, now and then I gained an insight into the situation which would be summarised in a report to Centre.

Fushun, industrial centre of Manchuria

Once, when I was on an excursion with Ernst, we encountered some Chinese soldiers in Japanese service and talked to them. This prompted me to send a lengthy report to my family:

> We are in the countryside near Mukden, on the edge of a small village. It starts to rain and we step into a small shop. There are about twenty houses there. The shop sells cigarettes, soya bean oil and empty tin cans. Three soldiers are sitting in the back of the shop on a large family bed, one playing a violin. The old shopkeeper leans on the counter, two bright little boys squat on the floor.
>
> Foreigners are such a rarity here that we are invited to sit down on the same bed. The soldiers are Chinese, pressed into the service of Manchoukuo: 'Are you Russian or English?'
>
> 'I am German.'
>
> One of the three says: 'The Germans are clever.' The second comments: 'The Germans have the best guns.' Then the third: 'The Chinese can only eat and sleep; they can't read or write.'

I ask: 'Are there bandits in this area?'

'No, now the Gaoliang (sorghum) has been harvested, the Redbeards can't hide. Did you know that Zhang Zuo-lin was a bandit once?'

The oldest soldier, playing the violin, laughs and says 'Zhang Zuo-lin was a redbeard bandit when he was too little to have a beard – when he got a beard he was a great general.' Zhang Zuo-lin was the former ruling general in Mukden.

I go on asking: 'And you work for the Japanese. Why? Do you like them?'

They laugh, and all three excitedly start to talk at once: 'The Japanese are very bad. We have one stripe on our sleeves and get eleven Machoukuo dollars a month. A Japanese with one stripe gets 60 dollars. If a Japanese with two stripes says "get that, do this," then the Chinese with two stripes has to jump to it. The Japanese are fat and walk like this.' The old soldier poses bandy-legged, pushes his chin forward and rams his fists to his hips. 'The Chinese does this.' He crouches and holds his hands in front of his face.

The young twenty-year-old soldier says: 'I hope the war will come soon, then we won't fight *with* the Japanese but *against* them.'

'Are there many bandits in Germany?' asks the old soldier.

'Where people can read and write there are not so many bandits,' answers the young one, and continues: 'Manchoukuo is now like India is to England.'

The third soldier says: 'How well you lady speak Chinese, congratulations.'

The others nod.

Outside there is lightning and thunder.

The old soldier says: 'Do you have that in Germany?'

I say 'Yes, and sun and rain too.'

'Is it the same sun as with us? Just as round?'

'Yes, the sun is the same, and the moon too.'

The young soldier nods, 'And we are all together on the round earth.'

One day I was shocked to learn that a newly arrived Nazi, a

representative of an armaments manufacturing company from the Rhineland, intended to rent the large villa to which my little house belonged. I got my water and electricity from there. He would be in a position to shut them both off, or he only needed to say that my presence did not suit him and the landlord would give me notice. And even if he did nothing of the kind, I did not exactly relish the thought of this prospective neighbour.

He moved in and evidently saw no reason to come over and introduce himself. But I had to know where I stood, and so I went across to see him.

The new tenant was sitting in one of the twelve large cold rooms. He received me with old-fashioned courtesy. Titled, perhaps in his mid-fifties, he had left his wife and four children behind in Germany. I have forgotten his name – let us call him Herr von Briesen. Our first conversation sufficed to tell me that the former German nationalist-turned Nazi felt more in sympathy with the era of Kaiser Wilhelm II than with Hitler. He was proud of his long line of ancestors and their military tradition. In a tactful and charming manner he intimated that he was opposed to anti-Semitism and that whatever happened, he wanted me to stay in the little house.

'Please don't allow my presence to oppress you in any way. I would feel hurt if you moved out on account of me.' Neither did Herr von Briesen want me to pay for my electricity. 'Those few coppers are not worth talking about.' I insisted, although it would have been fun to let chauvinistic German aristocracy pay the bill for nocturnal contact with the Soviet Army.

We had a good relationship for as long as we were neighbours.

'I value intelligence and I love temperament,' he used to say. 'That's why I so much prefer conversing with you than with the German philistines here.'

He drank too much. 'Neighbour,' he once said to me, 'if you meet me anywhere and think I've had enough, get me home, will you?'

One day he invited me to the German Club but I did not want to go there any more. He insisted. Afterwards he laid his fat, far from aristocratic hands on my shoulders and said: 'If a single

German so much as tries to harm one hair on your head, tell me at once.'

Herr von Briesen had some influence in the German community because of his firm's standing, because he drank a lot and bought other people drinks, and because in his own way he was a personality. Without particularly trying, I gathered information from him about the German business community and the Japanese with whom he dealt.

If I can describe him so well, and yet not recall details of much more important partisan campaigns, that is due to the letters which I still have in my possession. I wrote home about him:

> . . . This man has connections with the Prince Regent of Inner Mongolia, De Wang, who is very influential. My neighbour has just been to visit him in Mongolia and the prince wants to appoint him as his general adviser. He may be giving up his business to work solely for this prince, who has the following plan: he wants a monopoly to buy and sell the wool which Chinese merchants are at present buying up privately from Mongolians. (They give them a stable lamp in exchange for 200 kg. of wool!) My neighbour, who is to be the middleman, would then offer this wool to Germany at a very low price. 50 per cent to be paid for in goods. Fascinating, he should do a roaring trade. The point of the story is that he needs a secretary who wasn't born yesterday and who would of course accompany him through the length and breadth of Mongolia and deal with all his interesting correspondence. An attractive offer . . . But don't worry, somewhere along the line this vagabond life must cease. It's out of the question for me.

I was certain that there was more than wool at stake and I wouldn't have minded accompanying him for two or three months. It would certainly have been interesting. I believe I asked Centre, because Inner Mongolia and a prince of this ilk might have interested them too, but in the end nothing came of it.

My great delight at this time was Micha's development. His intelligent, pensive questions, his logic and powers of observation really were grounds for pleasure.

When, in January 1935, he went to stay with Rolf in Shanghai for a while, I wrote to my parents:

> Although I am busy from morn till night, I do miss the little person who dominates my life. Instead of enjoying not being woken for once at 6.30 a.m. and not having to be home for meals and being spared the little worry-pot on my lap while typing – I get sentimental and would love to have four like him.

Rolf brought Micha back to Mukden; he also came to visit us a second time. On both occasions he brought us parts for the transmitter which we badly needed. I believe he also brought us chemicals once.

Rolf's parents and my mother were not happy about the way I was living. I wrote to my mother:

> On no account must you worry about me. There is absolutely no need to. I live exactly the life I want to live and am very satisfied. I admit that I would have a much more protected, secure and carefree existence if I were simply living by Rolf's side as his wife, but only in theory; in practice I should be unhappy . . .
>
> Your erring but contented daughter.

I was sure that my parents, at any rate, could guess something of the political background to my life, after my long stay in the Soviet Union and the separation from Rolf.

After I had used the transmitter for some time, the valves failed. Ernst was annoyed. Perhaps it had been my fault. I had to travel the 700 kilometres to Tianjin and try to buy new ones. Micha and his teddy bear accompanied me. To cope with the customs control on the way back, I had decided to sew the valves inside the bear which was stuffed with wood fibres. I had not found the matching colour yarn for the toy in Mukden, and now tried in Tianjin. Pulling out a tuft of fur as a sample, I went to the haberdasher's.

In front of me a comfortably plump lady asked to see some lace mats. She took her time. Even in those days I could not stand waiting around in shops. When Micha began to whine, the lady turned round. It was Luise, Paul's wife! We were both speechless with excitement and joy.

Paul lived and worked in Tianjin. Luise asked me round to see them. How gladly I accepted and what a heart-warming evening it was. They had invited another guest – Paul's radio-operator Lutz – the seaman, my comrade from the school in Moscow. Those few hours together (Micha slept in Luise's bed until we went back to the hotel) boosted my morale for the next few months. After Mukden, those days in Tianjin seemed like paradise.

The atmosphere in Mukden is difficult to describe. The worst of it was the stupid petty spying on the part of the occupation forces, which was dangerous because it was so widespread. Even some Chinese entered this Japanese service and were consequently despised by their countrymen. They visited the houses of foreigners or invited you to attend the police station. I remember one 'conversation' there when a Japanese officer, who spoke to me in English, casually slipped in the Russian phrase for 'sit down'. Since I was always alert on such occasions, I asked, 'What did you say?'

I believe any occupying power would, during the initial period, act in a paranoid way. But with the Japanese this state of nerves never let up. Granted there was enough going on to justify a certain disquiet, as we knew better than anyone else!

The frequent use of our transmitter, the purchase of chemicals, their storage in our house and transportation, my meetings with the partisans – all took place under continuous Japanese surveillance, accompanied by what can only be called a hysterical fear of Communists, and were a permanent source of danger. Moreover, the use of bribes, which had helped in the case of the Noulens-Rueggs, simply did not apply in Mukden; the Japanese could never be drawn in this way. But you get used to danger as you get used to the climate of the country. Both Ernst and I were realistic in our analysis of the situation, but we went on behaving like normal people. I could be pleased with a new dress and annoyed over losing a pair of gloves. If I enjoyed dancing with 'Schlips' because he led so brilliantly, Ernst would be jealous. And

I suffered because Ernst flirted with a White Russian woman – better looking than me – who had a room next to his. So our lives were quite 'ordinary'. All the same, this was the period when I learnt a life-long lesson: not to ascribe undue importance to everyday irritations and to come to terms with them quickly.

There were many positive factors to set against the dangers. We were helping the only country in the world where the working class had been victorious. We were fighting Japanese fascism. Our hatred of capitalism, oppression and war was more than theory. We were witnessing their effects daily, with our own eyes, and we loved the Chinese people who had to suffer them – the coolies, the peasants, the children, the mothers.

In April 1935 – we had been working in Mukden for almost a year – I went to one of my regular meetings with Feng. For the first time he kept me waiting. Five minutes, ten, twenty. I told myself that his train might be late, he could be ill or there might be some misunderstanding about the date. I went to see Ernst, making some detours on the way. I never went straight to his address after a meeting.

Two days later Feng failed to turn up again.

The third time I did not take the written message along with me; we had removed the transmitter from the house, hiding it elsewhere. I thought I saw Feng. He was coming towards me. I could have wept with relief. But it was not Feng.

I noticed a Japanese who had been loitering around the last time as well. Like me, he waited exactly 15 minutes. I thought perhaps this was the end.

The Japanese did not follow me.

I still tried to push my anxiety about Feng into the background. Six days had gone by. If he was ill, that could take more than six days.

I fetched the transmitter back again and reported Feng's absence to Centre. Shortly after, we heard that he had been arrested: explosive materials had been found at his house. We knew his arrest meant death, and before that torture, which would only stop if he was prepared to betray his comrades. Feng betrayed no one. If he had, a number of comrades, myself among them, would not be alive today.

Centre ordered us to cut off all connections with the partisans, to leave Mukden and set our station up again in Peking. I thought of Feng's wife and his children. We couldn't even offer them any financial support. I was appalled at this harshness and found it unbearable simply to forsake comrades who relied on us. Their leaders would arrive at the appointed meeting-place and I would just not be there. We signalled Centre but they would not relent. I took sleeping tablets every evening, yet laid awake for hours. Only much later did I find out that new comrades had been sent to Mukden to replace us. I left Mukden without undue haste, in keeping with my legal bourgeois status. Herr von Briesen insisted on a farewell celebration which I could not refuse.

Ernst had inserted some of the parts, two valves and a rectifier, into our ordinary radio. He housed the transmitter itself in a gramophone which had no motor. I travelled with all my belongings, the radio and gramophone among them.

On the Manchurian border all went well. After that came the Chinese customs. Here too the suitcases were allowed through without any fuss. Suddenly the customs official said: 'You can't take the radio with you, it requires a special government permit.'

My objections got me nowhere. I demanded to speak to the chief customs officer. An official and a policeman directed me onto the platform. Micha, reasonable little fellow that he was, stayed in the compartment with our cases and our gramophone, waiting for me to return. A second official appeared, I tried to persuade him to let me take the radio. As always in China when anything unusual happens, a crowd gathers.

A train arrived on the other side of the platform and those who got out joined the growing circle of interested spectators. The official suggested that I should leave my address and post the permit from Peking, whereupon they would forward the radio at no cost. I did not want to give my name and address, as there were components in that set which had no business in a receiver. The dispute got more and more heated. I menaced with the German Consul, with my American firm and with complaints to the Chinese government about this frightful treatment of foreigners. The crowd around us grew.

Our train whistled, the driver shouted angrily that he would have to leave because the train was late. Micha stood at the window crying. The train on the opposite side of the platform whistled. I looked up and could not believe my eyes; leaning out of his compartment and watching everything with consternation was Niko, my Greek comrade from the school in Moscow. We gave no sign of recognition. His train left. I got on mine and went on to Peking without the radio.

We chose the hotel where foreigners always stayed. But I had no eyes yet for the beauties of the city. My first mission was to visit the customs authorities. It turned out that only Chinese citizens required permits for the transport of radios. I was given an officially stamped document to this effect, and was advised to send it to the frontier by post. Within a week I should have my radio.

Could I justify leaving the receiver with its extra parts at the frontier for a single hour longer than necessary? Besides, Ernst had fixed an immediate date to establish radio contact between us. Armed with the official paper I travelled the few hundred kilometres back to the frontier. Micha had to come along as well. Where could I have left him? This time, anticipating problems at the frontier, I was particularly reluctant to take him. On arrival I handed my paper to the custom official. His superior came and apologised for their mistake. No one had discovered the transmitter parts in the receiver.

The first telegram from Centre to reach me in Peking, in May, contained a worried enquiry as to what had happened to me at the frontier. Now I knew for sure that Niko had been no hallucination and that he had also arrived safely at his destination – wherever that was.

Even before the journey back to the frontier, I was plagued by a toothache and now it became unbearable. The hotel recommended a good Japanese dentist. I went to see him and, of course, Micha came too. A molar had to be pulled. The roots were lying crossways and the jaw bone had to be chiselled. Micha was fascinated. I did not utter a sound, but was bathed in sweat, as was the dentist.

When the effect of the injection wore off, the pain started in the damaged jaw. Because of the journey and the toothache I had not slept the previous night. For this second night we had arranged my radio contact with Ernst.

Today I ask myself: did we really have to test the connection between Mukden and Peking which we would never use again? It was reckless to transmit from a hotel room at 10.30 at night, when the place was full of guests. I dared not lie down, for fear of falling asleep. I did not want to set the alarm because of Micha. The whole of the right side of my face was throbbing and I had a sickening headache. The thought of not transmitting because of a sleepless night and pain would have been incomprehensible to Ernst.

At last the moment arrived. I set up the transmitter and when everything else was ready I plugged it into the wall socket – there was a bang, the hotel was in darkness. I groped about as fast as I could trying to hide all the transmitter parts without any light. Fortunately it was impossible for anyone to trace the cause of the short circuit to my room. The fuses were changed but I did not have the nerve to risk a second short.

The hotel had either direct current or too high a voltage. Although I had booked for a week, I needed to find other accommodation at once to contact Ernst, who would wait two more nights for my call. Again we packed our things. What an unnecessary risk! But I never questioned Ernst's decisions; I carried them out.

We moved into a boarding-house run by a German widow. The next two nights I sent my call-sign from the thin-walled room without reaching Ernst. Later, when he arrived in Peking, he expressed doubts as to whether I had even tried to transmit. He knew perfectly well that I always followed his instructions, that I was not a coward and, above all, that I would never lie to him. I was hurt by his reproaches, although I realised they were not seriously directed against me, but a result of his anger at our failure.

The accommodation problem was solved by one of the Wilhelm brothers. The sinologist, who was following in his father's professional footsteps, lived in a Chinese house in Peking. He was about to go on leave to Europe for several months and let me rent the house during his absence. When this was settled, I went on a visit to Shanghai. There I saw Walter again. Whether I met Grisha or Isa I do not remember now; anyhow, I was told – perhaps through Walter – that a comrade whom I knew wanted to see me. It was Kate, my good friend from the school in Moscow. She had come to Shanghai as co-worker and wife of a comrade. Kate was expecting a child and did not feel well. As far as underground discipline was concerned, it was not right for us to meet, but we were delighted to see each other and I was able to give her useful advice about her work and her child.

In May I settled into Wilhelm's house in Peking. It had four rooms which, in Chinese style, formed a quadrangle enclosing a courtyard. The windows were of parchment-like paper, broken up by wooden lattice-work, so that you could not see in or out.

To my parents. June 1935:

> Peking is heavenly. The sort of place to end your days in. It is unbelievably beautiful – I have never seen anything quite like it. A stroll through the gates or through the Forbidden City is always a fantastic experience, even the tenth time round. What I know of Italy, of Germany, or America or other countries simply cannot compare. It is unique . . . To Micha's delight we eat Chinese food for our main meal.
>
> Yesterday I spent two dollars on 140 flowering plants, asters, antirrhinums and wallflowers. They were planted out at once and now we live in a little flower garden in the truest sense of the word. Micha has his own small plot which may soon wilt under his over-affectionate care. The other day I took him to the Summer Palace, set in a wonderful landscape by a lake in the mountains. We took a boat and were rowed around for about an hour. I threw Micha into the water (with his rubber ring) and he swam among the lotus blossoms.

Ernst had arrived. I hardly remember any details of our work in Peking. I only know that at lengthy intervals we had radio contact with Centre, receiving and sending telegrams. Maybe we hardly worked at all. Quiet periods like that did occur when a group was temporarily withdrawn from action. But I do remember that I couldn't get over our sudden break with the partisans. Ernst felt the same. Logic did not help. However much I told myself that rationally Centre's decision had been necessary, I still felt that we had run away. Later I learnt that in similar circumstances relations were totally suspended, to be resumed again only after weeks or months of inactivity. Feng's murder threw a shadow over my life for a long time.

In Peking the relatively peaceful atmosphere did us good. Ernst loosened up and was less irritable. I enjoyed showing him the beauty of the city. In August we actually went on leave to Beidaihe on the Yellow Sea. We intended to enjoy every hour of those rare days free of danger. Unfortunately this was beyond me. I felt sick and did not want to swim or go for walks. Soon I knew that I was expecting a child. Before saying anything to Ernst or anyone else, I wanted to make my own decision. In China it was easy to have an abortion. Everything spoke for it, especially our kind of work. But Micha was now four years old and I yearned for a second child. In my line of business the time would never be right. If I was separated from Ernst, I might never be with anyone again from whom I would want a child. Now that it was on the way I wanted to keep it.

The timing was particularly inopportune. Within a few weeks Rolf, who had now completed five years in China, was to begin his home leave in Europe. His English employers would be paying the fares for the whole family. Centre wanted me to use this opportunity to come to Moscow and discuss my work. Besides, I was glad at the chance to visit my family in London. Whether Rolf should prolong his contract with the Shanghai Municipal Council for another five years remained an open question. Rolf was now a convinced communist and did not want to stay politically inactive any longer. I had informed Centre of this.

A second child, an infant that had to be nursed and cared for, would certainly complicate life still more, but so long as I did not leave my work, no one could reproach me. Indeed, a baby would provide excellent legal cover.

Before the European leave began, something happened that made my departure from China urgent and made it doubtful whether I would ever return. In Shanghai, a foreign comrade who had continued Richard's former work had been arrested. He remained silent throughout the interrogations and they never even learnt his name. His absolute refusal to speak became a sensation. The world press reported on him as Mr X.

This comrade was Kate's superior and companion. I did not know him personally and had never had anything to do with him, but Ernst and I were warned by Centre that the number of the Rhein-Metall typewriter connected with the arrested man could throw suspicion on Ernst. Neither he nor I had sold one to him or Kate. However, I was to leave at once and if Ernst found himself drawn into the affair, he could put any blame on me, as soon as I had safely crossed the border into the Soviet Union. He had sold me the machine and knew no more of it than that. We made out the appropriate invoice in my name. Ernst was to try to keep going in Peking for the present.

This made my future quite uncertain; the only thing I could be sure about was the separation from Ernst. I found the parting hard. We were not together merely because we happened to be doing the same work; our ties went deeper.

China too, I left with a heavy heart. I had lived here for five years.

When in 1949 the day of victory came, I considered it to be the most important milestone in the history of the international labour movement since the October Revolution of 1917. For me personally, it was one of the happiest events in my life.

In the 1950s, tourist trips to China became feasible and I started to save up for one. Then came the changes in China. As yet it was possible to travel there, but I felt I could not visit a country whose political development depressed me as much as the Cultural Revolution did.

Before my hasty departure in 1935, both Rolf and Ernst repeatedly tried to dissuade me from continuing the pregnancy – without success. Eventually Rolf declared that he could not leave me on my own in this condition; I was to meet him in Europe and to conceal the fact that he was not the father of the child. Ernst respected him for this, saying to me: 'If I can't be with you, then there is no one better than Rolf, and I shall feel much calmer.' I said nothing while the two of them bargained over my future. I did not want to lie about the child, and so far as the work was concerned, which country I went to and with whom – that decision was not ours anyway.

I was to receive my exit visa to the Soviet Union in Harbin. Ernst knew the exact date I would cross the border, after which he could blame me if questioned. In Harbin I found the Consulate closed and asked myself whether I might yet strike bad luck at the very last moment.

Everything went well. Ernst was not questioned. Mr X was later released. Kate must have conducted herself very well indeed. After her return to the Soviet Union she received a high decoration. Unfortunately she lost her baby in the eighth month. In 1937 or 1938 I met her in Moscow and also her husband, Mr X, without ever knowing his real name. He struck me as charming and highly knowledgeable about international politics. I was not curious to learn his name. Anyway, it would have been different from the one in Shanghai. I was glad to hear, years later, that within a short time Kate had two children, both healthy boys.

During the long journey by train I felt so ill that I was afraid for the unborn baby. Micha on the other hand loved these sudden changes in his everyday life and soon felt at home. On the journey his only disappointment was that he could not talk to anyone. He tried German, English and Chinese, but in vain. Once, when the train stopped, a cat came mewing along the platform and the four-year-old murmured to himself: 'Cats are cleverer than people. They all speak the same language.'

4

Poland, Danzig and the Soviet Union, 1936–38

On arrival in Moscow, I was collected from the station. At the Centre Comrade Andrei greeted me warmly, but remarked how poorly I looked. I weighed 20lbs less than when I had left Moscow eighteen months before. He wanted to send me to the doctor but I refused. We spoke about the work in Mukden, and he asked me in detail about Rolf and then made a suggestion. Would I go to Poland – with Rolf? Andrei did not know of my close relationship with Ernst and I did not tell anyone about the expected child. I had just spoken well of Rolf, and Andrei remembered that I had been against a divorce the last time I was in Moscow. From his point of view this was a logical, humane proposal.

While I was suffering from nausea and might continue to do so throughout the nine months, as with Micha, this pregnancy did not put me in a condition of needing support. I was not afraid to carry on the necessary work on my own. German emigrants – eking out some kind of living at subsistence level – were trying to settle in many foreign countries at this time. And all over the world there were families separated by Hitler's fascism. I could go to Poland alone. I felt that it would be too much to expect Rolf and me to share a life together under present circumstances. True – Rolf's profession would provide us with a more watertight legal cover and it would certainly be better for him to have me there on his initial task for Centre. Two things about Rolf worried me in particular. He was in many respects naïve and in his case one false assumption could snowball into a mass of erroneous deductions. That could result in wrong decisions. Moreover, he was soft-hearted and did not know how to use his elbows. This latter worry proved to be superfluous. He was never soft in political matters. He carried out dangerous missions calmly, without fuss, and lost his head less easily than many a more forceful person. His conduct in bourgeois circles, his charm and perfect courtesy, made him popular everywhere, especially with women, and opened many doors to him.

I agreed to Centre's plan that I should go to Poland. Rolf was to decide for himself. I do not remember now whether he interrupted his journey to Europe, which began later than mine, in order to pay his first visit to our friends in Moscow, or whether he came directly to London and I put the proposals to him there. He kept to his resolution not to leave me on my own until the child was born.

Although Rolf had brought parts for the transmitter to Ernst and me in Mukden, and over the years proved himself in intelligence work under difficult conditions, I never told him about my work in Shanghai. When Richard Sorge was murdered, he heard the name for the first time – and not through me. It was only from books about Sorge which appeared decades later that Rolf discovered the illegal connection between me and the owner of the camera shop where he had arranged the interior decoration.

My last call during my stay in Moscow was at the radio school where I saw Marek again, the only one of my group who was still in Moscow. Then I travelled with Micha to Leningrad and from there made a five-day journey by steamer to London. On the second day aboard a storm set in and the flowerpots in the dining-room were tied down. If only we had done the same with Micha's chamber pot! It raced from one end of the cabin to the other as though motorised, until it shattered. I was too sea-sick to care.

My parents greeted us at the dockside in London. I had not seen father, brother or sisters for five long years. Now, meeting them all again, our former close relationship was re-established immediately. Renate, the youngest, only twelve years old, proudly called herself a communist. Sabine, in contrast to the rest of us a gentle girl, had just turned seventeen. She was the only one to have inherited our mother's beauty, while I was the most disadvantaged in this respect. 'Weepy', the twenty-three-year-old, was intelligent, conscientious and ambitious. Brigitte, three years younger than me, had got her doctorate in history in Switzerland; she was, as always, full of zeal and enthusiasm for whatever she happened to be engaged in at the time. Jürgen now lived in London with his wife and child.

This was now 'home' for me. Compared to the villa in Schlachtensee, with its many rooms and the large garden running down to the lake, my parents' dowdy three-roomed flat in London NW3 seemed poky in the extreme. I am sure we all yearned for the house in which we had grown up, and for the landscape to which we belonged, but neither we children nor our parents were too worried about material possessions. Father's work lent its own special atmosphere to this place too. On his desk thousands of white sheets of paper were filled with his neat small handwriting. Father taught at the London School of Economics and published several books in Oxford and London in his special field of demography.

The walls, covered with father's bookshelves, left only little room for our mother's talented paintings. Every Sunday the family, now enlarged by sons-in-law and grandchildren, arrived for lunch. Sometimes there would be as many as twelve of us around the table. Mother cooked the way she painted. The kitchen was full of inspired disorder, just like her studio in the house in Schlachtensee.

It must have been daunting for my sisters' husbands when they came to their first Sunday dinner. The prospective son-in-law stumbled as a stranger upon a family clan which now suddenly included him – the chosen one. Banter and witticisms would fly past him from all directions. Perhaps he dreamt of joining in this repartee in order to be accepted. But how on earth would he get a word in – at that speed? While he was still smiling nervously at the last joke, the others were already listening to father's penetrating comments on some world event, around which a lively discussion would develop. The irreverence shown by these six children to their mother must have been equally shattering, until he sensed that it was a loving irreverence with its own brand of respect. Mother was the only one who would try to offer the future son-in-law a normal conversation. We were of the opinion that the intended would learn to swim fastest if he was thrown into the family waters at the deep end. Before long, he was one of us and all the siblings were on best terms with all the in-laws, and so it has remained.

Another very long-standing member of the household was Ollo (Olga Muth). Ollo is not a cover-name. I started calling her that when I was three years old. She came to us as a nanny after Brigitte was born, and soon became indispensable to everybody. Mother, happily married to father, loved life and was a beautiful woman with wide interests and a large circle of friends and acquaintances. Whenever the children had any serious problem, mother would drop everything and care for them lovingly. But with such a swarm of children there were also the daily worries to cope with and for those, as for all practical aspects of our lives, Ollo was responsible. Ollo washed and dressed and fed the babies. She saw to it that the older ones got to school on time. She nursed us when we were ill, dealt with cuts and bruises, helped to calm tempers, sang nursery rhymes with her lovely voice and sewed, crocheted and knitted for us all. Her parents had died when she was quite young. Her father had been a sailor in the Kaiser's navy and she was brought up in the military orphanage at Pretzsch, near the river Elbe. Ollo did not marry, we six were her life. She would have loved to have us all to herself. Sometimes she quarrelled with mother and then she would pack her bags and leave. We would miss our ordered life and Ollo's sure hand, until one day she would reappear, declaring: 'I can't live without the children.'

When Hitler came to power and the house searches in Schlachtensee began, Ollo courageously stood by the family. Our parents emigrated. Ollo could not bear the thought of separation and came along too. And so I met her again in England. Politically, although lacking any theoretical basis, she shared our views.

When I told the family that I was expecting my second child, they were all delighted. There was no need to lie because they naturally assumed that Rolf was the father. Jürgen was the only one who was told the true story; he thought I was impossible, but stood by me. Jürgen was a leading member of the party group of German emigrants in England and one of the founders of the Free German League of Culture, an anti-fascist organisation not bound to any party. They had over 1,000 members, including artists, writers, theatre groups, musicians. Guest speakers at their meetings included Wickham Steed, Stephen Spender, Kingsley Martin, and J. B. Priestley. Unfortunately because of my clandestine work, I was obliged to keep away from the party as well as the League of Culture.

Of the children only Renate, the youngest, was still living at home. Although she was deeply attached to Reni, Ollo felt that her task in mother's household had now been fulfilled, and she begged me to take her to Poland, as she was so much looking forward to my baby. Rolf and I gladly accepted her proposal.

The year of our arrival in Warsaw witnessed the death of Pilsudski, who in 1926 had established a highly reactionary dictatorship in Poland. Nothing much changed under his successors. The government remained anti-Soviet, the Communist Party was forbidden or only semi-legal. Pilsudski had signed a treaty with Hitler, directed against the Soviet Union. Chauvinism coupled with anti-Semitism ruled the land, and the economic situation was poor.

I am not dramatising if I describe the dangers which confronted us in each country. We took it for granted that we had to assess our position as quickly as possible and come to terms with it.

If our intelligence activities were discovered, something worse than a harsh sentence awaited us: deportation to Nazi Germany. That same year the Gestapo had managed to obtain the extradition of Olga Benario-Prestes and Sabo by the Brazilian government. When our house in Schlachtensee was repeatedly being searched in 1933, there had been enquiries after my whereabouts, always coupled with the threat: 'We'll catch her yet.'

The first tasks which Centre had set us for Poland were not very demanding and allowed us sufficient time to settle in the new country. We had to obtain residence permits, find work to legalise our existence, and set up our transmitter for radio contact with the Soviet Union.

We expected that the last item would be the easiest to arrange.

Obtaining a residence permit, not to mention work, was very complicated at a time when emigrants from the Nazi Reich were fleeing to all parts of the world and Poland was practically closing its border to them.

We began by trying to get to know people in useful places, preferably in Rolf's profession. The first were a progressively inclined architect couple, Syrkus by name.[1] They gave us friendly and sympathetic support without in any way suspecting how important it was to us. I particularly remember Mrs Syrkus as an intelligent and unusual woman.

By chance I heard her name mentioned a few years ago. Both played an important role in the reconstruction of the city of Warsaw after 1945. Maybe in this connection, I should mention another, more private episode in their lives, which illustrates the endearing qualities of this couple, who were so well-known in Poland.

Letter to the parents, 2nd February, 1936

> We were invited for lunch at the Syrkuses. He is Jewish and speaks broken German, his wife has studied in Germany. Another guest, a countess, informed us about the household. The main roles are played by the cook Veronica and the two dogs. At the last party, with 15 guests, the dog Clara devoured gloves to the value of 100 Zlotys. One day Veronica gave notice, confessing she was pregnant. The concierge was the guilty one. Mrs Syrkus would not hear of her leaving. She bought a pram, everything else a baby needs, and after its appearance baptised him 'Ricardo'. To allow the mother to continue as cook, a nurse was employed for Ricardo. We met all three, a pock-scarred, bandy-legged Veronica, a screaming 18–month-old Ricardo, and the father who polished the stairs. Actually the Syrkus couple considered a move to another flat to spare Veronica the sight of the father, who showed no interest in mother or son.
>
> When we left, the dog Clara was induced by a piece of chocolate to let go of my brand-new gloves.

And it was Mrs Syrkus who suggested the name Janina for my daughter, born nine weeks after our visit there.

Syrkus had found a professional partner for Rolf, if he managed to get a permit to stay in the country, but although we were not thrown out, our visa was extended for only ten days at a time. We decided not to let it bother us, but to begin a normal life, find our own home and set up the transmitter.

On 27th February, 1936 we moved into the ground-floor flat of a house in Anin, a suburb of Warsaw. An elderly couple lived upstairs, but only during the summer months. The man was a captain in the army, which did not exactly appeal to us.

For the first time I had to build the transmitter on my own and was very worried about establishing communication. Any direct contact with an official representative of the Soviet Union was strictly forbidden.

I built the transmitter in an empty gramophone case, as Ernst had taught me. I can well remember the night when I first pressed the key under a dim light in our flat. Once again the lower part consisted of that Chinese ruler with the beautiful proverb. It has journeyed with me around the world and I am still using it as a ruler today – to cross out (I hope) all the long-windedness from my manuscript.

I called for two minutes, tuned in the receiver and – what a wonderful feeling of relief! – the reply came at once. I was so pleased that when I confirmed reception I got my wires, or rather my keys, crossed – something I had never done before.

Of course from the beginning of our stay in Poland I took an interest in the politics and the economy of the country. I should have found it unnatural as well as boring not to become deeply involved in the country where I was living, quite apart from its usefulness for our work. I learnt Polish and forgot the Chinese language which I had taken so much trouble over. My experience in Mukden and Shanghai had taught me how much information can be gathered from individual people with a little effort, and careful reading of various newspapers was another way of making interesting deductions. But to begin with, we were hardly able to understand the Polish press.

A start had been made. We had found a house that was suitable for our work and established good contact with Centre. Moreover the architect whom Syrkus had found for us was prepared to take

The house in Anin, a suburb of Warsaw

Rolf as a partner in return for a small sum of money. Needless to say, he knew nothing of our mission either. The only remaining difficulty was that we were still without permanent residence visas. Again and again we had to apply to the authorities, to argue, to remain polite and patient, even when they treated us badly; each time we had to plead anew for an extension.

To my parents:

> . . . The twelve-month visa has still not been granted. They have only given us another provisional one. Rolf has to visit the authorities practically every day and has also asked some of our good connections (among them our friend Syrkus) who are willing to act as guarantors, to call there as well.

> Everyone tells us how difficult the procedure is, but Rolf cannot work properly until he has it.

Four weeks later:

> Our problem must be decided within the next few days – for the umpteenth time. Rolf has called at all kinds of offices some forty times by now – I am not exaggerating.

In this kind of situation Rolf was marvellous. I do not know whether I could have summoned such calm and skill in the face of those semi-fascist authorities.

Anyhow, after months of effort we at last received a visa for a year. Thus Rolf had succeeded under difficult circumstances in fulfilling two tasks that had been set us: to obtain the visa and to legitimise our position.

Apart from myself, a Bulgarian comrade whom I had met in Moscow had come to Poland. He had gone to Katowice or Poznán and was to establish some connections with Silesia and build up a group of intelligence workers in Poland itself. His wife and children had remained in Moscow and he found it difficult to settle. I met him once a month, and I was supposed to advise him and pass on his news to Centre. His work was only just beginning and I do not remember any details.

A second contact was to be taken up as soon as we had established ourselves, but as yet I knew no more about it.

Personally I did not find it easy to settle in either. I wrote home, '. . . We don't dislike Warsaw, but after China Europe seems boring.'

I had been torn away from all that had occupied me so intensively for five long years and there was little to substitute for it. Rolf and I got on in a comradely way and there were no quarrels; there were common interests, there was our son, but I was depressed and it surely must have been even more difficult for Rolf.

Shortly before the baby was born I had to travel to Kraków to meet the Bulgarian comrade. I always looked forward to this journey because Kraków was such a beautiful city. Every time I went, I visited the castle, the churches and the drapers' shops. But this time I was soon tired and had no alternative but to return to my small unheated hotel bedroom on the third floor. I struggled against my bad mood and thought how sad it was that my child was not being joyfully awaited by *two* people. In a building opposite my hotel room I saw a man's profile in a window; suddenly a girl slipped into his arms and I thought how lucky they were.

On 27th April, 1936, Janina was born in a Warsaw clinic called 'Opieka' in Chmielna 35. She was a strong and beautiful child. On 1st May, when Nina was four days old and I was feeding her in my room at the clinic, I suddenly heard the sound of music from the street. The 'Internationale', an illegal demonstration! I stood up and, child in arm, ran to the window.

Someone put their hand on my shoulder. It was the head doctor, Mrs Ukrainszyk. She looked out on to the street and said softly: 'My daughters are with them.'

In later years I asked myself more than once whether she and her girls had ended up in the Warsaw Ghetto.

Nina chose a good day to arrive. I was allowed home the day I was supposed to transmit and added a short item to my telegram that night, announcing the birth of a daughter.

To my parents:

14th May, 1936

> . . . You can't imagine what bliss it is to arrive home from the city and find a little crib complete with occupant standing in front of our house in the woods.
>
> . . . Micha is delighted with his sister and happy when I'm around as well. This morning I said to him 'Let's have a proper bone-lazy day today. His reply: 'I know what lazy is, but why bone?'
>
> Ollo is a wonderful help and crazy about Janina.
>
> Rolf very busy with a competition which he is entering under another architect's name. It won't therefore earn him any honours, but at any rate a bit of money!

Ollo's presence was a great relief to me. In the course of my work in China I had suffered too much worry and anxiety about Micha,

A baby basket complete with contents

Micha delighted with his sister

and now there were two children to look after. True there was also a growing conflict, whose ramifications I could not yet foresee.

To my parents, May 1936

> ... Micha, accustomed to claiming my company, is not at all nice to Ollo. He has suggested to her more than once that she should go back to London, because she now often takes my place looking after him. He cries and is naughty, but the moment I enter the room he beams. This goes so far that one day I found Ollo reduced to tears: she had so looked forward to Micha and now was 'unable to win the love of the child'.

In Poland the authorities would only issue a birth certificate for children who had been christened and so we had to take our Janina to church. Giving way to my pleas, Jürgen, who happened to be visiting us in July 1936, became her godfather and Ollo her godmother. We laughed a lot when we discovered that the church official had entered Jürgen's profession as 'statist' instead of 'statistician'.

The day I returned from the clinic with Janina, another good thing happened. Walter from Shanghai came to see us. He was just beginning his European leave and stayed with us for several days. I did not ask him about his work, nor did he ask me, but we spoke of the political situation in Shanghai and Poland and he gave us news of acquaintances. It was a pleasant get-together. I never saw him again.

The second contact, which Centre had asked me to take up before Nina was born, was with a group of comrades in Danzig (now Gdansk). I travelled there on a number of occasions and transmitted news between them and Centre. In the winter of 1936 I was asked to move there for a few months to give them more effective support.

At the end of 1936 Danzig was still officially a 'Free City'. In practice the situation was different. In fact the Nazis were carrying out a small-scale repetition of what they had done in the whole of Germany. 'Bringing Danzig into line' was the first step towards bringing her 'home to the Reich'. This was part of Hitler's preparation for war and, since it took place in the corridor between

Jürgen

Germany and Poland, it constituted a particularly dangerous threat to the Soviet Union. The process was brutal and methodical.

The President of the Senate was the Nazi Greiser, who stood under the command of Nazi Gauleiter Forster. German Nationalist and Centre Party deputies in the Danzig Parliament were shouted down, clubbed and imprisoned. In 1936 the Social Democratic Party was outlawed, and in 1937 the Centre Party was liquidated. The Communist Party had been banned since 1934, and hundreds of its members were in prison. The Swastika hung from official buildings, portraits of Hitler decorated the walls of public offices, Poles were terrorised, Jews intimidated, persecuted and arrested until they were prepared to leave Danzig 'voluntarily'. Before I sat down on a bench in the beautiful Oliva Park, or entered a shop, I had to make sure that it did not display a sign forbidding me to do so. A café in Langfuhr put the finishing touch: 'No Jews, Poles or dogs admitted.'

The Polish government, according to the constitution, had the right to be consulted about any decisions taken in Danzig, but did little to protect the Polish minority there. At the same time, many Polish postal employees, railwaymen, teachers and workers fought for their rights in Danzig and resisted Nazi persecution.

When complaints about the Nazis' outrageous violations of the Danzig constitution were lodged with the League of Nations, this body declared it 'inadvisable to interfere in the internal affairs of Danzig'. Hitler was given free rein. SA, SS, police and war veterans' associations were systematically training and preparing for war. German and Polish communists were working underground and offered active resistance. Not many survived.

At the founding of the German Democratic Republic in 1949, there were only around 65 German communists from Danzig still living; they had mostly settled in our old coastal towns of Rostock, Greifswald, Stralsund and Grevesmühlen.

Of course, in 1936 and 1937, I only had contact with our own group of about six comrades. All of them were workers whose homes were in Danzig. They collected information and prepared the practical campaign against the Nazis. German U-boats were being built in the shipyards of Danzig and war materials were being transported from there to the insurgents in Spain. Industrial production was geared to the needs of fascism. Any disruption was important. At that time the work was just beginning. I know of only one successful action which resulted in a minor target going up in flames.

The leader of the group came from the communist youth movement. He had a delicate face, brown eyes, brown hair. He had suffered from tuberculosis for some time and lived with his wife and daughter in a modest little house on a garden estate. He was now in his early thirties. I also met another couple who had grown up in the Danzig Young Communist movement. I remember him particularly because he, or rather his wife, could no longer bear the increasingly dangerous conditions of our work in Danzig. His wife insisted he give it up. He was unable to resolve this conflict in his marriage and asked to be allowed to drop his illegal activities. The other members of the group I did not meet personally, except one, forty years later. After the first (German) edition of this book appeared, Paul Ivertowski, a former crane driver from the dockyard in Danzig, told me that he was a member of the clandestine Danzig Group for which I worked temporarily. The group expanded and received special training in order to destroy certain traffic junctions when the expected Nazi invasion occurred. In 1939, shortly before the war began, the whole group was betrayed and arrested. Paul Ivertowski was sentenced to hard labour for life. He was freed from Mauthausen concentration camp in 1945. Four comrades were executed, including the group leader I described, who was called Karl Hoffman. Now, since he belongs on the roll of honour of those who died for the Red Army, I am glad to be able to name him.

My task in Danzig was to counsel the group and transmit for them.

In January Rolf went to Danzig ahead of us to find accommodation. Ostensibly it was to be for the whole family, since we needed a detached house for the transmitter. However, he intended to stay in Warsaw with the architects' firm, so as not to lose his legal status.

Early in 1937 I wrote to Jürgen from Danzig: 'We've found a charming little house, very comfortable, delightfully built with large garden and 15 minutes' bus journey from Danzig. Address from now on: Danzig-Oliva, Humboldstrasse 7.

Strange how I still have a record of that particular address because a week later it changed. When testing the transmitter and receiver we discovered that a loud humming made any signals inaudible. Nearby was an electric power station that I should have been aware of when renting the house. It had been very difficult to obtain and we did not find a substitute, at least not within the time at our disposal. I had to take an apartment in a new block in the same district of Oliva.

In comparison with the many other difficulties to be coped with in Danzig, this was of little significance. But anyone who has been through the ordeal of house removals will know what it meant – first to move with the family (Janina 9 months old and Micha 6 years) from Warsaw to Danzig, to find a house and then, just when we had settled in, find somewhere else, pack the household chattels and move again. In addition our sudden change of mind had to be explained to the landlord, which was not a pleasant task. We did not want to make ourselves conspicuous in any way. We had been glad to sign a proper contract with him and now, after only one week, we suddenly gave notice. What explanation could we offer? We were not leaving the city and stood to lose several weeks' rent paid in advance. We agreed that Rolf was to blame everything on his capricious wife, who had suddenly decided that the house was too much work for her and wanted a flat. When that was behind us he returned to Warsaw. Ollo, the children and I moved into the new apartment, where I prepared my transmitter-gramophone and sent messages twice weekly.

Our flat was sunny and the large living room had a deep double window intended for a small winter garden. Instead of flowers I filled the space with Nina's crib. There she slept and played for hours. Micha had his sixth birthday in Danzig and we celebrated by going out to see a children's play – 'Mother Holly'. It was his first visit to the theatre.

Discreetly I sought to inform myself about the other residents in the block. One floor above me lived a Nazi official. His bored wife seemed to enjoy gossiping, to me of all people, about who lived in the house and what went on in it.

One night when decoding a message just received, I thought it had been directed to the wrong person. Wasn't it quite feasible for such a mistake to occur now and again? And yet this was the one message which began by addressing me personally: 'Dear Sonya'. Quoted from memory, it went something like this: 'The People's Commissariat for Defence has decided to award you the Order of the Red Banner. We congratulate you warmly and wish you further successes in your work. Director.'

I had thought that this military order was given only for courage at the front line, during the Revolution or the Civil War and did not understand why I had received it. At first I felt quite numbed, but this slowly gave way to joy, though not without a degree of fear that my value was being overrated.

Shortly after this, while out shopping, I met the wife of the

Nazi. Her husband was away for a few days in connection with his work. We talked about the bitter cold weather and – inexhaustible theme – our fellow-residents. In the course of this gossip she asked: 'Do you get a lot of interference on your radio these days? Last night it was quite bad again.'

'I haven't heard anything,' I replied, 'What time was it?' She told me. 'Oh I don't listen that late. I'm already asleep by then.'

'My husband says there's someone transmitting secretly quite near us. He is going to arrange for the block to be surrounded from Friday on. He'll be home by then.'

I still had one opportunity to transmit before Friday. I watched everything closely. The man really did not seem to be at home. I had worked out to the second how quickly I could hide the gramophone and burn my message. But that would not have been much use. Interruption of my transmission would have given me away.

The appointed time for radio contact was approaching. The Nazi's flat upstairs lay in darkness. The house was not surrounded. That would in any case have been an unusual method. They were much more likely to use triangulated detection on the block. Reception was good and so transmission did not take long. I reported the reasons why I could not transmit again and that I would be listening for a reply on Thursday or Saturday. The next morning I took the gramophone transmitter to a comrade in our group.

Today it seems to me that I committed a number of errors and that I acted recklessly considering what was happening in the town. Even if it was difficult to get accommodation, it was wrong to move into this flat. Why did I not realise that with the current political situation in Danzig, the new blocks were largely occupied by Nazis?

I should also have fixed my transmission time for a much later hour at night, when no one in the block would have the radio switched on. And why, in my position, did I transmit from my flat again? No doubt I was anxious not to endanger anyone else. But wouldn't it have been better to take the equipment there and then to another member of our group, erect an aerial and transmit from his place just for one night? I only needed to ensure that I was not being shadowed on my way to the comrade. Or I could have gone back to Warsaw and called from there. I had brought the transmitter across the frontier between Poland and Danzig before, when I first came here. Of course there were controls but these were less of a risk than the alternative I had chosen and the equipment had to go back with me in any case. Maybe I did not want to leave Danzig without permission from Centre.

At the time such thoughts did not bother me and I was sure I had acted rightly. The prudence and experience I possess today would have helped in my work then. But today I have less resilience and slower reflexes.

The answer from Centre came on the Thursday and was repeated several times, since I was not transmitting and so could not confirm reception. I was to return to Poland.

Once again my household had to be wound up.

It was March 1937 – I had been in Danzig about four months. In Poland we moved to a different suburb, 40 minutes' bus ride from Warsaw. The address was Villa Joaska, Skolimow. Once again we lived in a two-family house with a garden bordering the woods. The flat upstairs was unoccupied.

Here I received news from Centre, it must have been in May, that a comrade would meet me in Novy Swiat, one of Warsaw's main streets, at a certain corner. Identification would be no problem.

As always, I arrived punctually. I was never late for a meeting, not even by a minute. Then, as now, I considered punctuality to be an essential part of underground work.

I had walked up and down for a short while. When I recognised an approaching figure, it was difficult for me to refrain from embracing him, my boss, Comrade Andrei. He had come to check on our work for himself, a good thing which should have been done more often.

Comrade Andrei stayed in Warsaw for a few days. He liked our house and how we had furnished it. He said he could now understand why we had needed such modest financial outlay. Not knowing how long we were permitted to stay in Poland, we had, rather than getting furniture at an ordinary shop, bought it

'Villa Joaska', Skolimow, outskirts of Warsaw

roughly finished from a joinery and Rolf had painted it himself in bright colours.

I regarded Andrei's visit as that of a friend and showed him Janina with pride. Now he learned that Ernst was the father.

We talked about my work and travelled to Danzig together.

During the journey Andrei said he wanted to talk to me, not only as my superior but as a friend; he hoped I would take it in that spirit. It seemed to him that I no longer radiated the happiness which everybody had so loved at the school in Moscow. Did the separation from Ernst depress me? How were things with Rolf? I told him that I valued Ernst highly and still missed him but did not want to return to him. I also told him how things were between Rolf and me. Andrei was the sort of person with whom you could discuss such things. I told him that there was nothing amiss. I merely had the bad luck of all lively people: when they weren't quite as cheerful as usual, others noticed it much more than with the quieter types.

He laughed, took my hands in his and said, 'Sonya, Sonya'. Later he told me that he was satisfied with my work and that the Director had asked him to tell me so as well.

I, on the other hand, told him how inexperienced I felt in my job; I found it difficult to follow the latest developments in transmitter construction and most of all would like to receive further training in the Soviet Union.

To my amazement Andrei agreed. I was to come to the Soviet Union for a few months and then return to Poland.

At times like these it was invaluable to have Ollo with us. Micha and Nina would be in the best of hands during my absence.

Comrade Andrei wanted me to signal Centre to tell them when he was intending to return. It was only a short message. In Warsaw I worked with batteries – two each of 120 volts, I think. Rolf was in the room when I set up the transmitter that night. I do not know what I did, but I received a severe electric shock. I screamed and could not pull my hand off the circuit. Rolf, who disconnected it at once, turned quite pale. There was a smell of burning and my thumb and index finger bore scorch marks. Finally I started transmitting, but that night the gremlins were loose. It hummed and buzzed and crackled continuously. I could not understand the person on the other end, neither could he take my message. And all I had to send were 40 to 50 groups. I tried for hours and got no further. It was embarrassing to confess my failure to Andrei the next day. He asked me angrily what would have happened in case of a really important message.

The next night I got through, although still with considerable difficulty.

Before saying goodbye, Andrei told me that the papers had reported sunspots causing atmospheric disturbances and resulting in widespread interference with radio communications.

In June 1937 I travelled to Moscow. We sent the children to Rolf's parents in Czechoslovakia. Ollo accompanied them and they rented a neighbouring chalet. When I thought of Rolf's mother with Janina, whom she believed to be her grandchild, I did not want to be party to the detestable deception any longer. Rolf, however, begged me not to cause additional grief to his mother during these hard times under Hitler.

From various letters I gather that I went to London first, to obtain a Soviet visa on a false passport or on a detachable page.

I stayed in the Soviet Union for three months.

A year later, in the summer of 1938, I spent a similar period there, before being sent to a new country. As it is difficult for me to distinguish between the events of these two visits, I will not try to recount them chronologically, but describe them together.

Soon after my arrival in Moscow, while I was waiting to see Andrei at the house on the Arbat, I met a German comrade who had also been called to see him. Our conversation was reserved, as was customary among those of us working clandestinely, but I learned that he had been married to my former room-mate Gerda. Only when I met him a second time did he tell me what had happened to her. They were sent out together to a colonial country. At sea, on their way to the new assignment, Gerda fell in love with an English police sergeant and declared that she could not live without him. An unsuccessful attempt at suicide followed. Under these circumstances her husband could do nothing but return to the Soviet Union alone. Such improbable penny-dreadful escapades did occur in the course of our work.

As soon as I arrived, Andrei sent me on leave to Alupka on the Black Sea. Karlosh was now working directly with Andrei. He saw to all technical matters involving foreign colleagues and took me to the railway station. Karlosh was a quiet and modest man. He did not overestimate his capabilities but one could sense what a reliable old Bolshevik he was.

I stayed in the rest-home in Alupka for four weeks. There were twenty of us in a dormitory and I made friends with quite a number of wonderful Soviet women. While I was in Alupka, I went to see the writer and comrade Berta Lask, who was living in Sevastopol or Yalta. Her husband was a doctor there. Between 1924 and 1928 I had visited her several times in her flat in Berlin-Lichterfelde, together with Gabo Lewin and Heinz Altmann. Heinz and Gabo had been two of my best friends in the

Communist Youth in Germany. When I was eighteen, I had once spent a week hiking on the island of Rügen with Gabo, who was a most cheerful companion. In 1924, when I had saved enough money from my wage as an apprentice, he bought an automatic for me. He and his friend Heinz Altmann taught me how to shoot in the Grunewald, a forest on the outskirts of Berlin. During the Nazi searches, my weapon was hidden among the roof timbers of our large house. Berta informed me that her eldest son Lutz, along with Gabo and his wife Herta (whom I also knew from Berlin), were living in Moscow.

I imagine that Gabo must have been especially pleased when we met again in Moscow. Other people had told him that my letters from China showed I had embraced bourgeois society and was lost to the movement.

Now Herta and Gabo had a baby. Today the little boy has children of his own and is a good comrade.

When I first returned from Alupka I lived in a Moscow hotel. Among the comrades who visited me there was Bruno Kühn. I had known him from Communist Youth days and now met him by pure chance – in the street. His red hair, freckled face and very blue eyes were unmistakable. In Berlin we had met at demonstrations and meetings and on week-end excursions, without knowing each other well. But what joy it was to meet a comrade from the German Youth movement in the streets of Moscow, knowing that he had been arrested by the Nazis. He had escaped and fought in the Spanish Civil War as a commissar in the 1st Partisan Battalion. We talked at length about Spain, the situation in Germany and about the communist children's movement, which had always been of particular interest to him.

He lost his life in 1941, fighting behind the fascist lines.

One day, as I walked along a corridor in the house on the Arbat, a young soldier came out of one of the rooms, and through the half-open door I caught sight of Paul from Shanghai sitting behind a desk. Elated, I rushed in and hugged him warmly – not exactly etiquette considering the military rules of the house. Paul wore the uniform of a high-ranking officer. He was as pleased as I was and invited me to his house that same evening.

Soon after my return from Alupka, Andrei told me to prepare

to receive the Order of the Red Banner. I put on my good grey suit, polished my shoes and gave my hair unusual attention. I cannot remember where I climbed on to an open truck whose rough-hewn benches were occupied by Red Army men. The wind ruffled my hair, and we choked in the dust. On arrival at the Kremlin, we walked past the guards and through endless corridors before reaching a small auditorium. We waited a few minutes until an elderly, grey-haired comrade entered the room. It was Kalinin. For me it was a special honour to receive my order from his hands. I had read many of Mikhail Kalinin's writings and admired him. Before the revolution, he had been in prison fourteen times. Later he became the Soviet Union's first President. Now he was already over sixty years old. Although the presentation of honours must surely have been routine to him, he was sincere, warm and friendly. Our names were called in alphabetical order. Kalinin held my hand for a long time. The Red Army men applauded loud and long, maybe because I was the only woman among them. I still remember, as though it were yesterday, the pure kindness on Kalinin's face.

The number of my Order was 944. At that time they did not have safety clips and I had to make a hole in the lapel of my jacket to take the thick bolt, which was held in place by a nut almost one inch in diameter.

Later that day I met Frida Rubiner. I knew her from Germany. She was an old revolutionary and a splendid teacher of Marxist theory. Frida had known Lenin personally and had translated a number of his works into German. She saw the decoration and embraced me. That was the only day I wore it. It stayed behind in the Soviet Union when I went abroad.

In Moscow I also met Erich Kunik again. He was a comrade who had influenced me during my first years in the labour movement, between 1924 and 1928. He worked for the Central Committee and must have lived in Berlin-Zehlendorf because I knew him through my party activities in the 10th district. Erich was a clever, good-looking communist with a deep understanding of young people. I visited him in his Moscow home, where he lived with his wife and son. We immediately resumed the good relationship we had enjoyed in Germany.

The Order of the Red Banner

Quite contrary to our rules, I had been trying to write a novel in Poland. From the age of fourteen, I had dreamed of becoming a writer. Many a manuscript had lain stillborn in the cupboards of my childhood and early youth.

The inspiration for this novel had been Sepp. A White Russian woman meets a German living in Shanghai. She falls in love with him and becomes his wife, not knowing that he is an illegally active communist. She only discovers this during a journey that is supposed to take them to Europe, when her husband discloses the truth: they are going to live in the Soviet Union. She trembles at what must seem to her a sinister future. But the impact of her experiences in the Soviet Union and the influence of her husband transform her. By the end of the book she is a communist.

With an uneasy conscience, I had brought the manuscript to Moscow. I had broken the basic code of illegal work, both in writing it and packing it in my luggage. I hoped very much that a publisher might be interested in it.

After I had left the Soviet Union again, I wrote to Jürgen about its fate:

> 11th October, 1937
>
> The manuscript is a total failure. Six people have read it and five share the opinion that, while its contents are very interesting, its style is clumsy and, above all, the ending must be changed completely to conform with today's conditions.
>
> *The girl must not adopt the man's views but, on the contrary, must bring about his ruin*!
>
> It could be published after a thorough revision. This decision was taken just before I left, but it would have meant about three months' work. The sixth person who read it was Erich K., whom I visited several times. After he had read half the manuscript, he suggested that I put a match to it. It was quite worthless. His wife (someone else told me this), called it a 'trashy thriller'. I can agree with the first five readers but Erich is too harsh and his wife's views I find downright stupid.

My manuscript was most kindly received by Frida Rubiner. She had offered it to a publisher who was prepared to print it with some alterations. But I did not have time to revise it, and my hopes of any sort of literary talent vanished. One thing is pretty certain: the manuscript really was worthless. I left it behind in Moscow.

It was typical of those years when mistrust was so quick to rear its head that all six readers insisted on the same point: this communist and the world's first socialist country must not be allowed to convert the White Russian, she must remain the enemy who draws the husband into her own destruction!

It was the time of the personality cult and the violation of socialist legality. It would be wrong to pass over this period, which had tragic consequences for many people.

When I visited my old friends in Sokolniki, I only found Lisa and her children at home. Her husband had been arrested. Lisa, quite calm and collected, told me that she knew one thing for sure – her husband had never committed a crime against the party or the Soviet Union.

We both had the same explanation: a serious mistake might have occurred in his work. At a time when the imperialists were stepping up their campaign to destabilise the Soviet Union by infiltrating saboteurs and agents, it was no easy matter for those responsible to distinguish between the mistakes of honest comrades and enemy actions. With so many guilty, it could happen that innocent people might sometimes fall under suspicion too; but this would all be cleared up. Capitalism in its death-throes was more dangerous, vicious and cunning than ever, and would stop at nothing in its efforts to damage the Soviet Union and destroy it from within.

When friends I trusted as I would myself were hit by the effects of this period, I was deeply shaken. I remained convinced that they were communists and not enemies, but they might have made mistakes that aroused suspicion. I myself worked illegally for a military organisation where a single error could endanger many colleagues, and the person responsible would have to be called to account.

Years passed before I knew that these condemnations were serious violations against the standards of socialist justice. Coming to terms with that was a painful process, particularly when we learned the then unthinkable – that Stalin was chiefly responsible for these crimes.

Karlosh had his worries too. Once when he was saying goodbye, he added: 'Oh Sonya, you, at least, always cheer me up.' I never saw him again.

For some time during my stay in Moscow, Comrade Andrei put me up in his home, where I met his family and enjoyed his intelligent discussions. Later I had a flat in a block belonging to the Red Army. Based there, I visited a radio school and learnt to build a more complicated transmitter, a 'push-pull' type. I was taught by a charming American comrade known as George, a good teacher and a good friend. Later his wife and two children also came to Moscow and I visited them several times during my second stay in 1938.

I also met Grisha from Shanghai again; we saw each other

frequently. The Moscow-Volga Canal had recently been opened, with a port in Khimki near Moscow. Grisha wanted to arrange a special treat and invited me on a canal voyage which lasted several days. He was delighted with my Order of the Red Banner and asked – clandestine discretion permitting – whether I could tell him what I had done. I felt embarrassed because, even if I had broken silence, which I never did, I could not think of anything heroic to tell. He never even found out that I was living in Poland, his home country.

I remember him laughing at me when we were in the cinema. A ship ran into distress: the radio operator tried to signal SOS but the set went dead. Water flooded his cabin and was rising fast. Gripped by despair, the operator seized the transmitter and shook it violently. I whispered to Grisha: 'That's just what I do when mine doesn't work properly.'

It was the last time I saw Grisha. When it was time to go abroad again, contact had to be broken even with your best friends.

Then came the war and conditions were even more difficult.

If Grisha had survived, he would have tried to find me and would have succeeded. He knew my maiden name. It would have been possible to reach me through Father or Jürgen, whose books were well-known to comrades. Others have used that method.

I was particularly happy to see Isa again. We resumed our close friendship immediately. Isa also knew Frida Rubiner well. When I left the country it was farewell for ever to Isa. In the 1950s a letter arrived, addressed to Jürgen in the GDR:

> Dear Professor,
>
> A short while ago I bought a copy of your book *On the History of German Imperialism*. From the preface (in Russian) I gather that you are at the University of Berlin. I am writing to ask you whether you could please let me have the address of your sister. For years we were the closest of friends but we lost touch with each other during the adversities of the war and post-war years. How happy I should be to make contact with her again.

It was some weeks before I was able to answer. I received no reply and went to see Comrade Frida Rubiner who, having returned to the GDR, had written to say that she now lived in Kleinmachnow near Berlin. She was pleased to see me again, had heard from Isa, but did not have her address.

I lost touch with Lisa's family too. In 1959, when I visited Moscow to gather material for my book on Olga Benario, I went to Sokolniki Park. The old wooden houses were still there, but I could no longer remember which one had been hers. Anyway, there was hardly a hope that I would find the family there after such a long time.

To my great regret, my superior and friend Andrei was given a new assignment around this time. I did not know what it was. His successor, Comrade Hadshi, was an Ossetian. He had fought in the Civil War in Spain and married a foreigner there. Hadshi was squarely built, his head was shorn and his eyes were dark. At times his round face bore an impish expression.

Ivan Vinarov, who was a very capable intelligence officer, describes him in his book *Fighters of the Silent Front* much better than I could.[2]

> Umar Dziorovich Mamsurov – Hadshi – had already gained considerable experience during the revolutionary fight against White Guard bandits in the Caucasus. In 1922, Umar was discovered by Mikhail Ivanovich Kalinin, who had journeyed through that still lawless region. Bandits attacked Kalinin in a village. Umar was one of the Red Army men wounded when fighting off the bandits. Kalinin took the young – barely twenty-year-old – communist along with him on the journey back to Moscow and recommended him to Bersin, then Chief of Intelligence of the General Staff of the Red Army. Thus began the career of this notable Soviet Intelligence officer.

Meeting his friend again in Spain, Vinarov describes a wonderful episode. Hadshi was involved in successful actions with the partisans and was later adviser to Durutti, one of the few reliable militant Spanish anarchists. Now Hemingway, the writer and journalist, was eager to contact a partisan leader and pursued Hadshi, who fled. Mikhail Kolzov and Ilya Ehrenburg, friends of Hemingway, finally succeeded in bringing the two together, but

Hadshi refused to talk. 'He drinks too much,' said Hadshi. 'I don't trust people like that. Anyway, when does he find the time to write?' Kolzov pleaded with him to be diplomatic and at least tell Hemingway a few of his experiences. 'Hemingway writes well,' said Kolzov, 'and his reports on Spain are the most honest and the best to appear in western papers. You can't refuse point-blank to co-operate with such a man.'

Hadshi, who respected Kolzov, at last gave in and became quite helpful, patiently answering Hemingway's many questions about partisan campaigns, dynamiting bridges and derailing trains.

And now I know why Hemingway's book on Spain, *For Whom the Bell Tolls*, was so realistic.

I did not get to know Hadshi as well as I had known Andrei, but I liked and admired him. He and Andrei were decent, hard-working people to work for, good friends and valiant comrades in uneasy times. I believe they held a protecting hand over me, too.

For years afterwards I often thought of these two comrades warmly, without knowing what had become of them. Then I heard that Hadshi had fought as a general on the West Russian front during the Second World War and died only a few years ago. Andrei had also been a general in the war. He died in 1972. How much I would have liked to have seen them once more.

In 1937 or 1938, during one of my visits to Moscow, the Chief of Military Intelligence called me to his office and asked about my experience in Poland. He was especially interested in our efforts to obtain a residence permit, what sort of questions had been put to us, how we had answered them, what level of officialdom we had negotiated with, what possibilities existed for legalisation in Poland, what would be appropriate for our workers there, what cover stories would be plausible. While I answered these questions, the Director was leafing through my passport with its innumerable temporary residence extensions. 'Sonya,' he said, 'I know what a battle it must have been for you both just to stay in the country.'

I was pleased for this opportunity to praise Rolf for his part in the matter. This Chief of Intelligence impressed me, but I did not see him again. Unfortunately comrades in leading positions changed frequently at that time.

I was to attend a school near Moscow which trained partisans as well as intelligence workers. Before I started, comrade Hadshi said to me: 'A good friend of yours is in Moscow and wants to see you if you agree.'

It was Ernst.

Hadshi brought him to me. The first words of that professional revolutionary were: 'Good, you're just as slim as ever.' I threw my arms around him without speaking.

Ernst and I were at the same school and we resumed our old relationship for the three months that we were there together – without any conflicts and without worrying about the future. Only once – after he had told me all that had happened to him – did Ernst ask me whether I would stay with him.

In spite of his undoubtable qualities, he was even more irritable, hard and intolerant than before. Once again I refused, although these shortcomings did not affect me personally during our time in the Soviet Union.

Ernst and I were doing the same course. I kept my flat in Moscow but a camp bed was put up for me in school, so that I could stay there when we worked late. All the other pupils, including Ernst, lived at the school. There were five other comrades besides Ernst and myself – former International Brigaders in Spain.

I remember one of them, Felix, particularly. He was a tall and powerful Pole who spoke German. He had been wounded in Spain and was unable to use his left arm which, despite treatment, was wasting away. He was courageous and intelligent. Another comrade who had fought in Spain struck me as rather limited, although good-natured.

The instructor who was training us for partisan work was a Soviet captain. He had taken part in the Spanish Civil War and had been awarded the Order of the Red Banner. He lived at the school with his wife and two children. We learnt what a partisan operating in enemy territory must know, especially the use of explosives. Chemistry seemed to be more in my line than the theory of radio communications, perhaps because of my practical experience in Mukden. I learned all the compounds that could be made from the so-called safe explosives, ammonium nitrate and potassium chlorate, and the different additives such as sugar, permanganate, aluminium powder and iron oxide. I have forgotten most of it now and may well be quoting them incorrectly. We dried the damp ammonium nitrate in huge frying pans over a fire and treated the chemicals rather flippantly. For instance, we prepared a highly sensitive explosive mixture of acetone, sulphur and hydrochloric acid (I may have got the ingredients wrong) which gave off dangerous caustic gases. We would then run out of the room until the gases had evaporated. This left a highly irritant flake-like residue which we stuffed, without more ado, into empty capsules. These carried electric fuses which we had soldered on beforehand. We laid a section of rail on a field outside and placed the explosive next to it. I learned to cut the detonating wire ready for use and set the contacts. Besides electric detonators, we also ignited fuse cords of different lengths, running away and throwing ourselves on the ground before the explosion.

Explosives were also detonated with an incendiary compound which took a predetermined time to eat through a layer of rubber.

We built explosive charges actuated by a clockwork mechanism, and others that went off on impact from a passing train. To ensure their anti-magnetic quality, we used wooden containers. All this happened fifty-three years ago and bears no comparison with present-day technology.

I liked learning at this school; the only trouble was that Ernst had no respect for our teacher and showed his contempt. Ernst was undergoing his second training in this subject and his fanatical thoroughness made him an indomitable learner. Perhaps he really did know more than our teacher. Anyhow, a strained relationship developed between them. Again and again I tried to calm Ernst down and avoid an open confrontation. Later, after I had left Moscow, Ernst was taken away from the school because of the difficulties he caused.

The school must have been in the vicinity of the new Moscow-Volga canal: I remember our group often went swimming there. It was a very dry summer and at first we were pleased to bask in

'Villa Maja', Zakopane

the unbroken sunshine. But when the grass began to scorch we joined in the general anxiety about the harvest.

The others knew that Ernst and I had met before, but we were discreet in their presence and no one knew that we had a daughter.

A postcard written to my parents on 24th September, 1937 describes my return to Poland via the Scandinavian countries. I flew for twelve hours. I found it hard to say goodbye to Ernst.

The house where we had lived before had been sold. Rolf's work frequently took him to Kraków, and since I was meeting the Bulgarian comrade there at regular intervals, we decided to leave Warsaw. We travelled to Zakopane and rented a log house that we liked very much. From 'Villa Maja', 900 m above sea level, we had views of mountains up to 2,000 m high. The landscape was beautiful and I learned to ski with the greatest pleasure. We used to go on long cross-country excursions on our snowshoes.

My letters no longer contained any political comments. They were exclusively concerned with family life and, as always, they were cheerful.

Winter 1937

Nina is delightful. She is a real 'hit', but unfortunately short of lyrics – in fact she doesn't speak at all yet. Micha is great fun. He has developed a new statistical flair which brings a flood of questions: 'How many children in the world are going to school today? How many are eating spinach?' And then suddenly: 'What does our house mean to a flea?' I found him busy measuring our kitchen stove. The result: 'The stove is to a flea the same as a house with 98 floors is to us. I can't tell how high our house seems to a flea until I know how to multiply numbers over ten.'

. . . I have had a touch of 'flu and was finding it difficult to sleep at night, and so I have been drinking sugar water. Our newspaper recommended this as a marvellous sleeping draught. Oh yes – our newspaper! There is a romantic serial running right now: 'I was an ugly girl.' This maid goes to the hairdresser, is permed and dyed back and front, plastered with every kind of face-pack and – lo and behold – she's beautiful.

'That's just what you need,' says Rolf. So off I go to the beautician. They stick paper under my eyes, they paint my lashes and brows with black goo. It smarts horribly but I keep my eyes closed and endure it. This is just what happened in the story about the ugly girl, so I sat there waiting expectantly for beauty. When I was allowed to open my inflamed eyes, black tears mixed with real ones came gushing forth – I hadn't become beautiful at all. I hardly dared to go home and when I did, Rolf gave one look and collapsed on the sofa in hysterical laughter. 'Like a tart,' he screamed. It took two evenings of pumice-stone and grease to get myself back to normal.

Soon after we had settled in Zakopane I was asked to go to Danzig again because a comrade there had problems in setting up his transmitter. It was the young comrade from the school in Moscow who had worried me because he was so slow on the uptake.

He had acquired a non-political wife from the countryside,

Micha learns to read and write

Nina, three years old

which did not improve his position as an illegal radio operator. I helped him build his transmitter. We tried it out and, when contact had been established, I left again, pondering why, with so many outstanding comrades from Spain, this one had been chosen. No doubt he had shown courage, but that alone was not sufficient for the tasks now demanded of him.

I felt that I was not accomplishing much in Poland. The Danzig people had their own radio operator, the Bulgarian comrade produced little information. I only transmitted once a fortnight. So I was glad when we were recalled a year later, in June 1938.

But parting from the beautiful landscape and the house was difficult. Here my philosophical Micha had first discovered the relativity of large objects to small ones, here I had taught the six-year-old the wonders of reading, and Nina had grown up healthy and carefree.

Thirty-eight years later I returned to Zakopane. The Kasprowy and the Giewont greeted me, but thousands of new houses had sprung up everywhere, making the landscape quite unfamiliar. It was a hopeless task trying to find our house here. I had an old photograph with me and started walking towards the mountains. Finally I wandered along an unknown street until I came to a bus stop, ready to go back. I walked on a few paces and then stood stock-still.

There it was – our house!

In the old days there had only been a meadow here, no paved streets. I counted the beams of the house, I counted the boards of the balcony; I counted again and looked – there was the name carved into the wood – 'Villa Maja'. My heart beat faster. I rang the bell. A very old man came to the door, put on his spectacles and murmured: 'A photograph of our house . . . That is the balcony . . .' And there above that roof we had spanned our aerial.

5

Switzerland, 1939–41

Before returning to the Soviet Union in 1938, I took Ollo and the children to England and found a room for them in Felpham on the south coast. They remained there for the summer.

I have already described my three months in the Soviet Union. Towards the end of this period in Moscow, in August 1938, Centre suggested two possibilities: Finland or Switzerland. Finland was tempting because it seemed more interesting, but it would be easier for me to make contacts in Switzerland. Father knew a number of people who worked at the League of Nations in Geneva. And I would not have to cope with a new language there. I left the decision to Centre, and they chose Switzerland.

By chance, I discovered my army rank while I was in Moscow. In China it seems I had been a captain, but now I was a major. I know that a few years later my rank went up twice more, presumably to colonel. But, as far as I can remember, I was never informed officially, and it was of no consequence to me either. I did not wear a uniform, nor did I know how to salute, let alone march in line. True, I was a good shot with rifle and revolver. Despite my lack of interest in rank and regulations, I was proud to be a soldier of the Red Army.

Before I left Moscow, Hadshi introduced Hermann, my future colleague. He was a German comrade who had fought in Spain and had just finished his military intelligence training.

Our work in Switzerland was aimed at Nazi Germany. As soon as I had a firm footing, Hermann would follow me to Switzerland and attempt to make contact with the Dornier aeroplane factory in Friedrichshafen, Germany. I was also to build up a group independently of Hermann, preferably of comrades whom I could send into Germany or who were living there. Rolf would stay with us in Switzerland until I had settled in. He too had come to realise that we could no longer live together as we had before. He wanted to return to China and Centre had granted this request.

I suggested that I visit England first, to prepare for my work in Switzerland. I would try to make contact with members of the British Battalion of the International Brigade, who might be willing to work for us in Germany. Despite Hitler's tirades against 'perfidious Albion', individual Englishmen still enjoyed a certain respect in Nazi Germany until the war broke out. It was not unusual for the odd well-to-do Englishman to travel the world and settle for a while wherever he happened to feel like it, and if he felt inspired to choose Germany, then this was not at all out of keeping with the continental image of the eccentric Englishman. Centre agreed to my plan, but reiterated what I already knew: no contact with the British party. I kept to that.

From Moscow I took a number of detours before reaching London. It is difficult to recall the various routes by which I travelled and the different passports I used during my years of work in Europe. I remember passing through Nazi Germany twice. Once with a false passport when I had to change planes in Nuremberg and another time when I had to change trains in Berlin and Cologne. On several occasions I stopped in Paris and on another journey, in Finland. In Helsinki I got a Swedish passport.

In London I was reunited with Micha and Janina. Ollo had made a perfect job of looking after them. My children travelled from country to country and never really came to rest. Micha, with his seven years, had lived in Shanghai, Peking, Mukden, Warsaw, Danzig, Zakopane, Czechoslovakia and England. During this time he had learnt German, English, Chinese and Polish. Now he had to start on French in Switzerland. A permanent home, where he could put down roots, would have been far better for his development. I was therefore always at pains to create at least a good atmosphere and a healthy life for the children, wherever my work took us. They had been in the Polish High Tatra mountains for a long while and now three months at the English seaside. I intended to give them a good home in Switzerland as well.

In London, after some fruitless efforts, I made contact with a comrade who had fought in Spain and whom I had known in Germany. Originally he came from Austria or Czechoslovakia. I told him only the essentials. My political work was directed against fascism. I needed one or two comrades who had given proof of their courage and reliability in the course of the Spanish Civil War; they must be prepared for illegal, dangerous work in Germany. I did not mention the Soviet Union.

This comrade knew the leading communists in the British Battalion of the International Brigade. After consulting them, he recommended Allan Foote. I obtained his biographical details and signalled them to Centre, who agreed to my recruiting him. It had been decided that I should contact him while I was still in London, but he was ill. So I went to Switzerland, leaving details of a meeting place for him.

In September, soon after our arrival, the western powers signed the Munich agreement which betrayed Czechoslovakia and gave the green light to Hitler's expansionist aims. I wrote home: 'Of course our spirits, just like yours, have sunk below zero.'

In early October, after boarding in Lausanne, we found a house similar to the one in Zakopane. It nestled in the mountains of French Switzerland at a height of about 1,200 m, near the village of Caux. Far below on the plain, we could see Montreux and Lake Geneva, with the blue ribbon of the Rhône. In the distance towered the 3,000 m French Alps and behind the house the Rochers de Naye. Our new home, La Taupinière (The Molehill), was a small renovated farm-house which stood by itself on a hill. There were three rooms to the front of the house; the back consisted of a stable sheltering a dozen cows, with a hayloft above. The cows grazed on lush meadows just behind the building. They belonged to François, the farmer who lived about ten minutes away along the footpath. Soon we knew every cow personally and the children gave them names. At night the chime of a cowbell or the sleepy lowing of cattle echoed in our dreams.

In spring, tourists came from far away to admire the renowned wild narcissus field behind our house. The flowers were so heavily

View of Lake Geneva from 'the Molehill'

scented that at night we had to close the windows. In winter, novices in skiing from the hotels in Caux practised on the gentle slopes of our hill. If they were thirsty, we gave them drinks; if they were tired they rested on the bench in front of our little house. At other times of the year it was very lonely up there. A car would have to stop half a kilometre below our house. The Molehill could only be reached by a narrow, barely discernible grass path.

I arranged for Micha to attend a nearby boarding school which took day pupils. In Poland, I had taught him myself for two years. Now I was proud to be told that he was well ahead of his age group. He soon spoke French fluently. In winter he skied across the meadows to school; before he left in the mornings I fastened a torch to his anorak so that he could find his way in the dark.

In La Taupinière I set up my transmitter, which now had to bridge a distance of over 2,000 km. My room had a built-in linen cupboard, and below the boards at the bottom there was a cavity. Rolf and I built the transmitter into this space, replaced the covering boards and stood my shoes on top. The set remained in place during operation. When it was not in use, the two holes bored for the banana plugs were stopped with pegs which looked like knots in the wood grain.

I was able to start my transmission schedule sooner than usual, and communication with Moscow was good. I suppose I had, after all, acquired some technical knowledge by then.

From the passage on the first floor there was a door which led into the hayloft. The farmer collected his hay from the entrance outside and never came near this door, for which I had the only key. The hay provided a ready hiding-place for illegal material. To my parents:

> After the restricted boarding-house atmosphere, where we had to insist on the children behaving demurely, they are revelling in their freedom to romp on the meadows. The view from here is better than anything you would expect from a holiday hotel window, and as good as any panorama you could hope to enjoy after a long climb to some outstanding vantage-point. In fact you can't help feeling that you're dreaming when you look up from your routine dusting and dishwashing. Father, thank you for the letter to B. I will delay my visit until the bulk of our luggage arrives with my elegant hat nestling in its tissue paper.

B. was an Englishman named Blelloch, who held a responsible position in the ILO (International Labour Organisation) of the League of Nations in Geneva. A useful connection for me. I met his wife as well. She visited me in La Taupinière and I went to see her whenever I was in Geneva. But most of all I enjoyed talking to her father, Robert Dell, an intelligent and principled liberal journalist, alert and lively despite his considerable age. He wrote for the *Manchester Guardian*.

If this letter referring to 'B' had failed to survive, I would not have included him and his family in my Report. I had forgotten

La Taupinière, front view. I transmitted from the room to the left upstairs

Back view

their existence and, on reading this letter, I could not even remember who 'B' was. It all came back to me when I discovered his full name in a subsequent letter.

Unfortunately there are many other people who are not mentioned anywhere, and who are now lost to my memory.

I also met Marie, the head librarian at the League of Nations. She enjoyed gossip and knew many people, and I discovered a great deal through her. She had friends among the foreign journalists in Geneva who were just as fond of chattering. Marie introduced me to my friend Katya, a left-wing journalist. We were both interested in politics and so we often discussed her news items. Of course, Katya knew nothing about what I really did. During my frequent visits to Geneva I stayed with her overnight, thus avoiding hotel registration. It was typical of Marie and her circle that when she heard this she began gossiping among her acquaintances: 'Is it as innocent as it seems? After all, Katya only has one room and a double bed!' I disliked rumour-mongering, but I had far less to lose by this version of my Geneva visits than by a suspicion coming closer to the truth. However, to be fair to Marie I should say that she was also very helpful. She was instrumental in obtaining a Honduras passport for me in Switzerland when I needed one, admittedly at a price, but then this was demanded by the consulate. Marie's ability to help us derived from her position in a Jewish emigrant organisation with Zionist tendencies which was under American influence.

In the late autumn of 1938 I met Allan Foote, 'Jim' in Geneva. At that time he did not know that his mission would take him to fascist Germany. He had merely been sounded out on his readiness for international work under conditions as dangerous as the war in Spain.

I met him in Geneva two or three times and we spoke for several hours. Intensive conversations like this were important. I took note of everything, every word, cadence, gesture, every facial expression; and I pondered his reactions for a long time after we had parted.

He grasped things quickly and asked sensible questions. He seemed resourceful and shrewd; that was an advantage for our work; in new and unaccustomed situations, Jim would react quickly. He had clearly proved himself courageous and a good fighter in Spain, otherwise he would never have been proposed for this task.

The facts I know today about Jim the traitor and his infamous *Handbook for Spies* must not colour my view of him at that time. Jim made a good impression on me and, with few minor exceptions, so it remained for the whole period of our work together.

From the beginning, I had noticed his taste for the good life and the gourmet approach to food and drink. During our first conversations he also showed a tendency towards cynicism but, as this was directed against our enemies, I did not consider it cause for criticism. At that time he must have been in his early thirties. He was tall and a bit overweight. His hair was a reddish blond, the eyelashes were fair, complexion pale and eyes blue. His appearance was very acceptable and he knew how to behave. To another Englishman, his accent would have betrayed a lower middle-class background, but in Germany this would not matter. Jim was to live in Munich, keep his eyes and ears open, seek acquaintances among Nazis and, if possible, establish connections with the Messerschmidt aeroplane factory. I do not remember whether we organised any form of postal communication. He knew neither my name nor my address.

Soon a second English comrade arrived in Switzerland. Len Beurton had been won in the same way. He and Jim knew each other from the British Brigade in Spain. I met Len for the first time in January or February 1939, outside the Uniprix shop in Vevey. He was then twenty-five years old, had thick brown hair, eyebrows that met and clear hazel eyes. He was lean and athletic, strong and muscular. Half shy, half aggressive, he gave the impression of boyish immaturity. Len was seven years younger than I was. Unlike Jim, he was not interested in material things and, again in contrast to Jim, he was extremely sensitive.

When I told him that he had been chosen for dangerous work in Germany his face lit up. I explained how difficult it was for the comrades in Germany and why an Englishman had advantages in this kind of work. He saw his new task as a continuation of his fight on Spanish soil, which had been the most important

Len at 25

period of his life. He had only one worry. Was he capable of carrying out such an honourable task? I was convinced that he would make a great effort. Intelligent, well-read and a keen observer, he was a little clumsy in organisational questions and did not possess Jim's self-assured poise. People would find him a nice, shy young man. Len was to settle in Frankfurt am Main and try to make contact with IG Farben. At the time I attributed his enthusiasm for dangerous missions, apart from his political conviction, to his youth. Later on I realised that this was an integral part of his character which would not diminish with age.

When English and American International Brigaders visited the GDR for the first time, in 1959, they told me of Len's blind fearlessness. It was so pronounced that an American psychologist in Spain had asked Len for a consultation; the case interested him professionally, as he had never met anyone so completely devoid of physical fear. But the negative aspect was Len's constant dissatisfaction with everyday life. It would be wrong to conclude that he was in any sense an adventurer. Later he was to devote twenty long years to working conscientiously for the GDR at an important but sedentary desk-job.

Len first joined the Spanish Communist Party while he was there, and transferred to his own as soon as he was back in England. Now he found it hard to destroy his membership card and leave the party without offering any explanation.

He travelled to Frankfurt am Main. Once there, he became a 'paying guest with family contact' in the house of a widow whose late husband had been a Privy Councillor. She had her son and his young wife living with her. The son held the concession for Blüthner pianos in Frankfurt.

Len thought up the following story. His father had been killed in the war. His godfather uncle was well-to-do and an admirer of Germany, so he encouraged his nephew to have a look around the country and learn the language.

The family took an interest in the young Englishman, introduced him to the theatre, took him to exhibitions and tried to teach him German.

Hermann was the last of our group to arrive, at the end of April 1939. We were to meet at the Universal Postal Memorial in Berne. I was expecting Hermann earlier, but a comrade's chemical experiment at the school had ended with an unexpected explosion, flinging Hermann through a closed window. The glass had cut his chin; he could thank his lucky stars that this drama had taken place on the ground floor.

A vivid red scar is not exactly an advantage to anybody involved in secret work. He was forced to wait until the wound was fully healed. Hermann had attended the school with five other Germans. All of them had been sent abroad but, according to Hermann, he was the only one to reach his destination. Those tense months just before the outbreak of war were difficult for our illegal workers. By the time Hermann arrived, Austria and Czechoslovakia had already been occupied by Hitler.

Hermann settled in Fribourg in western Switzerland. He was to live quietly during those first months, find himself suitable

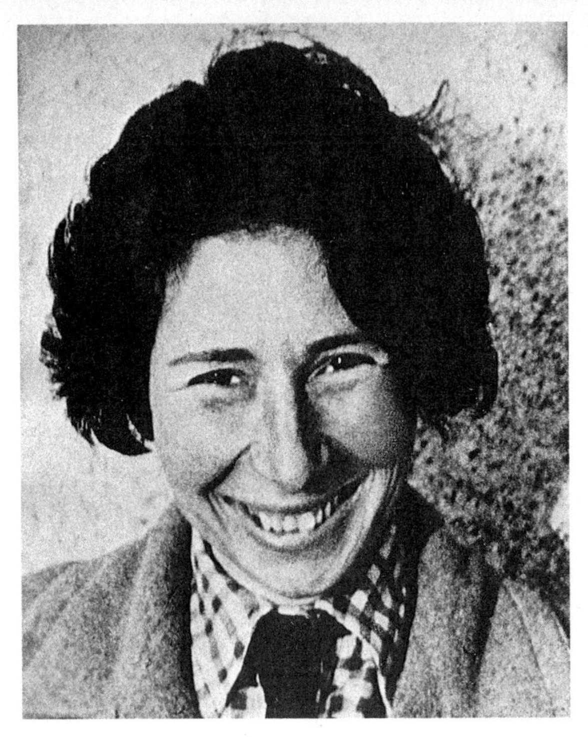

In Switzerland 1938

quarters and then build a transmitter. Hermann's history was similar to that of other communists from Germany. An active member since he was a young man, he had been arrested by the Nazis. Later he had fought in Spain. I felt perfectly secure with him, but not with his Finnish passport. Hermann did not speak a word of Finnish.

Our idyllic little house, the 'young mother with two little children' and the 'old nanny who used to nurse the mother' provided us with a respectable middle-class image.

For Christmas 1938, three months after our arrival, I invited two of my sisters and their English husbands to stay with me. My father also came to Caux. Apart from the fact that I was so glad to see them all, their visits reinforced my legal status.

I had received permission from the Swiss authorities to stay until 30th September, 1939. At the beginning of that year Rolf prepared for his departure. He had looked around in France and found a training school for radio operators in Marseilles, where he wanted to take a course before going on to China. He would be living inconspicuously, for learning a new trade was not unusual for emigrants, who had to make a living as best they could. After he had learned enough, he would disappear again.

It was lonely now, living on the very outskirts of Caux, which offered neither a cultural life nor much contact with people. I read even more than usual and tried to improve my knowledge of the language. Soon I was speaking fluent French. I knew English almost as well as my mother tongue, and I could make myself understood in Russian, Polish and Chinese. Today I have forgotten almost everything except English.

Before Rolf left, we had often spent time together with a German couple, Miriam and Werner. I cannot recall ever having had such good friends from bourgeois circles. They were emigrants living in Switzerland and waiting for their visas to leave for South America. They were my age and had two children. Werner was a good-natured, rather soft person; his horizon as a businessman had in many ways been broadened by his charming and vivaciously intellectual wife. We were soon inseparable.

Miriam also enchanted Father on several occasions when he visited Switzerland. I wrote to London:

> Miriam was pleased to get Father's letter. Although I am quite content to be his daughter, I must say that Father's letters to his daughter's girl-friends are considerably more amusing than those addressed to her!

Werner and Miriam lived in Montreux. We saw each other frequently and often spent the whole day together. Of course they knew absolutely nothing of my intelligence activities. I lived as they did, from 'my shrinking bank account'. In our many discussions I did however make it obvious that I had very left-wing views. Miriam was politically more radical than her husband.

I also made the acquaintance of Irene Forbes-Mosse. I do not remember how this came about, perhaps through my family. She was already well into her seventies. Her upright figure, blue eyes and white hair, her dignity and gentleness impressed me. She was a relative of Bettina von Arnim, the contemporary and admirer of Goethe. The economist Lujo Brentano, who died in 1931, had been Irene's cousin and close friend. Her house in Chexbres was furnished in exquisite taste.

Irene Forbes-Mosse was very like Bettina von Arnim: a progressive liberal who despised gossip, extremely well-read, and with a great many different interests. With my thirty-one years, I must have seemed very young to her. Perhaps she did not have much contact with other young people. Whatever the case, she grew sincerely fond of me and, later, of Len. It was touching how pleased she was when we visited her, and she spoilt us as though we were her grandchildren. When I once told her so, tears came to her eyes as she replied: 'But you really are like grandchildren to me.'

I mention my warm relations with Miriam's family and Irene Forbes-Mosse because they were part of my life in Switzerland, but also for another reason. Admittedly, I had to cultivate bourgeois acquaintances; but my friendship with these people was not a calculated one. We respected each other, and later on they helped me when I needed it. The same was true of my relationship with the wife of the farmer François. She worked very hard and had far more character than her husband, with whom she endured an unhappy marriage. We thought highly of one another and she too stood by me in time of need.

In every case they were people who hated war and fascism; otherwise they would not have been my friends.

I must have met Jim again by February 1939, and Len in March or April. After that I saw them together in June. Both knew that I wanted them to send me news based primarily on the mood, morale and opinions of people they met (many Germans were prepared to speak more openly to an Englishman), and that I was also interested in the potential for sabotage. Len's hosts had once taken him to Frankfurt airport, where the trans-Atlantic Zeppelin was on show in a huge hangar. A stream of visitors passed through the long gondola of the airship, which was divided into several compartments. Len noted all this carefully, the cushions on the seats, the curtains, the craft's impregnated canvas skin. He returned on a weekday, when there were fewer onlookers. It would be easy to conceal incendiary material there. Len proposed this to me. I thought it right that if Centre was in favour of the idea, Jim should also be involved. Len visited him in Munich. Jim was less than enthusiastic. He argued that with the Zeppelin standing inside a hangar, the draught would be too weak. Len and I were of a different opinion. Jim did not want to take this kind of risk in Nazi Germany. But to us anything which unsettled or damaged the enemy was important.

While Len was in Munich, he and Jim experienced an event which they reported to me. Today Len remembers it like this: as they approached Odeon Square, they witnessed by chance the end of an SS parade in commemoration of fallen members of the Condor Legion. This was the German legion which Hitler had sent to Spain in support of Franco. The Square was now being renamed 'Square of the Martyrs'. Ranks of the SS stood in formation on all four sides, each bearing a shield emblazoned with the name of one fallen soldier.

After the ceremony, Len and Jim looked for somewhere to eat. Walking down the Leopoldstrasse, they entered an inconspicuous restaurant on the right-hand side. Near their table sat a pretty girl, young, darkhaired; a tall blond entered; the two greeted each other coolly, sat together but did not converse. The door opened. Two large SS officers entered, behind them came Hitler. The owner greeted Hitler, who went into an adjoining room together with his entourage. Jim and Len were asked to put out their cigarettes, as the 'Führer' did not smoke. An adjutant appeared in the restaurant, bowed before the two women and escorted them to Hitler in the next room. Jim's German language teacher, a rather unwilling Nazi, told him later that the restaurant owner had supported Hitler before he came to power and since then the 'Führer' occasionally ate there. The brunette was Eva Braun, Hitler's girlfriend. The blonde was Unity Mitford, a supporter of the Nazis and friend of Hitler.

Later, after extensive conversations with Len, I reported to Centre that this presented an opportunity for coming close to Hitler and assassinating him. But before we could receive an answer, political events overtook us and eliminated this possibility. Len was disappointed. Neither of us believed in the effectiveness of terrorist attacks on individuals, a view that conformed with our party theory. But there were some people we considered so dangerous and bestial that we were both prepared to break the rules where they were concerned.

Centre showed interest in the Zeppelin. That was why I asked Len and Jim to visit me together in Switzerland in June 1939. I had acquired all the necessary chemicals and demonstrated their use. We assembled and tested the incendiary device. Within a certain period a chemical ate through a layer of rubber and ignited the inflammable compound. The whole thing fitted into a cigarette packet.

Len and Jim returned to Germany charged with making and testing devices like this on their own. This they did successfully.

In the early summer of 1939, as the danger of war increased daily, an expired German passport was useless to an emigrant. My Honduras passport did not give me real security either. Centre asked what possibilities there might be of obtaining another passport for me. We proposed that before Rolf left Europe, we should start divorce proceedings and I would enter into a pro-forma marriage with an Englishman. Both Len and Jim were bachelors. Jim's age was closer to mine and so we decided that I would marry him. Given the kind of life we were leading, it was of little consequence, since a divorce was possible at any time. Jim agreed.

In 1939, Rolf came to see us for the last time. When his return to China had been approved, Centre enquired whether he would be prepared to work under Ernst. Generous and principled as he was, Rolf had a high opinion of Ernst and agreed.

Ernst, coming from the Soviet Union, had little time to spend in Europe. He wanted to visit his mother whom he had not seen for years, but at the last moment he decided to come to me, since time was too short to do both. Here he saw his daughter for the first and only time. Janina was three years old and lovely to look at, lissom and high-spirited. Although I kept in touch with him, Ernst never asked about her again. I did not blame him, but neither could I understand him. Although I was glad to see Ernst, I deeply regretted that he had not gone to visit his mother instead. Having children myself, I felt sad that he had not granted her that joy.

Anyone unfamiliar with the situation in Switzerland at that time will hardly appreciate why I found the parting from Ernst and Rolf so hard to bear. There was scarcely any hope that a war could be avoided. Austria and Czechoslovakia were occupied by Hitler; would it be Switzerland's turn next? Would the war begin in our corner of Europe? Today, knowing that it did not work out that way, it might seem that Switzerland was a haven of peace, away from the storm of events raging over the world during those years. In reality, the atmosphere was terrible. Any emigrant with a valid passport did everything possible to leave the country quickly. There were rumours that emigrants whose residence permits ran out, including Jews, would be taken to the German border. According to my information there were cases where this actually happened. After the outbreak of war it became a tragic reality for many. The Swiss Federal Council was demanding 'the dispatch of refugees to their country of origin'. There was also a decree which laid down that Jewish emigrants were not permitted to work in Switzerland and would be 'expelled' for the slightest political activity.

The English passport was now important, but, as I accompanied Ernst and Rolf to the little train running from Caux to Montreux, it would still be a long time until I got one. Although I had chosen the separation from both of them and I did not regret my decision, I thought in my despair: war will break out and the only people who would do everything to help me and the children are leaving for good. I stood on the platform and watched the little blue mountain train until it had disappeared round the bend.

In August 1939 my sisters visited me once more. On 15th August we sent a light-hearted postcard to our parents at 25a Upper Park Road, London, NW3. Then the situation became so threatening that my guests left in a hurry.

On 23rd August, the day of the non-aggression pact between the Soviet Union and Nazi Germany, I met Hermann in Zürich. Shocked and bewildered we talked for hours: it was a relief to talk the matter over with an experienced comrade. We realised that the western powers wanted the communist Soviet Union and Nazi Germany to destroy each other, in which case they would emerge from the brawl laughing. A stop had to be put to that little plan. But even so, we had to suppress our emotions and rely on reason alone to take the pact in the right spirit.

Around this time I was expecting a visit from Jim. A fortnight earlier, Len had finally said goodbye to his hosts in Frankfurt am Main, on the pretext of a long holiday in London. In fact he had gone to the Tegernsee in Bavaria. He wanted to go back to Frankfurt, but only to set the incendiary device into position. He intended to leave the packet under a cushion in one of the Zeppelin's compartments. He would be a long way off before it went up in flames. Now he was waiting at the Tegernsee for Jim's return and for my final instructions.

I watched the political developments with extreme disquiet and Len also began to worry that the war could overtake him in Germany. His hotel was losing guests every day, and by now he was the only foreigner left. In Frankfurt things would be no different. He had been told to wait for Jim and then put the Zeppelin plan into operation. Meanwhile I had asked Centre whether the two Englishmen should remain in Germany in this situation. Jim was still with me when the command came to bring them both back to Switzerland, where I was to train them as radio operators. We immediately sent a telegram to Len and he arrived in Montreux just before war was declared.

On 27th August the Swiss Army was mobilised. The last guests left Caux in great haste. Hotels stood empty and shops were shut. Only the little grocery used by the villagers stayed open. Following the advice given to all Swiss citizens, we bought enough food supplies for two months.

On 1st September Danzig was occupied by Hitler's troops. I thought of my friends in that town. How would they fare? What importance their work would have now! How fortunate that we had prepared the transmitter in good time!

The invasion of Poland followed, with the declaration of war on 3rd September, 1939.

To my parents:

5th September, 1939

So now it has happened. As yet I can hardly believe it. Please write soon to let me know how you are affected by it all. This country has granted us further hospitality. I will stay up here. My permit will soon run out, but I expect it will be renewed since there is nowhere else I can go. It is lonely here. The railway service has been very much reduced and there are not many chances to go down to the valley . . .

Strange how the sunsets are still as beautiful and peaceful as ever and how the children seem almost alien in their untarnished joy of life.

October 1939 to London:

I don't hear much from you. I expect the post is slower now. I will send postcards in English between writing letters; I am sure they will reach you faster. I do nothing except join the haymaking now and again. Emigrants are not allowed to help the war effort. The Red Cross is organising things up here but I doubt whether I'll be given more to do than sewing pillowslips. You really feel like a parasite at a time like this. I have registered as a blood donor in case there are any wounded.

Last week I was in Geneva. The Blellochs invited me to stay overnight. It was very pleasant, as usual. Robert Dell was also there; lively as ever. He has amazing vitality for his age. The conversation was stimulating.

Haymaking was my 'day-time work'. Two nights a week I used the transmitter. Reports to Centre often followed visits to the Blellochs.

Was I deceiving people who were sympathetic towards me, who welcomed me warmly into their homes and trusted me? It would be wrong to see it in that light. I was interested in international events and followed them carefully; this meant that I could converse with a well-informed journalist like Robert Dell on the level that he enjoyed. Even if I had not had a special motive, my conversations with him would not have been very different. Naturally, with experience, I had developed a faculty for turning discussions to subjects and opinions that might interest the Soviet Union. I could, for example, find out much more about the interpretation which people close to the League of Nations were putting on the non-aggression pact and on the outbreak of war than could ever be gleaned from newspapers published in member countries. I did not have access to military information at that time, but political information was also important to Centre. When I was in Geneva I always tried to see as many contacts as possible, and if I went home empty-handed, at least my head was full.

Len and Jim had found quarters in Montreux, at the 'Pension Elisabeth'. I discovered an inexpensive toy at one of the shops which I bought on the spot for just 7 shillings. It was a Morse set, with key and buzzer powered by a torch battery and including the Morse code. Micha would play with it in the afternoons and, while he was at school, Jim and Len could use it during their regular training sessions at La Taupinière.

At the end of September or early October, Hermann needed to draw on my greater experience to build his transmitter. He came to live at our house for a few days. One morning while he was busy assembling his device upstairs, two officials of the Swiss Secret Service appeared at our front door. With Ollo's help I succeeded in warning Hermann. He concealed his transmitter parts quickly, but I could not conceal his presence. He had to show identification. I acted the young woman caught in an embarrassing situation with a young man while pressing her husband for divorce. I do not remember any specific questions about our radio. We hoped that this visit was a routine affair that might be expected in the deteriorating conditions following the outbreak of war.

The atmosphere in Switzerland was markedly tense. Counter-intelligence organisations were working overtime. Geneva, as the seat of the League of Nations, was an international meeting-place which attracted agents from all countries and a plethora of dubious foreigners; rumours abounded in the city.

Amateur radio communications had been forbidden when the war began, making detection of an isolated transmitter such as mine still easier. In Switzerland the technology of triangulated radio detection was more advanced than in Poland.

After mobilisation, a group of about thirty Swiss soldiers moved into disused barracks only 200 m or so up the hill from our house. This was not exactly convenient for us either.

Following the Swiss Secret Service visit to my house, Hermann and I went out after darkness fell to bury our transmitter in the dense forest below La Taupinière. We had a good hiding place in the wood, to the right of our house, but there a sentry on duty outside the barracks might have seen or heard us. There was no path down the steep hill; we moved as silently as possible. To bury two gramophone-sized transmitters among roots and undergrowth was hard work. Soaked in sweat, with wet feet and scratched hands, we crawled upwards, holding on from bush to bush. Suddenly Hermann stopped short, panting hard.

'Quiet Hermann, keep quiet,' I whispered.

When he had caught his breath, he said: 'On one lung that isn't so easy.' I learnt then that he had been wounded in Spain.

We had to reckon with a follow-up to the officials' visit and worried about Hermann's Finnish passport. We agreed to the very last detail what we would say if we were arrested.

The next morning two strangers walked slowly down the path that ended at our house. We first saw them a long way off. The transmitters had been hidden and no material was in the house. Ollo and the children would not come to any harm. As they approached, Hermann remained perfectly calm. I think he would say the same of me.

The strangers turned out to be soldiers. They walked around our house, stopped several times, and after a while went on their way again. Strange and inexplicable behaviour.

A few days later I was asked to meet someone from Swiss Security in a Lausanne café. An official appeared and asked me polite questions about the life I was leading. Eventually he said that they had received information that I possessed transmitting facilities. The delivery girl from the little grocery shop in Caux had denounced me. He actually used the word 'denounced'. Once, delivering groceries to our house, she had seen a Morse key. I laughed and insisted that we go to the nearest toyshop and view this sinister object or, even better, buy it, and show the girl how it worked. If the toy was no longer in stock we could go up to our house at once, although, since it belonged to my nine-year-old son, I did not know whether it would still function. The official indicated that there was no need for all this, although I repeated the offer a second time. After that I did not refer to it again as I did not want to attach more weight to the matter than the official himself had done. In answer to further questions, I told him that we were emigrants, that my father was a professor in England and that I lived on a small private income from my capital at a British bank; I also received financial support from my husband who had separated from me.

I was prepared for a question about Hermann. It never came. Before the official took his leave, I told him I felt offended that neutral democratic Switzerland should distrust Germans persecuted by Hitler, instead of concentrating on German Nazis of whom there were more than enough in the country. I said it in all sincerity and he replied, I believe just as sincerely: 'I would be a hundred times happier to do just that.'

My claim to have money in England was correct. I always put by three months' salary in a London bank account as a reserve for the children, in case anything happened to me and I had to leave them suddenly. An account in England was useful in other respects too. Centre used it to pay in money for me and my group. Soon after the war began, England blocked all transfers of sterling and we found ourselves in financial difficulties.

As far as I could tell, I was not under observation, and after a short break began to transmit again. This time Len helped me dig out the transmitter.

The hiding place in the wood was relatively safe, but getting to it was strenuous, awkward, and only possible at night. We therefore decided to prepare an alternative indoors for 'medium-risk' cases. The coal shed seemed suitable and Jim asked a carpenter to make a chest the size of the transmitter. Under the pretext of having to send valuable household goods to America, he asked for good workmanship and a watertight exterior for the long voyage. In those days everything required a foolproof explanation. The finished box was the masterpiece of a good craftsman. We were sorry we had to bury it one-and-a-half metres deep in a hole that Jim and Len dug beneath the shed. We put back the floor boards and shovelled coal on top. The shed could be entered any time without arousing suspicion; that box had to accommodate our transmitter on a number of critical occasions. With today's methods of metal detection, the deep hole with its protective heap of coal would be unlikely to escape a thorough search, but in those days it served us well enough.

Jim and Len came up to see me regularly, and with the help of the toy Morse buzzer, they made good, enthusiastic progress. Sometimes they stayed all day. Besides transmitting they were also learning the theory and practice of radio construction. I taught them everything I had learnt myself over many months at schools in the Soviet Union. It was general knowledge that my husband had left me and that I was thinking of marrying again. This helped to legitimise their visits.

Jim, robust and shrewd, was always cheerful, but I preferred the sensitive Len, who loved nature and took an interest in my children. Jim's ingenuity, his talent for organisation and his ability to make friends easily were useful attributes. He had, among other things, begun a flirtation with the Rumanian Foreign Minister's sister, who lived in Montreux. She was in love with him and told him whatever he wanted to know.

I noticed that when they were living at the Pension in Montreux, Len's relationship with Jim deteriorated. When I asked him about this, Len said Jim was now showing tendencies that had never had a chance to reveal themselves in Spain. He was an egoist and set too much store by pleasure. However, neither of us related this even remotely to the possibility of political dishonesty or a double game and I do not believe there was any reason to do so at the time.

Ever since the spring I had been trying to finalise my divorce. Rolf had left a letter to facilitate the procedure, and after a number of visits to the solicitor and the authorities, it looked as though success was in sight. However, as our 'marriage' drew nearer, Jim began to hesitate and then told me that he had a confession to make: before going to Spain he had promised to marry a girl in England; that was why Spain had come at a very convenient moment for him. If he got married now, this affair might be stirred up again. Would I consider Len instead? He was so shy anyway that the idea of marrying would never occur to him of his own accord. Len was a few years younger than I, otherwise I did not much mind who helped me become a British citizen.

I did not like Jim's explanation. Either it was true that he had actually promised to marry the girl (later I heard that she had been pregnant), in which case it was this, rather than any political reasons that had motivated him to go to Spain; or he had invented this excuse in order to avoid the pro-forma marriage which was so important for my security and accorded with the wishes of Centre.

Len agreed to the 'marriage'. I assured him that he could trust me to divorce him again as soon as he required. I did not grasp why he retorted with such uncustomary belligerence that he understood the meaning of a paper marriage perfectly well without further explanations from me.

Thirty-five years later – on a spring walk along the river Spree – we tried to recollect those days so that they would be recorded as accurately as possible in this book. I asked Len:

'When did you realise that you liked me?'

'In novels they would say "love at first sight". At our first illegal meeting in Vevey, outside Uniprix.'

Amazed, I replied: 'As early as that? I never had the slightest idea!'

'I didn't let on to myself for a long time,' he answered. We laughed about it together.

I only learned more about Len when he and Jim were living in Montreux and came up to my house regularly for Morse practice. Then, as now, I was always happiest out in the countryside and I went on a lot of hikes. Jim was physically lethargic; he preferred to stay on the meadow in front of the house but Len enjoyed coming with me. On these walks in the early autumn of 1939, he began to tell me more about himself. He was an orphan. His father had been killed in the First World War without ever seeing his son. His mother wanted to get rid of the boy. A railwayman's family took the child in for a weekly payment. His mother visited him a few times. He was barely six years old when she said to him: 'I'll come back in the school holidays.' The boy counted the days. The holidays began and he stood outside the railwayman's cottage every morning, watching the trains from London pass by and listening to them come to a halt at the station. Every morning he woke up with the fresh conviction that his mother would definitely come today. But she never came. Not in those holidays nor the next. She never came again and the payments ceased. The boy felt horribly betrayed.

I am not retelling this as a sentimental story, but because this treatment by a mother he never saw again, has been a negative influence on Len's attitude to his environment for the rest of his life. Over-sensitive and introvert, he has periods of depression when he feels betrayed by everyone.

At fourteen he went to work, at first on the land, then in a stone quarry, as a lorry driver and eventually as a car mechanic.

In a quarry in Jersey he worked beside a former seaman who had travelled the world in sailing-ships. An Irishman by birth, his name was Moriarty; he was seventy years old, broad-shouldered and six feet tall. For decades he had made his home in Seattle, which in the history of the American working-class movement had played a similar role to that of Hamburg in Germany or Clydeside in Scotland. There Moriarty joined the Industrial Workers of the World (IWW), the revolutionary anarchist trades union organisation of the United States. He told Len, who could have been his grandson, of sailors' mutinies on the whaling ships, of harbour strikes, of Joe Hill, the revolutionary murdered by the enemy, of demonstrations in Seattle, of meetings addressed by Jack London, whose books were among Len's favourites. The class-consciousness of the old man, his revolutionary ardour, his tales of the power and romance of working-class struggle influenced Len decisively.

In Caux I went skiing from autumn to spring. I had already had a lot of practice in Poland; in Switzerland I went into the mountains with Werner. From Caux, a thousand metres above sea-level, the train took us up another thousand metres and more, almost to the top of the Rochers de Naye, and we sped back down the slopes. I was certain that Len would love skiing, too. He did, and insisted too soon on taking part in one of these long excursions. This time his fearlessness had a bad ending. He shot down a steep slope, straight into a block of ice, hurt himself and broke his skiis. There wasn't a soul about. We had to work our

I read the book with much interest

way down slowly and carefully, in extreme cold; the descent, no problem on skis, became dangerous on foot. On this outing it dawned on me how much I liked Len.

Now, as an old woman, I take the licence of adding some lines about an incident that happened in February 1974. When I was writing these pages of my manuscript, I began to wonder whether I had allowed too much of my private life to slip into this account. Who, after all, is interested in my passion for skiing or the history of my relationship with Len?

I laid the manuscript aside and, as on most evenings, read for two or three hours. The book was *Christmas in Sorrento*. The Russian author Marietta Shaginyan writes about the friendship and the conflicts between Lenin and Gorky. I read the book with much interest because, like so many of my generation I had been greatly influenced by Gorky in my youth. His stories had awakened emotions in me as a fifteen-year-old that contributed to my becoming a communist. Two years later, Lenin's work reinforced these emotions with their appeal to reason. I owe it to Lenin that I remained a communist through all the tangles and turmoil of my life.

At the age of eighty or more, comrade Shaginyan recalls her youth in 1906 and writes:

> Summer in Switzerland, I climbed with my mother, who was still young, to the top of the Rochers de Naye from Montreux – or was it Glion – we walked all day . . . The Rochers de Naye! Ten years later, in December 1916, Lenin wrote to Inès Armand then at Clarens: 'Do you ski? You simply must. Learn, get hold of some skis and whatever happens, go into the mountains . . .[1]

I paused in my reading.

Everyone knows that Lenin worked prolifically and with intense concentration. Yet how wonderful – he also went skiing and advises a young woman: whatever you do, go into the mountains and ski!

And I had been on the point of deleting from my manuscript how much I enjoyed doing so!

It was not only Lenin, but also his wife who encouraged me. Comrade Shaginyan tells how 'Nadezhda Krupskaya was quite beside herself' when her life with Lenin in Shushenskoye was constantly portrayed as though they 'did nothing but translate the Webbs. What nonsense. They were young and loved one another.'

I see Marietta Shaginyan in the year 1906, climbing up 'our path' to the Rochers de Naye in bright sunshine. I follow her description of how, ten years later Lenin lived in Switzerland, working and preparing his country for the revolution.

I do not often speak of my past, but I would have loved to tell the old comrade that, twenty-three years later again, from a Swiss farmhouse below the Rochers de Naye, I transmitted messages to the imperilled country of Lenin.

The Rochers de Naye above our house (marked with an arrow)

Towards the end of 1939, Centre asked me if I could see some way of getting money to Rosa Thälmann.

I was sure that neither she nor her husband, Ernst Thälmann, had any connections with the Red Army. Moreover, it was clear from the tone of the enquiry that this was an act of support and solidarity and that Centre wanted to take advantage of any facilities which we had at our disposal.

I decided to send Ollo. She had a brother in Germany and could visit him for a holiday. Germans were permitted to travel between the two countries. Ollo was in her late fifties, small, grey-haired and in no way conspicuous. She would be of no interest to the Swiss or to the Nazis.

Ollo said she would go.

We had a clothes brush with a hollow wooden back which had served me in the past as a means of transporting money. Ollo and the clothes brush arrived safely in Germany. Rosa Thälmann was deeply moved. None of the comrades in Germany were allowed to go near her because they were working underground, and now this gesture of support came from the Soviet Union. Rosa said it would be difficult to spend the money because the authorities knew exactly what she had and recorded the numbers of her banknotes. But the fact that the gift had been arranged by the German comrades in the Soviet Union was an enormous boost to her morale, and worth more than the considerable sum of money she received.

In the winter of 1939, Centre gave me another task to perform. I was to meet a comrade. When I deciphered the message, I assumed that either this unknown person was to leave Switzerland or else we were to co-operate closely, otherwise so much detail would never have been passed on to me. I travelled to Geneva, went to the Rue Lausanne, pushed a letter through the door of number thirteen, and a few days later went back to Geneva to see the comrade.

Centre had given me a number of questions to ask. Did his office still function? What was his financial position? Might he be able to get messages to Centre via Italy or did he require a transmitter? Could he establish such contacts with his own resources?

The comrade was reticent. He did not seem enthusiastic about someone bursting into his flat with so much information about him and so many questions.

There was a pause. We looked at one another in silence. 'Albert' was thickset, verging on the plump; his movements were clumsy. He had dark hair, dark eyes and a melancholy air. I liked his work-room full of books and maps, the desk strewn with journals and papers. Albert struck me as a rather dry academic. He wanted to know how quickly his answer could be passed on to Centre and when a reply could be expected.

I was hesitant. Centre had asked me to support him but there had been no mention of my transmitter. And Albert had not yet answered a single question.

Only when I told him that this could be arranged quickly did he begin to describe his position. The route via Italy was not feasible. On the other hand he urgently needed contact with

Sándor Radó

Centre; this had been interrupted at the beginning of the war. Important information was lying idle. No doubt Centre had good reason for this interruption, but for him it was terrible. His transmitter had broken down and he had no operator.

To this I replied explicitly that transmission facilities were available and I would suggest to Centre that they should be put at his disposal until we had found other means.

And this was how I met Comrade Sándor Radó, who had been a political Commissar of the Hungarian Red Army at the age of nineteen. Two great passions filled his life: he was a dedicated communist and an obsessive cartographic scientist. His cartographical 'Geo-Press Bureau' in Geneva provided excellent cover for him. But comrade Radó himself describes all this much better in his book *Code-name Dora* published in Hungary, the Soviet Union, the GDR, Britain and other countries.[2]

On my next visit I also met Albert's wife, a German comrade whom I took to at once. Lene, in contrast to Albert, was vivacious, witty and communicative – in so far as the illegal work permitted. Their sons, ten and fourteen years old, and Lene's mother completed the family.

It meant a great deal to me to encounter a comrade like Lene, to spend a while in their home from time to time and enjoy the atmosphere of that harmonious marriage between the scholar and his exuberant wife.

When I think of Lene, I see us together in my mind's eye, recalling our younger days as communists, and talking about books. But most frequently I see us laughing. We were full of silly jokes; so much so that Albert, who was not the most lighthearted or frivolous of people would look at us disapprovingly. That only spurred us on to more nonsense.

Lene was interested in literature and was a talented writer. She came from a working-class background and did not have an easy childhood. She had made herself all she was.

In 1959, when Lene was no longer living, I wrote about her in *Olga Benario*. She was about seventeen when she began working as a clerical assistant with our Central Committee in Berlin. One day my friend from Shanghai days, Sabo, (whose husband Arthur Ewert was then a Communist member of the Reichstag), found her there in tears. Lene was sobbing her heart out, because a comrade had dictated to her in poor German, and her own grammar was not good enough to correct it. Sabo saw to it that Lene went to evening classes to improve her knowledge of the German language. In 1936 in France, Lene had played a vital role in the attempts to free Olga and Sabo when they were being deported in a German ship from Brazil into the hands of the Gestapo. The attempt failed since the ship changed its route and did not call at the scheduled French port. These details were given me in 1959, by Minna Ewert, Arthur's sister and a close friend of Sabo. She too had been involved in the escape attempt. In 1959, Minna Ewert lived near Potsdam, in an old peoples' home named 'Olga Benario'.

I was pleased when Centre assigned me the task of transmitting Albert's reports. Now my transmitter would be utilised to the full. During the first three months, Albert gave me his radiograms in ordinary text, which kept me busy. In addition to my own news I now had to collect Albert's, encipher it all, transmit by night and then decipher the messages for both of us that I received from Centre. I delivered replies to Albert and collected new reports from him. The journey from Caux to Geneva took about three hours. At the same time, I was still training Len and Jim.

It was Len's idea to prepare a torch for carrying Albert's messages. He hollowed out one of the two batteries and placed lead into the bottom of the empty shell to restore it to its normal weight. The rest of the space was for rolled up tissue paper on which we wrote the text. We then sealed the battery, which was outwardly indistinguishable from any other. We fitted a lower voltage bulb and it gave off a normal light from one battery.

There were no street lamps along the path to our house, so we naturally used a torch after dark. Later, when the Swiss also had to introduce the black-out, nobody went out without one.

The demand for a black-out in neutral Switzerland had come from Nazi Germany because, they maintained, the city lights gave bearings to British bomber squadrons on missions to Germany and Italy. Switzerland complied and also produced weapons for Germany in great numbers; large quantities of German war materials were transported through Switzerland to Italy. But I do not want to convey a false impression of the Swiss people themselves. Most of them rejected fascist Germany and hated Hitler.

With so much work to do, I would have felt happy if other worries had been fewer. I did not know how I could continue to support Hermann, Len, Jim, my own family and Ollo financially. Every channel for transferring money from other countries had now been blocked. I was therefore extremely relieved when Centre announced that a colleague would be visiting Albert with money for my group. He came in March and brought Albert his own transmitter but no financial support for me. I do not remember how I solved this problem, which was a permanent cloud on our horizon; we had to live very frugally.

But I had rushed ahead too quickly. In December 1939 we suffered a disaster far worse than any financial need.

After a reasonable period of quiet, Hermann collected his transmitter from me and prepared everything to begin radio work from his flat in the château 'La Rosière', in the Canton of Fribourg. I never went there. About a month later we met in Zürich, or was it Berne? He had some news for me which I passed on to Centre. From then on he was to operate his own station.

Hermann did not appear at the next appointment in December 1939. Neither did he keep the fall-back appointment. I waited a few weeks and then – contrary to agreed procedure – decided to ring him up at La Rosière from a kiosk in Geneva. A strange voice said he was no longer living there.

Hermann had been arrested on 11th December 1939. At the time I did not know that, but assumed this was the case and passed my fears on to Centre. They had of course already been informed of Hermann's meeting with the security officers at my house.

What could I do for him? I had no contact at all with the Swiss party and did not personally know any comrades. I decided to visit a solicitor whom I knew from Shanghai. He had been there to support our comrades the Noulens-Rueggs after their arrest. The address of his office was in the telephone book. I reminded him of our meeting in China and fortunately he remembered it. I told him about Hermann without mentioning our work or the Soviet Union. He promised to make enquiries and after some time he confirmed the arrest. He named another solicitor who would try to help Hermann.

Later, when it was discovered that Hermann was German, the Gestapo demanded his extradition. He had already been convicted of treason and condemned to death by a Nazi court. The Swiss authorities did not comply with the German demand because they had their own proceedings pending against Hermann.

We had to assume that his visit to me in La Taupinière in September 1939 was known to the authorities. I stopped transmitting for a time but continued to instruct Len and Jim. It would have been senseless to break off my contact with them suddenly. Len had become known as my 'fiancé' and it was natural that he and his friend should be with me frequently. For my part, I hardly ever went to their boarding-house.

No one came to enquire about Hermann. Nor, as I found out later, was he asked about me. Perhaps our hope that such cases were treated on a cantonal basis, without legal co-operation between our canton and Fribourg, had been justified. A fatal accident had befallen the security officer who questioned me in the Lausanne café. (Hermann was certain he read about it in the papers.) But this cannot explain what seems to amount to sheer negligence on the part of the authorities. Some sort of record must have existed. Perhaps the truth is that the official did not actually include my address in his notes. Where security officials are concerned, I have experienced so much incompetence alongside their thoroughness in every country I have worked in, that I have long since given up trying to puzzle them out.

Hermann had a difficult time at first. He was not ill-treated physically, but he was tormented in other ways. The electric light was left on continuously, he was interrogated to the point of exhaustion and threatened with extradition. His subsequent conviction was based purely on his violation of the passport laws and the punishment was mild. He remained in internment until the end of the war but had certain privileges. For example he could leave the camp once in a while and this enabled him to meet Len secretly during the summer of 1941, when I was no longer in Switzerland. Later Jim also met him once. These contacts were arranged by the lawyer, whom I had not met personally.

Before Hermann met Len, we had managed to let him know that when he arrived at the station in Geneva, he would watch out for a young man with a plaster on his cheek, as if he had cut himself shaving. The same comrade would meet him in the evening. Among other things, Len asked him on Centre's behalf whether he could do anything for Soviet officers who had escaped from Germany and were now interned in Switzerland. I believe that Hermann subsequently played an important part in helping to organise their complicated escape home.

In his book, Jim makes the interesting claim that he frequently provided Hermann with money. Len gave Hermann a hundred dollars. The one time Hermann met Jim he never got a penny.

According to Hermann's own reports he did, in the course of time, receive three thousand dollars, but from other sources. The Soviet officers required clothing, money and food for their flight. At the end of the war, Centre repaid this money.

Len's meeting with Hermann in the summer of 1941 had been our last contact with the German comrade.

The war continued another four years. I worried whether Hermann's health would enable him to survive such a long period of internment. It is difficult to convey to the younger generation of today not only how devoted we were to our cause, but what sacrifices it demanded and how much we took them for granted. What a life Hermann led! Underground activities in Germany, threatened with trial for high treason, armed combat in Spain, a year's training in the Soviet Union for the intelligence service, illegal work in Switzerland. Hermann was thirty-one years old when we worked together. Perhaps he would have liked to fall in love, to marry and have children? He renounced all that. He was shattered to find himself arrested in Switzerland before his work had begun properly, but even during internment he achieved a great deal. And then Foote in his *Handbook for Spies* dares to cast aspersions on Hermann for his alleged uselessness and for being such a financial burden!

In the autumn of 1958 in Berlin, when Len and I received our medals as 'Fighters against Fascism', we took our fifteen-year-old son Peter to the ceremony.

Suddenly someone behind me whispered 'Sonya'. It was Hermann.

We looked at each other and embraced, both with tears in our eyes. Peter, who had never seen me like this, looked away in embarrassment. I told him: 'This comrade was arrested during our struggle against fascism. He was tormented but he did not say a word. Otherwise I would probably not be sitting here and you wouldn't even exist.'

Peter's eyes shone: 'Can't he come home with us?'

Hermann came along and there was a second happy surprise in store for me. He told me that he was married and had five children. What beautiful moments there are in life. Later we met his wife too and liked her very much.

At the end of 1939 my divorce became final. Meanwhile I had begun lengthy investigations into how two people whose countries were at war with each other went about marrying. The procedure was complicated, to put it mildly. My German passport had expired long ago. If it was not recognised by the British authorities, I would have no papers. Could English citizens marry people without identification documents? On the other hand, if the authorities recognised the old passport, as a German I would be an undesirable alien. But if the British regarded me as an emigrant and a victim of Hitler, I would be equally unwelcome because so many single women in that situation gave their last penny to reach England by means of a marriage of convenience.

Ollo knew of the planned marriage. She hoped that it would help allay some of my worries. She was on good terms with Jim and Len and looked after them well, whenever they visited us. Her relationship with Micha had deteriorated, but Nina she spoilt as much as ever.

To my parents:

> 29th November, 1939
>
> ... If anyone says something nice about Micha, Ollo immediately contradicts and begins to talk about Nina. Werner told me he had asked Micha: 'How is Mummy?'
>
> Micha: 'Mummy is well.'
>
> 'And Ollo? Is she well?'
>
> Micha: 'Much too well.'

It is difficult to appreciate why, in such hard times, a self-sacrificing woman of almost sixty and a fairly well-behaved boy of nine should indulge in such conflicts. I tried again and again to do justice to both and began to worry about Micha, because a child can be damaged by this kind of tension.

By February 1940 I had at last collected all the documents I needed in order to marry and, although it was only a 'paper marriage', we wanted to choose an auspicious occasion. We decided on 23rd February, the birthday of the Red Army.

Our weddings rings seemed to be paper, too! We bought them for a shilling apiece at the Uniprix in Vevey. Romantics may remember it as the place where we first met. I was taken aback when we were asked about witnesses, but the porter and a clerk from the registrar's office obliged. Ollo made us pancakes for lunch.

Armed with our marriage certificate, I visited the British Consul in Geneva to apply for a passport; his response was distinctly cool. Ten weeks later, on 2nd May, 1940, I held the precious document in my hands, much envied by other German refugees.

Len moved up to the Molehill. He was a thoughtful, understanding partner. I am sure that becoming part of our family, feeling warmth and care in a cheerful, harmonious atmosphere (so long as Ollo and Micha were not squabbling), was a decisive experience for Len. We were comrades bound to one another through work and danger. We shared the same opinion about books and people. Every day we consciously enjoyed the beauties of the landscape. Len's understanding for the children, and especially for Micha, was quite amazing and has never altered, even now that the children are adults.

Although we had so much in common, there were difficulties. I did not realise then what a complicated person Len was and reacted wrongly to his difficulties. I underestimated his sensitivity and his unjustified mistrust. I was helpless against his frequent changes in mood, the depressions that I could not fathom. His nervousness was increased by my impatience when he fussed over things that I felt were unimportant, and by my quick and often vehement decisions, which struck him as dictatorial.

In the spring of 1940, Denmark, Norway, the Netherlands, Belgium and Luxemburg were all overrun by the fascist army. Each was a terrible blow bringing nearer the danger that a similar fate might befall Switzerland. Micha's school had to close: the parents took their children home. There was no other school in Caux. Although I found it painful to part from the nine-year-old, I decided to send him to an English boarding school in Glion, the next village below Caux. It was an expensive school but after seeing Micha's performance in the entrance examination, the Director was sufficiently interested in him to suggest a reduction in fees. I was now English and he assumed that the child's education would be continued in England.

Miriam and Werner had at last received their visas and left Switzerland in the spring of 1940. I wrote home:

> During the last few months – as ever – we have been very good friends. I am really very fond of them. It is amazing that I should have found such wonderful people here at all. No shadow ever dimmed our relationship.

Miriam's mother's visa had not yet arrived and for the time being she remained in Montreux. I had promised to keep an eye on her. She came from Poland and at the age of seventeen had been married to a Rabbi whom she hated and later separated from. Now she was elderly, ailing, and over-anxious about her daughter and grandchildren.

Before Miriam and Werner left, they expressed their fears for my future. Since they knew nothing of my work, they could not understand why we stayed in Switzerland, which might be occupied by the Germans any day. They advised us most urgently to go to England now that it was possible. Did I really imagine that the passport alone would save me from the Nazis?

I can't remember whether Ollo was present during one of these conversations or whether she herself conceived the idea that we might go to England and that she with her German passport would not be able to accompany us. Anyhow, this thought took root and soon became an obsession with her. She hardly ate or slept and declared in tears that she could not live without Nina. I managed to calm her down several times, but when I suggested she should take a holiday she refused and said: 'I am not going to let you out of my sight.' A sinister atmosphere developed. One day Ollo packed her things and moved in with the wife of farmer François, with whom she was on friendly terms. Sitting on a bench above our little house, she carried out her threat, watching us hour after hour through a pair of field-glasses.

Although we recognised Ollo's unbalanced condition as a possible danger, at that time we had no idea of the evil plan she had devised. She had decided to betray us in the hope that if something happened to me she could keep the child and take her back to Germany.

With this objective in mind she went to see the British consular representative in Montreux. Her ravings in broken English were so incoherent that no one attached any important to them. In those days, rumours and denunciations abounded. Ollo wanted to go back to the consulate but not without help. She went to Miriam's mother and told her everything. The old lady, who was suffering from a stomach ailment and lived only for the day when she could rejoin her family, had known nothing about our work, but she behaved splendidly. She tried to calm Ollo down and make her see that, if she denounced us at the consulate, she would regret it for the rest of her life, and that in so doing she would not be condemning us, but herself. Miriam's mother then came to tell me what was happening and even promised to talk to Ollo as often as she could and try to sway her. When we said goodbye, her eyes were sparkling: 'Please don't laugh at me. I admire you. I always thought you had something of Rosa Luxemburg about you.'

While this comparison embarrassed me very much, I mention it here because it shows how amazing this woman's reaction was. As a very young wife, she had rebelled against her husband and brought up two children on her own. Besides, she was an enemy of Hitler. Although she was desperately keen to get her visa, she undertook, at no small risk, to keep me informed and influence Ollo in the right direction.

What did Ollo know? Although we had never spoken about it, she was surely aware that I used a transmitter. She had not met any of my colleagues in Danzig or Poland. In Switzerland she knew Jim, Len and Hermann, but not Hermann's name or address. Neither did she know of his arrest.

When Ollo told the same tale to the wife of François, with whom she was staying, our position became untenable. But now the farmer's wife also came and declared her affection for me, saying she knew that I would not do anything wrong and that she too had been against Hitler for a long time. On no account did she want me to suffer. Of course she would not talk. She was outraged by Ollo and did not want her in the house.

And so these two very different women helped me in my hour of need.

I told the wife of François the same as I had told Miriam's

mother, that Ollo's rantings were mostly fantasy, but I did not deny my wish to combat fascism.

Miriam's mother received her visa and departed. She promised never to speak about this affair, not even to her children. For many years Miriam affectionately sent me parcels at my father's address in London. In the winter of 1946, as soon as I thought my position was sufficiently safe, I wrote to her and received an answer. I quoted part of Miriam's reply in a letter to my mother:

> 'You simply cannot imagine how I felt when I saw your handwriting on the envelope. I was so happy.' And Werner writes: 'Your letter is one of the most wonderful things that has happened to us in a long time. After such a long interval and from so far away, let me assure you that you are still as dear a friend to me as ever.'

Again I was unable to answer because my position took a turn for the worse and I feared that a letter from me might have compromised them.

I often had to go to Geneva. Albert did not take the events with Ollo so seriously, but I was deeply worried that she would get hold of Nina while I was away and take her to Germany. If she did, the child would be lost to me. Len, who helped me throughout this period in his fearless, considerate way, kept Nina near him all the time when I was gone. François's wife promised to keep an eye on Ollo. But something had to be done, because by now Ollo had also informed her hairdresser. He proved to be an opponent of HItler and refused to be drawn in. I looked for a safe place where Nina would be out of Ollo's reach, and found a German boarding school called Les Rayons in the neighbouring canton. They applied the modern teaching methods of the Salem School, whose director, Kurt Hahn, had emigrated to Britain during the Hitler period where he founded the famous Gordonstoun School. In Les Rayons the political atmosphere was clean.

Len and I decided to leave Caux and look for a flat in Geneva. Albert's increasing workload had also made this necessary.

Micha had settled down in his English school. The teachers thought he was gifted and took pains with him, but I could not leave him there. No one could foresee what Ollo might do to

Micha once she found out that Nina had been taken away. I also thought it best that if Nina was going to be separated from us so suddenly, she should at least have her brother with her, for she was very attached to him. And so the poor boy had to uproot himself again.

No one in Caux knew where I had taken the children. When I said goodbye to Nina in her strange new surroundings she clung to me tightly and screamed. Micha, himself near tears, cuddled and comforted her. I experienced one of my rare moments of despair. What was I doing to my children? Switzerland under siege, Hermann's arrest, Ollo's betrayal – would I ever see the children again?

Only after we had packed the last of our things in Caux did I speak to Ollo. She had aged and showed growing signs of hysteria. I told her that I had taken Nina and Micha away and that she would have to get used to the separation. The children were safe, and it did not matter what happened to me now. She should know me well enough to realise that I was not afraid. This was the first indication I gave her that I had heard anything about her betrayal. Ollo collapsed on the floor, rigid and blue-lipped. She had suffered a similar attack a few months before. Crying bitterly and regretting all she had done, she left a few days later to join her brother in Germany.

I have often wondered how all this came about and whether I was wrong to put my trust in somebody who proved so unreliable.

Ollo's political conviction was not based on any knowledge of theory or even class-consciousness; it was rooted in her close attachment to our family. When she concentrated this attachment exclusively on my youngest child, doting on her to the point of illness, total collapse set in.

After Ollo returned to Germany, she took it upon herself to visit an acquaintance of our family, who found her some work in a children's home. The headmistress of this place had also taken in children who were in danger for racial or political reasons. When one of her instructions annoyed Ollo, she also attempted denunciation here, but again her abnormal behaviour gave her away and the headmistress was able to send the children into hiding before it was too late. I heard of this only after 1945.

We left La Taupinière. The mountain landscape had become part of my life. It was close to me at all seasons and in all moods: the fragrance of spring, the sunsets behind the snow-covered French Alps, Lake Geneva, the lights of Montreux, the fir trees on the nearby slopes and the meadows full of flowers around our house. The landscape never palled. It was my daily joy and I found it very difficult to tear myself away.

Albert was pleased that we were moving to Geneva because, apart from transmitting, I could train his future radio operator as well.

He was a Swiss by the name of Edmund Hamel, who owned a little shop in Geneva where he sold and repaired radios. Over the shop was his simple flat. Edmund was a decent, good-natured man, and his wife a vivacious beauty with thick jet-black hair and black eyes to match. It seemed inconceivable that she could be satisfied with her lot. When I came to know her better she told me that she was from the country and had worked in a city bar where she soon grew sick of her male customers. Then Edmund came along, decent, reliable, quiet and shy; that had appealed to her.

They were both communists. Olga served in the shop and Edmund was the radio expert. He was a slow learner and did not have much spare time because of his work. We decided to train Olga too. She applied herself to the task with great fervour. Lessons took place in the evening. There were times when Edmund would come into the kitchen in pyjamas and slippers, half asleep; 'Aren't you finished yet?' he would say. 'When are you coming to bed?' She brushed him off impatiently. But it would be wrong to ridicule Edmund. He started transmitting, which by then was very dangerous, and later, when the time came, he proved himself to be courageous and level-headed in difficult circumstances.

I spent many evenings in their clean, tidy flat and enjoyed teaching both of them. Sometimes Len would stand in for me. The Hamels did not know our names or our address.

At Albert's request, I did not transmit from our two-roomed furnished flat in Geneva, but from the Hamel's kitchen or other places suggested by Albert. I remember a lonely week-end house in a wood near Geneva. I worked about twice a week sending through my reports and his. The latter were of greater significance.

In the late autumn of 1940 Centre suggested that Len and I move to England. Albert opposed the idea. When I accepted, I believe he regarded it as near desertion, but then it was a desertion into a country at war which was being savagely bombed by the fascist Luftwaffe, still in unchallenged command of the air.

Albert's work was important and he wanted to retain Len and me. On the other hand, Jim was fully trained, Olga and Edmund would soon be functioning as operators and Len was for the present at his disposal. As a former member of the International Brigade, Len could not travel through Spain and had to stay in Geneva until we could find a different route for him.

England could only be reached by the most improbable detours. At that time just one narrow road was open in France. This crossed the region 'governed' by the Nazi puppet General Pétain, and led to the Spanish border. From there the route lay through Spain and Portugal. From Lisbon it was supposed to be possible to reach England by plane or ship.

I prepared my departure for the end of December.

When I visited Olga and Edmund for the last time, Edmund walked around with tears in his eyes. Olga looked at him severely. Suddenly she sat down, threw up her apron peasant-fashion to hide her face, and sobbed.

Len took over as their teacher. Later Jim was put into touch with the Hamels. They both became good operators. For three years they worked hard, overburdened by Albert's important reports until, in October 1943, their transmitter was detected by radio triangulation and they were arrested.

Albert (Sándor Radó) describes in *Code-name Dora* how seventy (seventy!) police with dogs carried out the arrest in a raid directed personally by the chief of the Confederate Swiss Police.

To give some idea of how a transmitter was detected in those days, I quote from a report of the Swiss police, printed in Radó's book, which refers to the discovery of Jim's transmitter.

> In the course of our monitoring operations in Geneva [on the Hamels] . . . we monitored a third transmitter . . .

9th October, 1943: We knew for certain that it was in Lausanne . . .

20th October: We knew which quarter . . .

25th October . . . which house . . .

The police set up special listening stations and recorded the texts of Jim's telegrams for several days.

On 19th November, 1943, he too was arrested during a transmission.

In December 1940 I had said goodbye to Jim. Later, as a traitor, he was welcomed with open arms by the Anglo-American secret service. I have little to add to his story. I do not think that he played a double game from the beginning. Some of the things described so cynically in his *Handbook for Spies*, he saw differently at the time they happened. Incidentally, after his treachery he was far from the superior being he made himself out to be later on. In 1947, the Austrian comrade who had introduced us to Jim asked to see me urgently. He reported the following: the bell rang. He opened the door: in front of him stood an agitated individual he did not immediately recognise and took for a beggar or a sick man. It was Jim. He refused to come in, trembled and stammered incoherently: 'Len and Sonya, great danger, not to work, destroy everything.' Then he ran away. The comrade was even more shocked by Jim's appearance and demeanour than by what he said.

At that point we knew nothing of his desertion, and only later could we interpret his behaviour. It would seem that with all the damage he had done, there had remained a spark of the British sense of fair play. Having nothing against us personally, he risked a secret warning before the security officials could visit our house.

Jim was let out of prison in 1944, by which time Switzerland no longer doubted the defeat of fascism. It is possible that he began to waver while in Swiss custody and began his treacherous activities from that time on. I think it is much more likely that he decided on this course in 1945 while in the Soviet Union, where he had fled with Radó's help. Jim had not joined the Communist Party until he came back from Spain, and he did not have a firm ideological grasp. During 1944 and 1945, in the Soviet Union, he witnessed the effects that those distrustful years were having on other comrades and, when he was sent abroad again, he ran away at the first opportunity.

In contrast to such wretched characters as Jim, there are comrades like Gabo, Rolf and hundreds of others who experienced harder times than he did in this period of deviations and mistakes – and never wavered. As soon as they were free, they worked on as communists.

In running away, Jim showed that his ties to the revolutionary movement were superficial; what was so abominable was that he went on to become a complete traitor. This final step must have been studied calculation. Merely to abandon his work for the Soviet Union would have meant an uncertain future, but by telling everything to British Counter-intelligence he obliged them to take him in and offer him a good job. This is what happened. In addition, the publication of his lurid spy-thriller memoirs assured his prosperity.

December 1940. It is even harder to say good-bye to people you love and respect when you know it may be farewell for ever. Irene Forbes-Mosse told me how disappointed she was that I had to leave just then. She had planned to surprise us all with a Christmas visit and give each of us – Len, Micha, Nina and me – a bicycle. So now I would have to accept something else from her, and although I tried to refuse she insisted on giving me forty English pounds. She must have realised how frugally we lived. This gift was a great help to me, but her warmth and friendship moved me even more.

I did not know how the journey to England would work out. I could not take much luggage and therefore sent my books to Irene in Chexbres. I had already been forced to leave behind a fairly large and valued library in Shanghai. In Switzerland I had accumulated another one. Books helped me to feel at home in foreign countries while they were being burnt in my German homeland.

My books remained in Chexbres for eleven years. In early 1951 a friend of Irene Forbes-Mosse, who had been living with her since 1939, wrote to me in the GDR explaining that the household was now being dissolved. Irene had died a few years before. Where should she send the books? The letter went to my brother's address as she did not know mine. At that time I was working as a department head in one of our government institutions and conditions did not make it appropriate for me to correspond with the capitalist world and even less to receive parcels. She wrote a second time. It was not easy for me to leave her enquiries unanswered and I would have liked my books back again.

Farewell to Albert and Lene.

I met Comrade Radó again when he visited the GDR in the 1960s. Lene had died of cancer in 1958, at the age of fifty-eight. I also met Radó in Hungary. It was good to see how much he enjoyed being in his homeland again, and to witness a comrade pursuing his scientific work with such dedication.

6

England, 1941–50

Our journey from Geneva to England began on 18th December, 1940. At seven in the morning we got on the bus. Len helped the driver to stow away our cases. The bus started. Len was left standing at the side of the road. We did not foresee that twenty months were to pass before we would be together again.

To my parents:

Lisbon, January 1941

At eight o'clock we crossed the French border. The currency control was strict: we had to half undress. The fares were high and so I took just one seat for the two children. All in all, Nina had to sit on my lap for 28 hours. The bus was not heated and after scarcely an hour's journey we were stiff with cold. In front of us sat the former finance minister of Lithuania. He benevolently asked Nina where we came from and where we were going to. The journey through France was sad. The country looked desolate. There was nothing in the food shops and they were locked up. 11 p.m. in Nîmes. At six in the morning we travelled on; in the evening we stopped at the French/Spanish border in the Pyrenees. Here we had to stand outside in the dark for three hours with icy winds blowing. I saw to it that the children kept moving about. Nothing to eat, no toilet and one small customs hut; we were called in one by one.

200 metres on, we were at the Spanish border. Here we

waited another three hours. The children behaved marvellously throughout the journey.

Spanish customs searched each piece of luggage very thoroughly. Instead of arriving at 7 p.m. we got to Barcelona at 3.30 in the morning. The night journey through Spain was very beautiful. Bright moonlight, little towns asleep, houses with curved balconies, a few hills and on our left the Mediterranean. In Barcelona I realised what I had been missing these two years past: the people. The poverty here is heart-rending. No bread, no sugar. They look hungry but their vivacity and their interesting faces, their charm and their conversation – the whole atmosphere! I towed the children across market places and through narrow streets.

The train journey from Barcelona to Madrid went smoothly. With our transit visas we had to leave Madrid for Portugal by the next train, due to depart at 11 p.m.

It was 23rd December. Thousands were waiting by the five locked platform barriers. When they were opened, I managed to push children and hand-luggage through a compartment window; but I could not board the train myself. A man threw me off the steps. I was afraid the children might suffocate inside the carriage. Someone handed them back to me on the platform. My luggage stayed inside. A scuffle ensued, soldiers appeared and drove the crowds away from the train with pistols drawn. I tried to reach the international sleeper compartments but they were guarded and no one was allowed through without a reservation. I said that I was only bringing in the children, the parents would follow with the tickets. They believed me. We looked into the full compartments and found the Lithuanian finance minister again. He hid Micha in his bed and his wife took Nina. I hid somewhere and only appeared again in the morning. While the children were still asleep, the couple told me how they had been practically the only 'lucky ones' to escape before the Bolsheviks came.

On 24th December we arrived in Lisbon, all three of us ill. Nina had a high temperature. I called a doctor to the hotel and, before I too succumbed, went out to buy a doll for Nina and some building bricks for Micha. After all it was Christmas.

In Lisbon the British consulate explained to me that passengers were not flown out according to the length of time they had been waiting, but in order of importance, and I was about the most insignificant person on the long list. There were many citizens without means who had to be transported home, since Britain forbade any export of money, even to its own nationals.

I moved from the town to Estoril on the coast. The climate was so mild that we were able to sun ourselves in deck-chairs as though there were no war on and no worries. The children recovered magnificently. It was wonderful to have them with me all the time, but I was not feeling as carefree as they.

We had to live very frugally because we had no idea how long we would be staying. As transferring money was becoming more and more difficult, I had tried to draw as little as possible on Centre's Swiss account for the journey. My reserves were dwindling and I would not be able to hold out much longer.

What awaited me in England? Judging by the manner of my reception at the Lisbon consulate, I might well be considered a second-class citizen. Or had Ollo succeeded in arousing suspicion against me?

While in Lisbon, I also tried to find some means by which Len might travel to England. Franco's Spain had refused him a transit visa. The same happened to other British citizens eligible for military service. It was a friendly gesture towards Hitler by Franco. Len already possessed a French transit visa. But the African route that we had planned also proved impossible. I went to every shipping agent I could find to organise a passage for him by freighter from Marseilles, but in vain.

After about three weeks, the consulate informed me that we would be taken to England by ship.

Our steamer sailed in convoy with twelve others. First we went in the opposite direction, to Gibraltar. The voyage to England took almost three weeks. The cabins were blacked out; the porthole had to be kept shut, every passenger was given a life-belt to carry at all times. Since they were for adults, Nina's was much too big for her and she had to keep a constant hold on it, with only her legs and head peeping out. The English people on board kept aloof from us.

On arrival in Liverpool I was the only one to be interrogated: Where is your husband? Why didn't he come with you? Why didn't you stay with him? Where do you want to settle here? What are you going to live on? What is he living on?

The children were very cold and tired, and Nina began to cry. When the interrogation was over, the official gave them a penny each. It was late. We had difficulty in finding a hotel room. The children were hardly asleep when the air-raid sirens began to howl. I shook them awake and we ran down to the cellar as we had been instructed to do.

The next morning we travelled to Oxford. I described this journey to Len:

> In the train from Liverpool to Oxford, a soldier shared our compartment. Nina immediately won his heart. He made her a cannon out of her Plasticine, and she was allowed to put his beret on her head. When he took off his jacket, the children sighed with admiration. He was tattooed all over. Nina could not take her eyes off the naked woman with a snake wound round her and she asked the most awkward questions. Micha, being a decent little fellow, preferred two doves that were pecking at a heart. Nina kept begging to be tattooed as well, so the soldier spat on her arm and painted a lovely picture with indelible pencil. It reached right up to her elbow and I had to promise not to wash it off under any circumstances. Micha and the soldier played cards for hours . . .

How glad I was that after our unfriendly reception, something nice was happening to the children in this new country.

Because of the air raids, for the time being my parents were living with friends in Oxford. Soon after my arrival they had to go back to London because their room was needed by their friends' relatives. We tried to find a place in Oxford but house-hunting in towns that appeared to be relatively safe from air attacks was hopeless. Nor could we find anything in the bombed cities, because so many buildings had been destroyed. At last I found a furnished room large enough for the three of us, but the landlady only wanted to let to one person. So once again I had no choice but to send the children away. I found a little forest school and kindergarten with a progressive head, near Eynsham not far from Oxford. Nina did not know any English at all, and the first words the little four-year-old learnt in her strange surroundings were 'stop it' and 'go away'.

A few days later the landlady asked me to move because she could not endure my foreign countenance. The owner of my next room did not allow any visits from children.

Letter to Len:

> Yesterday I had exactly one hour with the children. I miss them so. The school does not approve of parental visits and makes this pretty clear. My landlady does not allow them into my room. The school appears to be of the opinion that handkerchiefs are perverse and that children should have runny noses. But the teachers and the head are nice and the food is good. Micha feels at home there, but Nina has lost her cheerfulness and adds to her own misdemeanours all the tricks she can pick up from the other children. I wish I could have her with me.
>
> It is noticeable that people who have not yet suffered from the war are colder and more intolerant than those who have been hit by it.

My landlady decided that she would prefer to take in a 'gentleman' and I found a room at the vicarage in Glympton near Woodstock, out in the country. The vicar's wife asked: 'Are you a member of our Church? Isn't Chamberlain a wonderful man? Do you pray? Will you play cards with us in the evening?'

After I had passed this examination I was allowed to move into the beautiful house with its park-like garden and little brook.

Every two weeks I travelled to London and afterwards would send Len my impressions:

> Of course I hate the noise of the aeroplanes and the bombs; but – maybe due to lack of imagination – I feel quite calm during the alarms. I have no fear for myself.

The underground stations with their night life! Hundreds sleep there, in wooden bunks. They have already been coming here for months and a kind of community has developed. They unpack their supper from big bundles, their Thermos flasks of tea, the knitting and the newspapers. Father smokes and mother gossips with the neighbours. Children play hide-and-seek. Lovers sit enraptured in the corners. Noisy trains arrive. People stream out of the compartments, careful to avoid treading on those who have not managed to find a free bunk and are stretched out on the platform . . .

Yesterday I wandered through London for a long while. The debris of the great department stores bothers me less than a little home in ruins . . . a line of washing still hanging over the kitchen stove . . .

I saw Charlie Chaplin's film *The Great Dictator* and could hardly bear to sit through to the end. Chaplin makes a joke of everything. But at the end he delivers a very fine and moving speech.

I had gone to see that film with Father and could not understand why he found it so good. I was no longer able to laugh about the Nazis, even caricatured by Chaplin's genius. In England people could. The country was in an extraordinary situation. Since the beginning of the war, the British army had experienced nothing but defeat. It had been driven out of Norway and France. Three hundred thousand retreating British and French soldiers had flooded into the now famous harbour of Dunkirk, waiting for evacuation to England. Because this succeeded – with the loss of all equipment – it was called 'The Miracle of Dunkirk'.

After these blows Britain, a vulnerable and badly prepared island, was confronted with Hitler's threatened invasion. In September 1940 the terrible bombing of English cities began. It was to continue for many months.

Why were the preparations so inadequate? The ruling class and its party, the Conservatives, had allowed Hitler's power to grow right up until 1939, in the hope that he would make war, not against the Western powers, but against the Soviet Union. Only when they found the knife at their own throats did they decide to act. War production was now given total priority. Conservative Prime Minister Churchill demanded 'blood, toil, tears and sweat' from the people, and the people made the sacrifice. They hated Hitler and fascism. The whole country rose to defend itself and so a more positive atmosphere developed than in 'neutral' Switzerland, fenced in by fascists and in many respects appeasing Hitler. Hitler's air force did not break the British people. The opposite took place.

Later, when Britain's war effort was running at full speed, she produced first-class planes that were superior to Hitler's Luftwaffe. The British pilots were idolised by the people for their skill and daring; their losses were high.

Although I did not yet have my own home, I was impatient to begin work.

Arrangements for my first meeting, together with fall-back appointments, had already been transmitted to me in Switzerland. I was to meet a Soviet comrade in a street near Hyde Park not far from Marble Arch. Recognition signs and passwords, essential when strangers meet, had been agreed upon. It would be superfluous to describe them.

The first meeting in a new country is always exciting. Will someone be there? What sort of work will Centre want me to do? Will I be capable of carrying it out? What if no one turns up?

One or two dates had already passed, as I had not foreseen the delay in Portugal, nor the weeks at sea. My partner would probably also be pleased to make contact at last.

I waited long beyond the appointed hour but no one came. I waited the next evening – in vain. And again a fortnight later. I do not recall how often I travelled to London and how many times I walked up and down that street. The area had been badly chosen. It was a favourite haunt of prostitutes, who did not appreciate my frequent appearance. I felt increasingly uneasy. Had there been a misunderstanding about the arrangements? Had I confused the location? I was not allowed to go to the Soviet Embassy, and anyway I would never have done so.

It could be that I had unwittingly committed an error, that something had happened in Switzerland as a result of Hermann's arrest or through Ollo's betrayal, or – quite independently – in

Albert's group. I knew that contact could be broken off with comrades if their situation jeopardised the work. I would have accepted that without feeling hurt. In illegality, protecting the work was the most important thing. If I could not continue, I would find myself a job, join the British party, and carry on working as a communist.

Soon little hope remained that anyone from Centre would meet me.

We had arrived in England with the bare essentials for clothing ourselves. I possessed no furniture, had no claim to any housing and had to support two children at boarding school. I could not meet my commitments much longer. But I did not reveal these worries to my family. None of them had much to spare, and besides, moving in with any of them was out of the question. My parents were staying with friends in an overcrowded house. Weepy was herself looking for somewhere to live. Brigitte had a one-roomed flat. Sabine, wanting to marry, needed accommodation. Reni was studying in Cambridge. Jürgen's home was just large enough for his family of four. They lived modestly on an income of £250 a year.

There was no prospect of being able to pay for the children's school much longer, of finding anywhere to live, of meeting someone from Centre or of bringing Len back to England.

I was worried about Rolf, too. He had written to me from China now and again, either direct to Switzerland or via my sisters in London, and he always remembered the children's birthdays. Then he had informed me that he was going into the interior. For many months there was no news of him. Finally I heard that Rolf had been arrested by the Chinese, and I knew his life was in danger.

Later I heard the details. Ernst and Rolf had been unable to establish a basis for their work in Shanghai. Rolf had hoped to make better contact in Chongqing, the seat of government. He was arrested while he was building his transmitter or sending his first radio message. I believe he was freed through the efforts of the Soviet Union.

At last, in April 1941, I found a furnished bungalow. It was one of a row in Kidlington, two and a half miles outside Oxford. The rent was very high and I was down to the last of my savings. But I enjoyed not having a landlady and – above all – I could have my children with me.

When I went to the London meeting place in May, I had all but given up hope. A man approached me, not the first in this accursed street, but this time he was the one I wanted. He greeted me with the code words I was waiting for, and I glided down the street and along two more as if on wings to the place where we were to talk. The Soviet comrade Sergei (my cover-name for him) brought me greetings from Centre and congratulations on my arrival. He also handed me enough money to allay all my financial worries. A car accident had delayed his appearance.

With the unflappable serenity of the Russian people, he would never have understood how oppressive those months had been for me. I decided that from now on I would not let myself be shaken by things like this, but bear in mind the philosophic words of the harbour pilot on the quay at Vladivostok. I would try to think of the vast distances between the stars and the earth, and that would calm me down.

Sergei explained the significance of our work in a country that was at war with the Nazis, but where influential reactionary circles were always ready to come to an understanding with Hitler against the Soviet Union. Centre needed news. What contacts could I take up? With the military? With political circles? I was to try to establish an information network. When could my transmitter begin to function?

As always I was given plenty of time. Centre never pushed me for deadlines. I was the impatient one, and more likely to rush into something than take my time over it. I had already bought all the transmitter parts and worked on them between praying and playing cards in the Rectory. It could be in operation within 24 hours.

I hoped that Jürgen, and perhaps Father too, would help me obtain information. Father, who was very tactful, had never asked me about my work. Now it seemed right to tell him something about it, but without mentioning its military destination. He was the only member of the family who knew about my decoration.

Father had no head for such things and therefore did not recognise its military character, but when I told him that Comrade Kalinin had given it to me in the Kremlin, he was moved.

I had only to let him know that I was interested in political and economic facts for my work. He nodded and that was all. It hardly had any effect on our conversations since they usually took the form of political discussions in any case. Mostly Father mixed with left-wing economists and Labour politicians; at that time many of them had some sort of job connected with the war effort, and Father told me what he heard. But as I said, there were no big secrets, but political talks we would have had anyway.

Hitler's attack on the Soviet Union in June 1941 made a powerful impact on Britain. I am sure I need not describe how shattered I felt by the event. But there wasn't much time to brood.

I listened to Churchill's speech promising full support to the Soviet Union, made notes and tried to evaluate them. As usual with Churchill, in rhetoric and style his speech was brilliant. I went to London to talk to Father, who told me that Britain's leading politicians and soldiers were counting on the Soviet Union's defeat within three months. Father had these views confirmed by Sir Stafford Cripps, a leading member of the Labour Party and Ambassador to the Soviet Union from 1940 to 1942.

'The German Wehrmacht will slice through Russia like a hot knife through butter,' Cripps added. Later this opinion became general knowledge, but at the time of my report to Centre, neither they nor anyone else in the Soviet Union appeared to have heard of it. I received a telegram of thanks from the Director. This was a rare occurrence. Perhaps that is why I can remember this particular report while I have forgotten so many others.

The governments of capitalist countries had long made the error of underestimating the Soviet Union. They simply could not get it into their heads that a workers' state with communists in power could 'hold out'. Their error began with attempts at military intervention after the October Revolution in Russia; it continued with their non-recognition of the Soviet Union over so many years and was still current, as the words of Cripps testified, at the beginning of the Second World War.

Hitler began to deploy the full might of his army and air

force against the Soviet Union. This brought significant relief to England; the threat of invasion came to an end and Nazi bombing attacks also diminished.

After Hitler's invasion of the Soviet Union, several days went by without response to my call-sign, but then they came on the air again. I used the transmitter twice a week. Every fortnight I went to London. At first I only talked to Jürgen and Father. Jürgen was as always enormously productive. Apart from articles in several journals such as the British *Labour Monthly, Labour Research*, and pamphlets on *Labour Conditions in War and Peace* and one on *Hunger and Work*, he had embarked on his life's work on labour conditions under industrial capitalism. This was to grow to 40 volumes. Jürgen was also preparing economic analyses for the Soviet embassy. He passed on to me useful information outside the field of economics. From my conversations with Father and Jürgen I drew up four to six reports a month, but Jürgen informed me more consciously than my father did.

In accordance with the rules, I kept strictly away from the British party. Nor did I take up any contacts with the emigrant German party in England, except for Jürgen, who was at that time the group's political organiser. I talked to him about the possibility of obtaining more information, especially military, and he arranged for me to meet the German comrade Hans Kahle. As a divisional commander, Hans had been a leading light in the International Brigades in Spain, where he had been well respected for his courage and ability to make quick decisions. In England he worked, among other things, as a military correspondent of the magazines *Time* and *Fortune*, which belonged to the famous American Luce company. I do not know the background of this particular occupation, but in any case it was a fertile source of information. Centre agreed to my contact with Hans Kahle and so I began to see him, too, about twice a month.[1] This resulted in some useful reports to Centre, who frequently asked follow-up questions which gave us some idea of what was important to them. I enjoyed working with Hans Kahle. After victory he returned to East Germany and took over responsible work, but – sad loss for our country – he died soon after.

In London I stayed with my parents or one of my sisters. At

times I would meet Hans Kahle there. My sisters were out at work and knew nothing of this. Apart from Father and Jürgen, I spoke to no one about what I was doing – neither then nor afterwards. Even my children, long after they were adults, knew nothing of my Order of the Red Banner until thirty years later, when a Soviet General located me in the GDR and awarded it to me a second time. (It was my original medal, number 944; the certificate was also there. How carefully it had been preserved through all the ravages of war!)

Apart from radio contact with the Soviet Union, I continued to meet Comrade Sergei. After I had succeeded in making some military contacts, I received material that could not be sent by radio. At one of these meetings, Sergei gave me a little parcel measuring about eight by six inches. It contained a small transmitter. Although I was still as unenthusiastic as ever about theory, I became attached to this reliable, handy and technically superior instrument. I dismantled my own transmitter, which was six times the size, and hid the parts for emergency use. Altogether I transmitted from England for five or six years. Amateur radio activities had – as in Switzerland – been strictly forbidden for the duration.

While I was in England the 'Sergeis' changed two or three times. I looked forward to our appointments which, apart from the initial failure, were always kept to the minute. The comrades were friendly, experienced and competent. We met in the street during the black-out, preferably at a time when we were unlikely to be surprised by an air-raid siren, and never for more than a quarter of an hour.

I have mentioned several times that my illegal work did not frighten me, but I must confess that in the blacked-out city, without street lamps or even a glimmer of window light, I was afraid. There was hardly a soul on the streets and anybody who did pass by was invisible. I stood in the pitch dark, expecting somebody to grab my face or throat at any minute. Whenever I heard gentle footsteps, I would hold my breath in fear and be relieved if they belonged to 'our man'.

We felt at home in our little house, but I missed Len. My letters to Geneva were a portrait of our life:

Spring 1941,

Tomorrow my parents are coming. I am on particularly good terms with Father, but then every one of us is on particularly good terms with him. Since he is now 65, he has had to retire from the university. He has practically no financial reserves, which means that he must find some other work. He is much too modest and much too proud to be a good job-hunter. His professional stature is beyond all question. He is always receiving honorary invitations. He is world-famous in his field. All his life he has worked and been scientifically productive. Now, at 65, he does not know whether he will find anything to earn his bread by. Government and scientific institutes overwhelm him with requests, but none of them are paid. It really is a scandal . . . The world situation doesn't look too rosy; it overshadows everything at present. The events in Crete have come in for sharp criticism. But at least it has the advantage of exposing Britain's weaknesses and the urgent need to reinforce home defence. Without the lesson of Crete, it is doubtful whether the difficulties involved in island defence would have been recognised quite so concretely.

. . . Have been reading a biography of Noël Coward. His reactions as a soldier in the First World War are exactly the reactions of a liberal intellectual incapable of disciplining himself, incapable of giving up his individualism, of subordinating himself and of standing up to physical effort. I do not despise him for not enjoying being a soldier, but rather for his reasons for not enjoying it. However, I admire his honesty . . .

Am just reading a book on China. Will I ever lose my longing for that country? . . .

Nina's reaction to her first air raid, just when she was away in a children's holiday home: 'How the house wobbled! And the terrible noise in the walls, under the bed and in my ears!' Since then she has kept on talking about death. She needs my daily assurance that I shan't die before she has grown up. For her, anything nice is related to 'when the war is over . . .' – 'then I will eat an egg every day; then I needn't go to school any more, then the aeroplanes will fly so high that I can't hear them any more.' Micha finds it easier to cope with the change of country . . . I haven't found any friends yet but am on good terms with our neighbour in the next bungalow. She is the wife of a bricklayer. Simple, balanced, friendly, she has a wisdom that does not come from the brain but from her warm heart. She is expecting her fourth child. How I envy her . . .

Although there is nothing much to report, I would like to write to you every day because there are so many small things I want you to share . . . This morning I raced off with the pram to fetch a sack of coal. Had only just heard in time that some was available. That means our first bath in weeks . . . Sunday I went walking with the children. Nina by a bush in blossom and a bird in song. The grace of her movements – strange how some are born with it and others not.

I am wearing a new dress; the first that you do not know. Red with little white polka dots on it, white belt and white collar . . .

Write me a long letter. Let me know what you are doing. Are you learning? A language? Mathematics? I would love you to go on learning . . .

It is after midnight. The sirens have begun to wail and in a few minutes people just like us, who are bringing up their children and who enjoy nature, will have had the life blown out of them by bombs.

Len must have reported that he was still needed in Switzerland and that he would not be able to join me in England. I answered:

. . . Now that it is all off, I realise how much I counted on your coming – in a hundred ways – 'We must do this walk together.' 'We must discuss this book.' 'When I have heavy things to carry home, you will fetch me from the bus stop.' 'My evenings will never be lonely.' Now I shall have to get used to the fact that such things are not for us.

Soon afterwards I heard from Len that he was still trying to come to England. Only later did I learn what had happened. Comrade Radó wanted to keep Len in Switzerland. With all the news that had to be passed on, this was understandable. Radó maintained that England was of no interest, while the German-Swiss connection was most important.

Len had received the same order from Centre as I had: to go to England. But Radó's arguments influenced him. Although he found our long separation difficult, he felt obliged to stay on. Alongside the messages he sent for Radó, Len still used our old code for his own communications to Centre. He asked them: 'Shall I try to reach England as Sonya instructed or remain in Switzerland as Albert wishes?' 'Do as Sonya says,' came the reply.

Len remembers as little as I do of the information he sent to the Soviet Union from Switzerland. But he does recall one connection. We had got to know a Chinese journalist by the name of Wang who was accredited to the League of Nations. He was married to a Dutch woman. General von Falkenhausen, a former military adviser of Chiang Kai-shek who became High Commander in Belgium during the Nazi occupation, often stayed in Switzerland and was well acquainted with Wang and his wife. Through Wang, Len occasionally learnt something of the General's opinions and comments.

Len was still applying fruitlessly to the British consulate for help to reach England. They were extremely busy with other British citizens of military age who could no longer travel through occupied France, issuing them with false passports and using all kinds of pretexts to channel them home. Top priority was given to British prisoners-of-war who had escaped from Germany or Italy. Maybe the consulate also remembered Len's German wife. Nor was his past in the International Brigade exactly a recommendation to them. In any case, like me in Lisbon, he was told that there were many more urgent cases to be dealt with before his.

I had meanwhile discussed the matter with Hans Kahle and Jack Brent of the British International Brigade Association. Jack was a comrade who had been seriously wounded in Spain. He continued working conscientiously, overcoming his physical suffering until his premature death. Neither Jack nor the Spanish Committee knew anything about Len's work. They did what they could for him, simply as a former member of the International Brigade. Finally, with the support of the Committee, I wrote a letter to Eleanor Rathbone, the left-wing Labour MP. The matter was taken up in Parliament, as she put a question in the House of Commons. It must have been published in Hansard during 1942. It went something like this: 'Why is a British citizen and anti-fascist with military experience in the Spanish Civil War, who is abroad and wants to volunteer for the British Army, not being given the support of His Majesty's Government in order to return to his home country?'

Mrs Rathbone was assured that the case would be looked into. And indeed, the Permanent Secretary to the Ministry of Foreign Affairs informed the Consul General in Geneva, who now asked Len to come and see him at once and smoothed the way for his journey. The consulate issued him with a passport in the name of John Miller, as well as a doctor's certificate confirming that tuberculosis had incapacitated him for military service.

Late in the summer of 1942, twenty months after I left Switzerland, he arrived in England. For the moment he really was of no use to the military because a nervous stomach condition had caused him to lose a lot of weight. We had not deceived Eleanor Rathbone. Everything she had said about Len was true.

He had been home for just three days when he received an OHMS letter from the Treasury, demanding repayment of the money he owed the government for his transport back from the Spanish border to London as a member of the International Brigade, four years before, in 1938. At that time the 'Non-Intervention Committee' formed by the western powers had arranged with Franco and the Republican Government that both the International Brigades and the fascist Condor Legion would be withdrawn from battle. The Republicans honoured their undertaking. Franco broke it and the Condor Legion remained active.

This bill testified to the speed and efficiency of the British Treasury. Moreover, it told us that the authorities – and we assumed not only the Treasury – had taken note of Len's return. The army, on the other hand, worked slowly and Len was only called up a year after he had volunteered, possibly because of his past activities in Spain.

In the autumn of 1942, the owners of our bungalow gave us notice as they required it for their own use. Once again, we looked for a detached house where I could transmit. This time we found 'Avenue Cottage', 50 George Street, in the Summertown district of Oxford. It was a funny little old house dating back several generations, with a grassy patch for a back yard and a lot of old sheds. It seemed totally out of place among the rather ordinary suburban dwellings in that road.

In days gone by, the sheds had been stables which belonged to a large villa in the more fashionable avenue running along behind. The coachman used to live in our house. The relationship between the coachman and the big house was still, in some sense, preserved. Now the wealthy and influential family of Judge Neville Laski lived in the villa. He was the brother of a leading member of the Labour Party, Professor Harold Laski. The stables were still part of his property.

Mrs Laski was a plump, good-looking woman. I once visited her at 10 o'clock in the morning. She lay in bed in a lace-trimmed nightgown, taking breakfast from a silver tray, just like rich people in the films. Mrs Laski had a social conscience and worked for various welfare organisations. She had taken an endangered Jewish child from Germany into her home.

My visit had a purpose. I needed her permission to erect an aerial leading from our roof to one of her stables. She was always friendly towards us and agreed. The aerial looked rather like a normal one for any radio receiver.

I was pleased that Len was there to put the aerial up this time. In our bungalow in Kidlington I had been obliged to clamber about on the roof alone.

Beside the house stood a thick wall of Cotswold stone which had surrounded the yard for a century and a half. We loosened a stone where the mortar had crumbled, removed the one behind, put our little transmitter into the cavity and replaced the outer moss-covered stone. No one could have detected a change in the wall.

Our house had four rooms and a spiral staircase. The largest room could not be used, it was completely filled by a Morrison air-raid shelter. Herbert Morrison, a leading member of the

Labour Party, was Home Secretary in the coalition cabinet, and this family shelter came into use during his term of office. It looked like a big wire mesh cage and was covered by a heavy iron top. The government supplied them free of charge; however, Oxford was never bombed.

I remember the cage in another connection. Immediately upon arrival in England I had bought a cheap second-hand bicycle. Len, who made its acquaintance twenty months later, declared it to be a danger to life and limb. One day when I returned from a meeting in London, the front door was locked. I had to ring the bell and heard the excited whispers of the children who opened the door and told me to shut my eyes. After two minutes I was allowed to enter the room. On top of the shelter – decorated with flags and illuminated by all the lamps and torches to be found in our house – stood a beautiful new bicycle. I used it a lot and it also served me well for getting to various illegal meeting places. Later on, when I moved to the GDR, Len took the bicycle to pieces, and it came with me on the plane. At first Nina used it to ride to school in Berlin. Now it is resting in the cellar. None of us could bear to hand it over to the junk collection.

In the year 1942, before Len came to England, I had taken up an important contact with an RAF officer whose wife and child had been evacuated to Oxford. A welder by trade, he was one of the few officers to come from the working class. By the age of sixteen, he had already adopted progressive political views, and he had never lost them. I got to know James through his wife. Since he was interested in world politics, he was eager to discuss things with me. I sensed his respect for the Soviet Union and his anger about Britain's reluctance to open the promised second front and provide the USSR with constructive support against Hitler. James did not come to Oxford often, and it took a while before I knew him well enough to ask Centre about his co-operation in our work. They agreed. Again I was sure that, even if he did not want to take the risk, he would not betray me. We talked for hours; I approached the vital question by degrees, until he could practically guess what it would be and consented.

James belonged to the technical branch of the Air Force and had access to some of the newest developments in aeroplane construction. He got hold of exact data for us, weights and dimensions, load-carrying capacity, special characteristics, and even contrived to let me have blueprints of machines that had not yet flown. I remember a new invention, a small mechanical device, of which he gave me the original. As parts like this were all numbered and kept under lock and key, its disappearance caused an uproar.

James was modest and cheerful. He became our friend. I met him once or twice a month – his family had left the town. Every time I saw him, he produced something useful for me. James would not take any money from us and did not consider himself to be a 'spy'. He was aiding the allied country that was fighting the hardest and bearing the heaviest sacrifices in the war against fascism.

Amateur radio transmissions were forbidden. We had to count on my transmitter being discovered at some point. Centre wanted me to train somebody new as my operator, and I found Tom. He had not been called up due to some eye trouble.

Tom was a fitter in a car plant. He did whatever was required of him without hesitation or fuss. He was tactful, witty and sensitive. He was reliable, too, and, when the work demanded it, he could be hard. You could always depend on Tom. In order to teach him Morse either Len or I had to visit him at his house or he would come to us. Tom, likewise, refused to accept any money. He wanted to have more time for learning and found a job that did not demand a full working day (he became a bill-sticker).

Towards the end of 1942, another unexpected event happened. As far as I understood, a comrade with worthwhile military information had lost touch with the Soviet Union for quite some time. He had turned to Jürgen, as a leading party member, for advice. Jürgen told me. I sent a coded message to Centre and received the reply that contact should be established. The name of this comrade: Klaus Fuchs. I did not know then that he was an outstanding scientist, working with a group that was to build the atomic bomb in co-operation with the United States. This was of course top secret, and not known to Jürgen or to me.

I knew that Klaus Fuchs lived in Birmingham and, probably

through Jürgen, he arranged a meeting near Banbury, which lies between Birmingham and Oxford.

When I met Klaus for the first time we went for a walk arm-in-arm, according to the old-established principle of illicit meetings. We discussed many things that had nothing to do with the main objective. It was pleasant just to have a conversation with so sensitive and intelligent a comrade and scientist. I noticed that very first time how calm, thoughtful, tactful and cultured he was. We spoke of books, films, and current affairs.

At our subsequent meetings he had questions for Centre which gave me a vague hint as to the nature of his work. I coded them and passed them on over my transmitter, and decoded Centre's replies for him. In order to meet, we used a 'letterbox', though the word isn't really applicable in our case. I found the hiding places and, as far as I could, arranged our meetings outside the town in secluded areas, so that I could use my bicycle. This cycle had a comfortable wicker seat for a child, which my daughter had almost outgrown. When I was expecting my youngest child, I embellished the seat with a new, colourful cushion of daisies on a green background – I can still see it today.

Meeting in the countryside also helped us to move about more freely and become better acquainted. Klaus once said to me that it did him good to be out of the city and to be talking to me. I thought him reserved and modest. I don't think he would have been conspicuous anywhere.

I also arranged to meet outside the city not only because it was more difficult to tail us in the open countryside, but also because I found it easier to find my way about there. I remember how I followed a small path across some meadows and discovered a spot in the undergrowth near the edge of a wood where we dug a small hole between the roots of a tree. Klaus stood beside me and watched me through his spectacles. I thought this quite all right, because I was more of an ordinary person and more practical than he. I looked up at him once and thought, 'oh, you dear, great professor'.

Klaus never came to my flat and I never went to his. We didn't know each other's addresses. I don't believe he even knew that I was Jürgen's sister.

Once, it must have been in 1943 when I still lived in Oxford, in Summertown, Klaus gave me a thick book of blueprints, more than a hundred pages long, asking me to forward it quickly. To get in touch with my Soviet contact outside the regular arrangement, I had to travel to London and, at a certain time in a certain place, drop a small piece of chalk and tread on it. This chalk sign indicated that same day in the evening. Two days later I cycled the few miles from Oxford in the direction of Cheltenham to what is today the junction of the A40 and A34. After about six or seven miles I turned into a side road. I was to do this every other day until 'Sergei' came. But the first time I went, his car was there.

I cycled on, hid my bike, and went to sit in the car beside him for a moment. I hoped very much that he and the complicated formulae and drawings would arrive safely in London.

Klaus and I never spent more than half an hour together when we met. Two minutes would have been enough but, apart from the pleasure of the meeting, it would arouse less suspicion if we took a little walk rather than parting immediately. Nobody who did not live in such isolation can guess how precious these meetings with another German comrade were. In this respect he was even worse off than I. Our common involvement in trading in danger also added to our feeling of closeness.

Centre twice acknowledged his messages with 'important' and 'very valuable'. Jürgen had arranged the contact but I never talked to him about Klaus and our meetings. Though my brother and I got on so well, I kept strictly to the rules.

About two years after we had started working together, Centre asked me to arrange a meeting for Klaus in New York. I had lived there for a few months in 1928, and racked my brains to remember landmarks in the city. I recalled two places, the Prosnit bookshop, uptown, where I had worked, and the Henry Street Settlement at 256 Henry Street, a popular street for poor Jews on New York's East Side. I'd lived there at the time. Instead of paying rent, we did social work twice a week under the guidance of the progressively-minded and much respected Lillian Wald. I chose the settlement and found methods of identification and code names. I believe they were used by Klaus Fuchs and his partner.

Henry Street Settlement

Of course I was delighted with this additional task. The more I had to achieve, the better I felt. When Klaus Fuchs went to New York my contact with him ceased.

I was aware of the significance of his material, although I did not know that its ultimate goal was the atom bomb, but my role was relatively small. I was the person in charge of the technicalities of communication, that's all.

Soon after Len came back, he made his own contacts, but I never met them. By chance he ran into an old acquaintance who had previously shown sympathy with our movement: he was a specialist in sea-borne tank landing. Apart from information on tank-landing operations, he supplied us with an important instrument that was used for submarine radar. At that time radar was quite new and Centre was very interested in it. Usually we buried such treasures until the next meeting with Sergei, but, if they seemed exceptionally important, we would ask for an emergency meeting by means of the chalk crumb signals.

Len also had contact with a chemist who gave him information.

Although I am listing all these new contacts of ours so breezily, the process of establishing them was actually quite a long-drawn-out business. Len, too, had to probe the ground more than once and prepare people gradually before he asked for their help. Equally, I did not recruit Tom overnight. After several conversations we would send whatever details we knew about these comrades to Centre, and they would accept or reject. James and Tom knew what country they were working for. Len's friends probably guessed it. Up to the end of the war, there was no great difficulty in winning people, because in that period work for the Soviet Union was work for an ally in the war against Hitler.

The British people were sympathetic towards the Soviet Union. If the word got around in an arms factory that something was destined for Murmansk, productivity rose noticeably; in some cases it doubled. Even upper-class ladies succumbed to this mood and knitted gloves for the Red Army!

The British and American delay in opening a second front on the continent caused indignation, or at least a feeling of considerable unease, among many people. In spite of all their promises, these two countries allowed their ally, the Soviet Union, to fight and bleed – practically on her own – for a long time. Later, too, their contribution was limited. (In a survey of 1972 the *Observer* gave the following figures of Second World War dead: Soviet Union 20 million; England 386,000; the USA, including Far East operations, 259,000).

In the cities of England in 1942, the peoples' demand was proclaimed on walls in large red letters: 'Second Front *Now*!'

Even the children were infected. In January 1942, Micha drew a picture for the *Magazine of Peoples' Writing* with the two captions: 'An Everyday Life Scene of an English Soldier: polishing his shoes.' and 'Everyday Life Scene of a Russian Soldier: defending an aerodrome.'[2]

By Micha – 10 years old

Now, nearly fifty years later, we can see that this popular demand, and our own help for the Soviet Union, were more than justified. We have only to read what one of the most prominent military experts in the USA, Hanson W. Baldwin, wrote in *The Crucial Years, 1939–41*.[3]

> The German invasion of Russia offered the United States alternatives short of all out war . . . It was certainly not – as the post-war decades have shown – in the American interest, or world interest, to help one menace [Nazi Germany] to replace another [the Soviet Union]. The destruction of both . . . could only have benefited not harmed . . .

I need hardly recount here how closely we followed the battles of the Soviet Union from one day to the next; how we feared for Moscow and Leningrad; how we marvelled at the resistance of their citizens and mourned their dead. Every success in our work seemed twice as important as before. Then, as now, we would have refuted any suggestion that we, or the comrades working with us, were betraying Britain by our actions.

Len had volunteered for air-crew duties with the RAF. Before he embarked on that danger, I wanted a child from him. Nina was already six years old. I wanted this very much and, as before, I had the excuse that infants provided a good legalisation. When, at the end of 1942, the encirclement of the German army began at Stalingrad, foreshadowing victory on this important front, I began to insist. In the end Len agreed because he felt that the decision had to be mine. Later he was to prove a proud and infatuated father.

One evening in August, a month before Peter was born, I was in London for a meeting when a great storm blew up and the skies roared with thunder. Sergei was there but had hardly expected to see me under the circumstances. He brought a special message from the Director praising me for a report I had sent. Either Sergei had been in Moscow or he had been instructed to convey the exact words to me. The Director had said: 'If we had five Sonyas in England, the war would be over sooner.' I didn't believe I was quite such an asset as that, but I was very happy. He had expressed better than anybody else what we were working for: the destruction of fascism and an end to the war for the sake of all humanity. Every hour counted.

To my mother:

> 8th September, 1943, 5 p.m.
>
> ... At 12.45 I was still out shopping. And now the baby is already two hours old. So you can see what an easy time I had. It's a boy, and he only weighs six-and-a-half pounds. He arrived two or three weeks early.

The next appointment with Sergei had been fixed for this very day. Len went to London instead of me. Immediately after his return, late in the evening, he came to the clinic, looked at me and said: 'I have never seen you so happy. You look like two Sonyas.' Then he went to the little cot and contemplated his six-hour-old son.

My parents were living in London again by this time, but if

father's research work took him to the Oxford libraries he stayed at our house. When he came to visit me in hospital the day after Peter's birth, my first question was: 'What do you think about Italy?' The cease-fire that sealed Italy's final defeat had been signed on 8th September.

Father beamed: 'Glad you brought up the subject. I had been afraid it might not be the done thing to talk politics with a woman in confinement.' We talked about the effects of this defeat and about the whole war situation while Peter slept by my side, woke up, whimpered and fell asleep again.

Soon after Peter was born, Len was called up. He was not happy with his training.

To Mother:

> January 1944,
>
> Rather gloomy letters from Len. After his Christmas leave he finds everything particularly depressing. The only thing that keeps him going is the chance that he may be able to start training as a pilot. Len has never had much time for the petty bourgeoisie, but even he is shocked at how little interest the people around him show in world events. For six weeks he has spent the whole time with the twenty-five men in his barracks, but has not heard a single word about Churchill, Russia, Italy, Teheran, Hitler or anything to do with the course the war is taking.

Despite a recommendation from his commanding officer and the highest possible grade (A1) on completion of his initial training period, Len's application for pilot training was refused. With rare exceptions, International Brigaders stayed in the ranks, especially if they were workers. Still hoping for active service, Len applied to train as a radio operator. When he was turned down again, he asked to be transferred to a fighting unit of the army. To our amazement he was posted to the Coldstream Guards, one of the most feudal of all British regiments. The regiments of the Brigade of Guards were the troops of the royal household. Here he had infantry and armoured training. As with the RAF, he got an A1 for each of the training courses.

To Jürgen:

> Believe it or not, Len is developing into an exemplary soldier. Just listen to this! He is getting an extra week-end leave as the best of 800 soldiers. Moreover, he has beaten all existing camp records for long distance running.

During his RAF service Len was stationed only twenty-five miles from Oxford and I cycled over to see him whenever possible. With his tank training completed shortly before the end of the war, he went to Europe to the front. Len's tank unit was the reconnaissance troop of the 1st Armoured Battalion Coldstream Guards.

The workload increased, including more meetings in London, and with Len gone, I had no one to look after the children during my absence. Mother used to come to Oxford to help me out, until she fell ill.

To Mother:

> For the first time I regret that among your five daughters you don't have a spinster who thinks of nothing but household duties and takes all your worries off you. I found them all very busy indeed in London. And *you* have brought up Father so badly that now you have to worry about his helplessness. Whatever happens, you should stay in hospital as long as the doctors think fit.

I had to find a solution. Then there was the additional problem of concealing my nocturnal transmissions from Micha. I decided to send him to boarding school at Eastbourne, especially as he had already won a scholarship. I also sent Nina, who was now seven years old, to another boarding school in beautiful rural surroundings near Epping Forest.

She had not been there long when I received a telegram. Nina's life was in danger from peritonitis. I spent three days and nights at her bedside in hospital. Weeks later, when I was allowed to bring her home, I swore that I would never send her away again. I could not keep my word. Nina suffers to this day from the effects of her operation.

When I had to go to London I was now forced to take the baby along. Travelling was not easy in war-time and mother didn't think much of my trundling the infant around with me. As soon as her condition allowed, she resumed her visits to Oxford when I had to travel. She helped me out many a time, though I never spoke a word to her about my work.

In 1943, after the Soviet Army won its decisive victory at Stalingrad, King George VI presented a magnificent sword of honour to Stalin, but there was still no second front.

At the first Teheran Conference, in November 1943, the Soviet Union insisted that an attack on Hitler should be launched from France. Churchill was more inclined towards a march on the Balkans! Roosevelt supported Stalin.

On 6th June, 1944, when the Soviet Army was already assured of victory, the long promised second front was at last opened as British and American troops landed in Normandy. Seven weeks later, 37 divisions were fighting against Hitler in France.

Laurence Thompson, an English journalist, commented on this in *Picture Post 1938–50*: 'For the first time since the invasion of Russia, the Germans were forced to divert substantial forces from the Russian Front.'[4]

In July 1944, the first German 'Wunderwaffen' (the 'miracle weapons' by which Hitler set such store), the V1 flying bombs, were falling on London, and the V2 rockets followed in September.

On 7th November, Sergei brought me the Director's greetings on the anniversary of the Russian Revolution. I had a little present for him too – a book. There were no red roses to be had, and carrying them to a meeting on such a date would hardly have been sound clandestine practice. Len wasn't there, so I couldn't celebrate the day with anyone. My thoughts returned to the past.

Years later I learnt that Richard Sorge, condemned to death by the Japanese, had been executed on that same 7th November of 1944.

That autumn, Jürgen was offered a position by the US Army because of his knowledge of economic conditions in Germany. He had published a great deal on the subject. He was to work in the Office of the United States Strategic Bombing Survey with the rank of colonel. He asked for time to think it over, so that I could consult Centre.

Work against Nazi Germany with an American secret service organisation only made sense if Centre was in favour and sent instructions. The reply came quickly. They were interested. Now I regularly obtained useful reports from Jürgen. Like me, he cannot remember exact details. One thing he does remember. During the war Dick Ruggles, Professor at Harvard, was researching the methodology of espionage for the Office of Strategic Services (OSS). He had worked out a system whereby careful monitoring of the serial numbers of all destroyed German tanks, aircraft, etc. could reveal the level of current enemy arms production. This fortnightly estimate was restricted to a very small, select readership: Roosevelt, Eisenhower, Churchill, the Chief of the British General Staff, the Head of the OSS, and the Chief of the Office of the United States Strategic Bombing Survey. Apart from this, a single copy circulated among approximately five members of the survey who were involved in analysing the figures. Jürgen regularly supplied me with this estimate, which I passed on to Centre. I have reason to believe that the Commander-in-Chief of the Soviet Army, J. W. Stalin, was acquainted with its contents just as regularly. This highly confidential little record, which regularly published the statistics calculated by Ruggles, was in fact part of the 'United States Strategic Bombing Survey'.

Jürgen's office had connections with the OSS, the forerunner of the CIA. Here he got to know a young American lieutenant called Joseph Gould, who had been assigned the task of recruiting German emigrants for espionage missions in Germany. They were to be trained and dropped by parachute. He knew Jürgen to be in close contact with anti-fascist movements, and asked him for assistance.

Centre was interested in this use of Germans by the OSS and asked me to work with Joseph Gould, warning me to be on my guard. I passed this message on to Jürgen and, with Centre's approval, he put Joe, as he was soon called, in touch with a German comrade who was to be responsible for all work relating to the future parachutists. From there on, Jürgen had nothing more to do with that affair, and I took over, never meeting Joe directly. The comrade who was chosen as our go-between was Erich Henschke, a member of the London branch of the German Communist Party.

Erich had fought in Spain and I knew him from the Communist Youth Movement. In 1928–9 the Berlin regional committee of the party had entrusted me with setting up a Marxist Workers' Library (MAB). Since no money was available, we had to start from scratch. We rented a cellar in Berlin's Jewish working-class quarter, Grenadierstrasse, where pigeons had formerly been sold. To recoup the rent we charged a fee of 10 Pfennig (1d.) per loan. We collected the books by hand-cart from comrades and publishers. Erich Henschke, Max Kahane and Gerd Degenhardt were the first voluntary helpers in the library. Subsequently it was linked to the Marxist Workers' School (MASCH). Its early history is described more fully in my book *An Unusual Girl*, published in 1958.[5]

And so I met Erich again in England. He was a slow thinker who found it difficult to reach decisions. He was over-careful and hated taking risks, but he was no coward. He had plenty of party experience and was very conscientious and reliable.

I repeat I did not meet Joe Gould, and he knew nothing of my existence, but all the German anti-fascists who had anything to do with him respected and liked him. He accepted Erich as a colleague and agreed to his suggestion that the parachutists should be chosen from among the German communists. After all, they really were the most dependable in the fight against fascism. During Roosevelt's administration and the war against Nazi Germany, a number of progressive Americans were to be found in the military administration and the intelligence apparatus. This changed later on.

In recording what follows, I draw on a conversation I had with Erich Henschke in 1968, since he remembered these things better than I did.

We could not commit our comrades to these missions without the consent of the German party leadership in England. Erich spoke to Wilhelm Koenen. Assuming that Erich kept the silence demanded of him, my existence was never mentioned. The party leadership delegated Erich Henschke, Hans Kahle and Wilhelm Koenen to draw up a list of suitable comrades. Erich Henschke withdrew temporarily from party work in order to devote himself fully to his tasks of co-operating with the OSS and passing on material to me. He supplied me with photos and biographies of a number of comrades. After I had relayed these to Centre and received their agreement, the names were proposed to the OSS. The comrades knew that this had been approved by the Soviet Union. Two were rejected by the OSS, which left Adolf, Walter, Peter, Paul Lindner, Werner Fischer, Kurt Gruber and Anton (Toni) Ruh.

Erich did not become a proper employee of the OSS. They gave him five pounds a week for expenses and he received a similar amount from Centre. In fact Erich's work with the seven comrades, passing their news on to me and maintaining contact between them and the OSS, was a full-time job which took him two or three months.

The chosen comrades signed a contract with the OSS. They were well-paid and their lives were insured for a considerable sum. With Joe Gould they underwent two months' intensive training, including parachute jumping and the use of a 'walkie-talkie' that had been developed specially for them and proved to be a sensational invention. They also had to learn a numerical code system by heart. Their passports, clothing and life stories were prepared with great care. Invisible ink, poison capsules and food concentrates were part of their equipment. I reported all the details to Centre, and the Director confirmed his interest, especially in the code.

Each of the comrades was to be parachuted into Germany on a predetermined day, at a specific time and place. Immediately after landing, they were to hold their walkie-talkies in readiness so that a US plane circling the area could establish contact with them.

The OSS had asked Erich to supply addresses of anti-fascists in Germany where the comrades could call if they had no contacts of their own. For this purpose – after obtaining Centre's consent – Erich flew to Paris in a US plane with Joe. Here the Free German Movement, an organisation of German anti-fascists, was bigger, and Paris was also geographically nearer to Germany; he brought back all the addresses they needed.

Joe was also interested in direct contacts with the Free German Movement in Paris. Centre agreed and Erich put him in touch with them. In this work with the OSS, the American espionage organisation, I did not take a single step without consulting Centre, because it was too complicated for me to judge the situation. I imagine they were able to control developments through their Paris connections. I had no direct contact with any of our chosen comrades, except via Erich.

As Erich recollects, Adolf was the first or second to jump. Toni Ruh and Paul Lindner flew out together. After their jump they successfully contacted the aircraft. This was, as already mentioned, the first walkie-talkie ever used in ground to air communication and I hoped they were able to save it and eventually pass it on to Centre.

(In the 1970s, I learnt of the fulfilment of my hopes from Walli Schmidt of Berlin. She and her sister Dora Selchow knew Toni from the Communist Youth League, before 1933. Toni visited them after his jump and they buried the instrument between a plum tree and a chicken coop on their allotment in Kolonie Falkenhöhe, in the Wartenburg district of Berlin. When the first Soviet troops arrived, Walli unearthed the walkie-talkie and handed it over to an officer who gave her a receipt for it.)

The detailed preparation for their jump, their new 'biographies', the Nazi papers needed, are wonderfully described in *Piercing the Reich* by Joseph E. Persico. This book could surely not have been written without Joe Gould's assistance. It tells of his thoughts when Toni and Paul climbed into their aeroplane at Watton airfield, knowing the deadly danger of their mission. Joe himself tells how 'he had committed the professional sin of getting too close to these men'.

Paul and Toni parachuted successfully, landing 30 miles from Berlin. They made their way to the home of Paul's parents, well aware that they were putting the old couple's life in danger. No need to describe the surprise and joy when the parents recognised their son and his friend, and of course they supported and helped them. Later, Toni moved to his sister, Mrs Tredup, who also acted courageously. Paul's parents lived near the Teltow Canal. Before the Red Army marched in, Toni and Paul tried to save two bridges near what is now the Baumschulenbrücke. They came under fire and the bridge was blown up. At the other bridge they succeeded in cutting the contact wire and prevented the bridge's destruction by the Nazi army.

As I live not far from there, I remember those two communists whenever I cross the bridges.

After completing their mission, they returned to England, and later to the German Democratic Republic. Toni became our ambassador in Rumania, and before that, he had been director of customs. After 1951, we frequently lunched together in the government guesthouse on the Thälmannplatz. So strong is the ingrained discipline of conspiracy that I never hinted at our paths having crossed before, in England, under different circumstances. I was convinced that he did not know of my role in that scheme.

About the other men much less is known to me. Peter and Walter parachuted somewhere over Bavaria. There was not much news from Peter. Walter's reports, when he returned, were factual and interesting.

Kurt Gruber, a Westphalian by birth and a miner by trade, had been an underground party worker in Berlin from 1933 to 1936. Later he went into exile and worked in a coal-mine in Scotland, where he married a Scotswoman. He became a member of the Scottish Union of Mineworkers and wrote a pamphlet called *I am a German Worker*.

The plane from which he was to jump exploded in mid-air. From *Piercing the Reich* I learned more about Kurt Gruber's death. The United States had lost interest in those missions. Joe was replaced by another officer. Kurt Gruber and an inexperienced crew took off in stormy winds and rain in a plane that had not been properly serviced. The ensuing crash killed them all. Kurt's wife received news of his death with courage and dignity. The families of the parachutists knew nothing of our work.

Werner Fischer, as far as Erich can remember, carried Nazi papers under the name of Lauterbach when he jumped. He almost certainly lost his life. I asked Centre if they knew anything about him, but in vain. The German party leadership investigated without result and the English lawyer D. N. Pritt's efforts to obtain information were also unsuccessful. Werner Fischer stayed on record as missing.

I think the time has come to honour these comrades. In August 1990, forty-five years after all this happened, an elderly man from the United States announced that he would like to visit us. It was Joe Gould, whom I had never met before. Apparently, after hearing of my book, he contacted Jürgen, whose address was more or less internationally known, and asked for my whereabouts. He had come to Berlin in the hope of meeting some of his parachutists, but I had to give him the sad news that by now none were alive. His friend Erich Henschke had died only a short while before.

Prior to the end of the war Toni Ruh had handed Erich a small part of an aircraft. Erich and I deposited this into the pram with my son Peter, wheeled it to the edge of a wood near Great Rollright, and buried it.

For some reason I had no contact with Centre for several weeks. When I eventually needed to unearth the part I couldn't find it. I spent hours searching, unable to locate the exact spot again. That only happened to me once in twenty years – once too often.

Work with the OSS was terminated a few weeks after the end of the war, when the Americans demobilised our comrades. My other contacts continued. Information on the post-war policies of the allies was important for the Soviet Union.

In May 1945 street parties were held all over the country to celebrate peace. Tables stood end-to-end along the road with places set. Residents gave of their meagre flour or fat rations or even an egg – the allocation was one egg per person per week – biscuits were baked, tea and lemonade provided.

Mrs Laski organised the celebration in our street. A photograph of the occasion is still in my possession. I shared everyone's joy about the victorious end of the war; I felt the same relief, because the anxiety about relatives at the front had come to an end. Everyone hoped for a better world, but here our visions of the future differed.

Before my contact with Erich finished and his connection with

Street party to celebrate peace, Oxford 1945

the OSS terminated after the end of the war, he lent me some interesting papers. It was a file on an American sergeant who was suspected of communism. This was one of those occasions when an emergency meeting with Sergei was called for. He had the contents of the file, about 200 pages, photocopied immediately. They were worth it.

If I worked at Centre in Moscow, I would translate these records and make them essential reading for all intelligence officers. It would take the place of any theoretical teaching on the need for strict protective secrecy.

It is important to bear in mind that these records concerned an ordinary person whom no one had heard of apart from a rumour that he had communist sympathies. He was a sergeant who had not played a significant role either in the army or in civilian life. But the suspicion that he might be a communist was enough to lead to such painstaking investigations that the results filled all of 200 pages. Nothing was missed out. It began with a report on his parents and all his relatives, on his schooling and apprenticeship. Every address he had lived at, statements from his landlords and many of his neighbours, his colleagues, his friends, the books he read – it was all there. His correspondence, his holidays, his relationships with women, his marriage – nothing, not one item had been left out. I myself, with all my experience, would not have thought such a thing possible.

After the war, the Labour Party won the General Election and formed a new government. Harold Laski, brother of Neville, was at that time chairman of the Labour Party.

The post-war state of Britain's economy was catastrophic. An enormous loan from the United States was supposed to help; it put the finishing touches to Britain's dependence on America. The US and Britain began to wage their cold war against the Soviet Union. And if anyone still doubted that this was a systematic policy, they were soon put straight by Churchill's speech at Fulton, Missouri. Unfortunately, as so often, the Labour Party followed the anti-Soviet line of the Conservatives.

In May 1945, the owner of Avenue Cottage wanted her home back. We had to move once again. Len was still in the army in Germany. He was demobbed 21 months after the war had ended.

I was thoroughly fed up with furnished dwellings whose landladies would inspect their property at regular intervals and promptly extort extra charges for every spot on the carpet. But, as before, finding anything furnished was impossible enough, and an unfurnished place remained a Utopian dream. By pure chance a neighbour mentioned a farmhouse in the Costwolds that she wanted to let. It was called 'The Firs' and situated in the isolated village of Great Rollright. The gentle Cotswold hills begin within twenty miles of Oxford. I looked at the two-storeyed house with its seven rooms, the enormous kitchen and miscellany of utility rooms. The whole thing was much too large for us: there was no electricity and no refuse collection; the bus to the nearest town went once a day. But the surroundings were beautiful and the 250–year-old house with its thick wooden beams and low ceilings, the yard and barn and the wild garden appealed to me. Besides, the rent was only a third of what we had been paying in Oxford. I took the house. Perhaps I could let a few rooms in order to have someone at hand for the children when I had to travel. On the other hand, the presence of tenants would not be very suitable for my radio work.

Great Rollright

I bought some second-hand furniture and my sisters gave me what they could spare. The long corridor was decorated with my Chinese paintings from the Ming period. Strange how well the silk scrolls suited the old farm house.

It was not easy to make friends with people in the village. Opposite us stood the Squire's mansion, inhabited by wealthy landed gentry – the Lonsdale family. He was a well-known retired naval commander. As a young man, Prince Philip had served under him. In fact Philip visited the house during our time there, together with his wife, who later became Queen Elizabeth II. The other villagers were agricultural workers or smallholders who did not think much of a 'foreigner' like me.

So I was very much on my own; but I had my work, and I had Nina and Peter. During holiday time, Micha came home from his boarding school and Len would also obtain leave from Germany once in a while. I knew he loved the Cotswolds. We had cycled

'The Firs', Great Rollright

through the countryside on several occasions in the past. I was looking forward to showing him our first real home. Nina, now nine years old, prophesied before he came on leave: 'I bet he is so excited he can't sleep all night. He won't be able to lie in his bunk. He will want to jump off the boat and swim the last bit . . .'

But when Len arrived from Travemünde at last, he had no eyes for our house or the idyllic village. He came from a Germany desolated by poverty, conflicts, tension and difficulties. I was saddened, and when he went back I tried to keep him close to us by writing down everything we did in my letters.

February 1946

I bought Micha a tie for his birthday. He has long been admiring it in a shop window. Bright yellow with horse heads

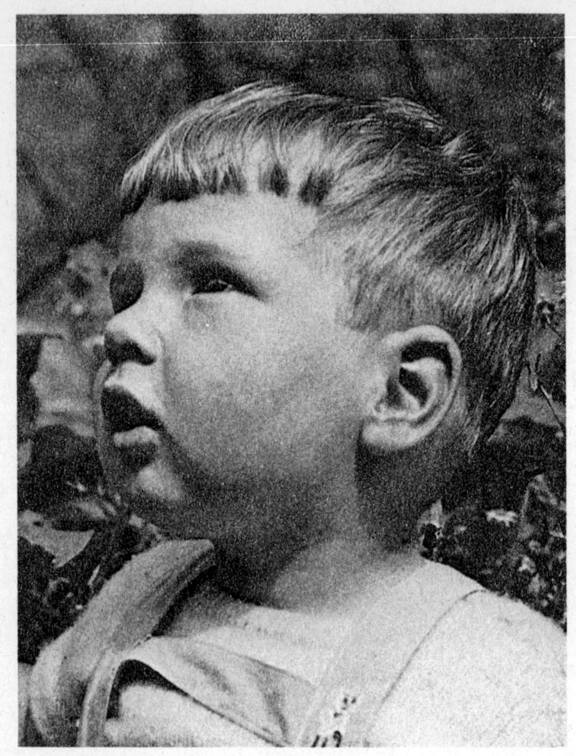

Peter in 1945

printed all over it. A Gigolo horror, but that's how they are at fifteen. If you would like to send him something, make it a bright yellow silk handkerchief to go with it; the gaudier the better . . .

Summer 1946

. . . The children and I were in Stratford-on-Avon from nine in the morning till seven at night. It was *the* summer excursion that I have been promising them for some time, so they were each allowed four fizzy drinks, three ice-creams, and two complete inspections of Woolworths. And highbrow activities such as a visit to the house where Shakespeare was born and a tour of the theatre. Then a boat trip on the Avon and a few hours in the beautifully situated swimming pool.

December 1946

Christmas was quite extraordinary. I invited two German

With the children, Oxford 1945

> prisoners of war who are working here on the Lonsdale farm, to celebrate with us. They have been through a 'democratic education camp'. Hardly had we sat down to coffee and real gingerbread, when someone knocked on the door. Eight bell-ringers trotted in and, following an old custom, played Christmas carols by ringing 14 handbells of different notes. It was quite beautiful. The villagers seemed surprised about my visitors and I thought it right to make a little speech about Christmas, peace on Earth and the need to overcome the enmities of war.

That same year was the first time I heard from Ernst again. He was in a bad way, wanted to return to Germany – and asked me to help him. The German emigrant organisation in China required confirmation that he was forced to leave Nazi Germany as a refugee. I knew this was so and could provide evidence for him. His doctor had calculated that he had survived the last 30 months on 400 calories a day. He was still just about alive.

Using Marguerite's address instead of mine, I wrote to the organisation for German emigrants, 696 Tong Shan Road, Shanghai.

Ernst did not manage to return to Germany. I am still convinced that if he had succeeded in doing so at the time, there would be one more hard-working honest and devoted comrade with us in the GDR.

After I myself returned to the GDR I heard nothing from him for ages. In 1966, after 20 years of silence, a letter arrived from South America, addressed to Jürgen. Ernst wrote that he longed for Europe and wanted to come over. His political views were the same as ever. In the late autumn he wrote that he would visit me if I agreed.

Ernst arrived at the beginning of January 1967. We had last met 28 years before. I opened the door and saw that he was close to a break-down. He could not speak – nor, for that matter, could I. I led him to an armchair. He trembled and complained of feeling cold. I made him coffee, fetched a pullover and asked Len not to join us until Ernst had pulled himself together. But he could not relax properly at all. He was worn out and a nervous wreck. At last he was able to tell me his story:

His connections with Centre had broken off soon after Rolf's arrest in China (probably partly due to Ernst's own obstinacy). He could not find any work. In 1949, after the liberation of China, the government asked all foreigners to leave the country. Ernst went to Argentina and earned his living as a mechanic. He married an Argentinian. Now, after so many years, he was home-sick for Europe. He had come on his own but his wife would follow as soon as he had saved the money for her journey.

He would like to live in the GDR, he said, but if that was not possible, he could also earn his living in West Germany. He did not need much. Wherever he was, he would live as a communist. He talked for a long time and I did not interrupt. While I was listening, I forgot his awful physical and nervous condition.

Only when he had finished did I ask him how he felt about China. It turned out that he approved of China's development. He told me that he was prepared to work honestly for the GDR and would not enter into any polemics. But if asked a direct question or if someone 'started on China', he would have to say something.

Len and I talked to him at length, but he was as obstinate and inflexible as ever. Certainly the world did not look the same from the GDR as it did from South America. Len and I bore that in mind and took a broad approach, but Ernst waved all arguments aside. He was not prepared to consider other opinions. It was like talking to a brick wall.

This was the first time that Len had met Ernst. If we could have dismissed him as a worthless human being, neither of us would have been so sad. We would probably have taken swift leave of him. But all his good qualities were still there; his will-power, his self-sacrifice, his compassion for the oppressed whose poverty he witnessed daily.

The next day we took Ernst along to the traditional demonstration in commemoration of Rosa Luxemburg and Karl Liebknecht, which ends up at the cemetery for outstanding revolutionaries. He knew this demonstration from his youth in Germany. The red flags and slogans, the masses of people, moved him. As we entered the Friedrichsfelde memorial grounds, he saw the leading comrades standing on the tribune return the greetings of the marching demonstrators. His eyes shone: 'That's how it should be,' he said.

We continued our discussions when we returned home, but got nowhere. That evening Ernst departed. Len was just as depressed as I was. Later a letter arrived from West Germany. Ernst wrote that the European working class gave no grounds for hope and that in the GDR, too, middle-class values prevailed. That was why he had decided to return to South America.

In the summer or autumn of 1946, Centre broke off contact with me. It cannot have been because of Foote, since he had not yet turned traitor. Perhaps, unbeknown to me, something had occurred in another country. Jürgen was already living in Berlin.

Len's army unit was stationed there. I asked him to tell my brother of our situation. Jürgen let me know that he had also heard of other interruptions and at the moment this seemed to be happening everywhere.

We had a special arrangement to cope with loss of contact. A few miles from Great Rollright, the Oxford to Banbury road passed under the railway; beyond the first crossroad after the underpass a message would be found under a hollow root of the fourth tree on the left. A monthly date for collecting had also been fixed. I cycled there every month but never found anything.

I can deduce more or less when contact was broken from the financial difficulties mentioned in my letters.

To Marguerite:

> Autumn 1946
> I can buy very little now . . . Do you want some of my clothing coupons? When Len is demobilised, Micha can have his army coat. We will dye it. He badly needs a winter coat . . . From the middle of February onwards I am going to start letting rooms with board. If you know anyone who might be interested, do recommend me as a 'perfect housewife' with 'home-grown vegetables'.

When Len was finally demobilised, he took a job in London which Marguerite recommended to him. It was in a factory that had innovated a method of spraying patterns on to plastic material. Toni Ruh was also working there. So the two of them met.

Around Great Rollright there was no hope of finding employment for Len or for me. And in any case, who was to look after our three-year-old Peter while I was out at work? I couldn't think of giving up the house; we would never find anything as cheap again. In bombed-out London there was nowhere to live either. My various sisters took it in turns to put Len up.

The winter of 1946–7 was the hardest that England had experienced in a hundred years. It snowed for weeks. Icy winds blew the snow into drifts, coal became scarce, and transport was almost at a standstill. There were over two-and-a-half million unemployed.

With open-grate coal fires it was difficult to keep even two of our seven ice-cold rooms warm enough to live in. The village did not yet have electricity and I was thoroughly fed up with smoky oil lamps, cooking with coal, and ironing with an old-fashioned flat iron, heated on the kitchen stove. The water tank froze and burst pipes ensued.

To my parents:

Winter 1946–7
It looks as though I'll have to shovel snow again for three hours tomorrow just to dig a path out of the house. No buses running. I feel lonely and cooped up. The farmers are downhearted. It will be a bad year for food and I believe a bad year politically. American foreign policy is catastrophic. We knew their line, of course, but I never expected action so brutal and flagrant. They don't even try to hide their desire to strangle the left in any countries they can lay their hands on, to build military bases against Russia and to dominate as many strategic points as they possibly can. The Greece/Turkey affair – the way in which it was announced and the timing of it – is a considerable step towards the next war. I am depressed and horrified. So far I have only read the reaction of the *News Chronicle*, which is weak and irresponsible. It argues that there will be a more democratic government in Greece because America will insist on it!!!

P.S. We are now totally cut off. The most famous snowdrift in the village is leaning against the wall of our house and reaches right up to the roof.

P.P.S. Three cheers for the Co-op. Four strong men have made their way to our village on foot. Each was carrying an 80-pound sack of bread on his back. I will give them this letter to post.

Spring 1947
My first paying guest has been and gone. I found it a bit odd carrying a tray laden with food in to a young woman so that she could have her 'breakfast in bed'. But it helps financially.

I had decided, as far as possible to be self-sufficient. Our garden was large enough for that.

To Jürgen:

May 1947
To my greatest amazement everything that I have sown in the garden is beginning to grow, even if not at the same rate as the weeds I thought I had got rid of.

We soon had a flourishing vegetable garden. Unlike housework, which I have always hated, I enjoyed gardening. My cauliflower heads were even praised by experts. I bought some chickens and let the hens brood. I bought a five-week-old pig, too. The children loved it and I had to promise that I would not slaughter it under any circumstances.

About Len and his work I wrote to Jürgen in 1947:

Len is doing very well in his job, although he is so run down that he can do nothing but work and sleep. So, morally we are both stuck in a mire which is not exactly improved by his mire being in London and mine 80 miles away. After his three years in the army, seeing each other twice a month is just not good enough, especially when you are fond of each other. Marguerite, my bed is now my university. Every evening I read one of Jürgen's lectures there. I do like the way he uses language.

In June 1947 my parents came to see me during father's holiday. Shortly before the end of their stay, I heard groans coming from their room at two o'clock one night. Mother was having a heart attack. The medicine did not appear to help. The only telephone in the village, on the green, did not function. I pedalled as fast as I could to the doctor in the nearest town. He drove me back in his car. It was too late. Mother was dying. He could not have done anything even if he had arrived earlier. Before I had left mother to fetch the doctor, I heard her say in great pain, 'Oh my little boy'. She was thinking of Jürgen, her eldest, whom she had probably loved most of all her children.

Mother was buried in the beautiful old village graveyard. Her name is carved on the gravestone above the names of those who mourned her – father and her six children.

My parents had been happily married for forty-five years and father was loath to return to their empty flat. He stayed with me while he continued to work on his extensive study – the demography of the British colonies. I accompanied him on his walks as often as I could. Father frequently visited the cemetery. He was a free-thinker and smiled at himself in embarrassment, but he kept going back. I told him that I thought the view of the countryside was particularly beautiful from the cemetery. He was grateful to me for that.

Len's firm did not have much work. Plastic was then still regarded as a poor substitute for leather. Our separate households proved expensive and I urged him to come to Rollright. In the summer of 1947 he got a job in Banbury in an aluminium factory with 3,000 employees. It was 13 miles from Rollright and he bought a second-hand motorbike for the daily journey.

It was more than nine months since I had heard from Centre. I must stress once again that I had no bitter feelings. I had never looked upon my work as a way of earning a living but as a communist commitment. There must have been a good reason for Centre to act like this – as was confirmed later. All the same, it was depressing. I had lived for this work for years and now my days were empty. I also found it hard to tell James and Tom that the contact with Centre was no longer there. Tom had been trained and could have worked as a radio operator, and I had collected information from James that I could not now pass on. James might have left the Air Force and returned to his own trade, but at our request he had prolonged his service. I have said far too little about James and Tom here. When I think of the best in the British working class, I see them before me.

James died of leukaemia. He was still young. Sometimes when people die, you simply cannot accept it, and not just because they are close. He was so genuine, so full of the joys of life, so optimistic.

We did not want to make the final break with Tom now that our work together was finished. But we could not permit ourselves the pleasure of this friendship for much longer, as we soon realised that we might endanger him, even without our work.

Len and I did not want to remain politically inactive any longer, so we decided to join the British Communist Party. But my branch, based in Banbury, was too far away for me to establish real contact. Len did not fare much better. There were eight comrades in his factory who worked different shifts. At most they could meet three at a time and that only in winter.

In August or September of 1947, as I mentioned before, I heard from the Austrian comrade that Jim had appeared on his doorstep to warn us against further activities. Unfortunately our work had already stopped by then in any case.

One day in August or September, at any rate during the time when Father was still living with us (he left in October), there was a knock on the door. I opened it. Two gentlemen greeted me politely, and before they had even entered the room one of them said rapidly, without pausing for breath: 'You were a Russian agent for a long time, until the Finnish war disillusioned you. We know that you haven't been active in England and we haven't come to arrest you, but to ask for your co-operation.'

This 'psychological' attempt to take me by surprise was so funny and inept, and so far from throwing me off balance, that I almost burst out laughing. I said, 'Would you like a cup of tea?'

The two agreed somewhat sourly and, at my request, identified themselves.

Len was busy somewhere in the garden beyond the yard. Father was sitting in the room above us, working. The gentlemen mentioned some incidents in Switzerland which strengthened my suspicion that Foote had betrayed us. They kept stressing again and again that they knew of my disillusionment with communism since the 'invasion of Finland by the Soviet Union'; they knew that I was a loyal British subject and would not engage in any blameworthy enterprise here. I therefore had nothing to fear. Was there any reason why I should not co-operate with them and tell them about my time in Switzerland?

I confirmed my loyalty, but said this did not oblige me to talk about a period of my life before I became a British citizen. I was quite prepared to talk about my years in England.

Once again they repeated that they knew I had not been guilty of anything in this country. They asked in astonishment why I refused to say anything, since I had, after all, recognised the real worth of communism.

I thought for a bit. We took the English party paper and were party members. Father had been president of the left-orientated Free German Movement. Jürgen's political books were well-known. I replied that while I had experienced disappointments, I could not describe myself as anti-communist. Besides, I was of the opinion that there was no contradiction between being a loyal British citizen and holding left-wing views.

My guests wanted to talk to Len. I called him and asked whether I should leave the room. No, that wouldn't be necessary. The first thing they said to him was that they knew of his close acquaintance with Allan Foote. Len replied: 'Footie? Oh yes. What is he doing nowadays?' They were annoyed and I poured them fresh tea. Len of course also refused to talk about the period in Switzerland. They treated him too as though he was anti-communist. Without having been able to talk it over beforehand, Len behaved as I had done and said that despite disappointments – I believe he even used the same words, 'despite disappointments' – he did not hate communists.

They left us calmly and politely, but empty-handed. As they said goodbye, one of the gentlemen remarked: 'It is beautiful here. I shouldn't mind living like this.' I replied: 'That could be arranged, I am letting rooms.'

The visit kept our minds busy. Had the traitor Foote really 'protected' us and reported our 'disappointment' about the Finnish war to MI5? (In his book, which at that time we had not yet seen, I seem to remember that he mentioned the non-aggression pact between the Soviet Union and fascist Germany as our disappointment.)

Did MI5 really believe him or did they use this trick to lull us into a sense of security and catch us out? We were not under observation either before or after that visit. We were well-trained enough to know that.

I do not remember now when Foote's book came into our hands, but since that visit from MI5 we were sure that we would not be able to continue working for Centre in England. However, it appeared that Centre had already taken that decision in any case.

In October father began to feel ill, went back to London and into hospital. He had cancer.

To Jürgen:

November 1947
The others will have told you about father's death. I have not written much during the last few weeks. It seemed senseless to describe to you the tragic details of his daily deterioration . . .

Father was marvellous right to the end. In some ways unexpectedly wonderful. He had, after all, never been seriously ill before and he proved himself to be courageous and patient. he never had any complaints, was touchingly grateful for every one of our visits and even during the last days he smiled whenever one of us came. Until three days before he died he discussed current events, such as the new budget and the dismissal of Hugh Dalton, the Labour Chancellor of the Exchequer.

He lived long enough to experience the joy of seeing and holding in his hands the first printed volume of his *Demographic Survey of the British Colonial Empire*. Brigitte read him your letter about the 7th November celebrations when we visited him together. Monday evening he was still talking about everything under the sun. Tuesday he slept and only woke up once, between six and eight in the evening. Then he went to sleep and did not wake again. Of course we had known what to expect for some time, and during the last two weeks we could only wish for the end. All the same his death has been a great shock.

The obituary in *The Times* acknowledged my father's role in developing the study of demography and added that he was 'at no time content to be merely a theoretician . . . Special authority was thus lent to his reiterated demands in later years for radical changes in the drawing up of census schedules to conform with the requirements of modern communities.'

Jürgen received many letters when father died. One letter of condolence was signed by Wilhelm Pieck and Otto Grotewohl, the then President and Prime Minister of the GDR. I quote from it:

Berlin, 12th December, 1947

. . . His passing is a great loss for the German people. Professor Kuczynski embodied not only modern progressive science and research, which he consciously placed at the service of the working class, he also felt deep ties to his German homeland during his English exile. His unimpeachable objectivity, and unswerving tolerance towards those whose ideas differed from his, made him a focal point among the progressive democratic Germans in Britain . . .

My letter to Jürgen:

29th January, 1948

I was moved by reading through the letters. How nice it would have been if mother and father had experienced the kind of affection and honour now being accorded them, while they were still alive.

Jürgen had intended to bring our parents back to Germany.

7
Return to Berlin

I was wrong to encourage Len to return to Rollright. The job in Banbury was monotonous and physically exhausting. He hated it and there seemed to be no chance of a change. Len would never have left me in the lurch, but chained to this treadmill of a factory, having to feed a wife and three children, and being unable to see any way out of the situation – that was not how he had imagined his life would be. With deep longing he recalled his period of action in Spain.

As a tank driver Len had suffered from gunfire which left him with a damaged acoustic nerve in one ear, causing a constant ringing and headaches. His job was tiring and the shift work increased his chronic insomnia. His depressions became more frequent. He withdrew into silence for days on end. I suffered, too, and could not help him. My own life had also run aground. Things could not go on like this.

To Jürgen (undated):

> There is absolutely nothing to say about me. Apart from making a home for my husband and children, my life seems fairly useless at the moment. Not that I am so very important that this is a terrible misfortune, but any human being is too precious to be left to sink into such an existence.
>
> . . . Writing? How much I should love to do that. I often wonder whether I could write a few articles for you over there. Something about the mentality and attitude of the local prisoners of war; something about the way ordinary Labour

> Party members are reacting to the crisis; or about the USA? Have you any topics to suggest? I have written an article in English. Len thinks it is good and finds my style 'lively and attractive'. Sometimes I dream that it might get accepted and that I could then suggest a whole series of articles for publication.

(My article was returned to me).

Even so, it was not as if we were living in an atmosphere of constant depression. The children broke the monotony and cheered us up, and we had a close affinity with the countryside. If I felt low I would just wander to a favourite spot nearby where I had a view across the fields and hills.

What with the family, our big house, the garden, lodgers and animals, I did not have much free time, but whenever I did, I used to read long-neglected works of Marxism-Leninism, and I also attended the Workers' Educational Association in the nearest little town, Chipping Norton. The WEA had close links with the Labour Party.

I was trying to make life more interesting, but as soon as I was sure that Centre would not re-establish contact with me, I wanted to go back to Germany. That meant that I needed to see Jürgen before I could do anything else. In January 1948 one of my attempts failed.

To Jürgen:

> My application for permission to visit you has been turned down by the American military office. They say that entry to Austria and Germany is only granted in urgent cases.
>
> The secretary, a little underling, did not hold out any hope. She put me into a file and said I could enquire again in the summer. Although I had not been counting on it, I am very disappointed. I feel like a fish out of water here. In Germany I could contribute something. Anyway, I want so much to be there from a personal and emotional point-of-view too.
>
> Politically the world looks quite exciting. I have every confidence in the future and sometimes find myself quite exhilarated by the prospects before us. Right now, people are mistaking the violence of the reactionary forces (and there is

> far worse to come) for strength. True, I often feel depressed at the thought of how much suffering they will yet bring upon the world before they are destroyed.

The problems of reconstructing a new Germany interested me from the first day on and Jürgen sent me a constant flow of material.

To Jürgen (undated):

> I do not understand the poems in the volume you sent me, or at least the majority of them. Is that my fault or the poet's? Yesterday I received *The Land of Happy Confidence.* I read it the same day, or rather into the night, and am so impressed that I suggest you concentrate exclusively on writing for children. It really fills a gap I should very much have liked to fill myself, but the book is so much better than mine would have been that I am quite relieved *you* have written it.
>
> Many thanks, especially for the copy of *Die Wirtschaft.* Since the Workers' Educational Association has asked me to speak on the German post-war economy in relation to Europe, these latest production figures were particularly useful . . . By the way, I found your article in *Die Arbeit*, 'German Foreign Trade and Investments', extremely interesting. For me at any rate it clarifies a lot of questions and makes a refreshing change from the empty banalities printed so often in our press, whatever the country.
>
> Your idea of writing a family history seems completely crazy. But perhaps my views will soften if you can give me some more details. Apart from father and you, we have no one in the family we can boast about. One grandfather was a rich banker and the other gambled away half his worldly goods. One great-grandfather sold shoe laces from a barrow in Galicia and the other, I suppose, was something of a free-thinker? But perhaps you intend to make it a bit more of a social and historical document? It is 10.15 p.m. and I must make Len's evening meal. He is just coming off the late shift.

At last, in January 1949, I managed to meet Jürgen in Prague. He had arranged for me to stay with some Czech comrades who welcomed me warmly. Perhaps I had looked forward too much to meeting him. At any rate, as soon as I saw him, I felt overwhelmed by my present situation in England; the abrupt interruption of my work by Centre, Len's dissatisfaction with his life, the financial worries, and the uncertainty of the future. What a relief to be able to pour my heart out at long last and receive some good advice! I hugged Jürgen with tears in my eyes and kept saying: 'I'm so happy. Now everything will be all right.' I had quite forgotten that Jürgen never had any time for soul-baring or displays of emotion. He wanted to know my plans, briefly and to the point, and whether he could help me in any way. Besides, he was busy throughout his whole stay in Prague and could only see me twice for half an hour. He also commented that it would be very difficult for me to stay in Germany without Centre's agreement.

I therefore decided to go to the Soviet Embassy in Prague and leave a letter there for Centre. I addressed the envelope to the 'Military Attaché'. The letter itself was addressed to 'The Director of Military Intelligence of the Army, Moscow-Arbat'. The sender was given as 'Sonya, Brazil'.

The message itself was coded. I mentioned the broken contact and asked for permission to go to Germany. I repeated once again the exact hiding place that had been arranged in case we lost touch.

To Marguerite:

> 6th June, 1949
>
> The Gerhart Eisler affair was most refreshing. On the very day when Jürgen's latest parcel arrived, there was an appeal in the paper to send Gerhart books. So I immediately forwarded the contents of the parcel, including Jürgen's own booklet in the new SED series.[1]

Eisler had visited Shanghai while I was there. After being persecuted in America he had fled to England, where he was promptly arrested. The matter was widely reported in the British press. Later he was freed as a result of mass protests.

Books were even more important to me now.

To Jürgen:

Winter of 1949

The annual battle with the draughty windows and burst waterpipes has begun. Even Nina's mice have frozen to death. A blow that hit her hard, especially as the mummy mouse was expecting babies and Nina had already prepared a list of names for the happy event.

I read Scheer, *Encounters*, and liked two chapters very much. I read the Kollwitz volume. How much more she comes to life through her pictures than in her diaries.

One of the short stories from the Arctic is outstanding (Gorbatov, 'Birth on Cucumber Island'). Without a word of propaganda, without sentimentality or clichés, he expresses what so many other Russian novels try to ram home with a sledge-hammer. Outstanding is not the right word. Len, for whom I immediately translated it into English, said, 'moving and enchanting'. That is right. By the way, you must read Elliot Paul, *Ghost City on the Yellowstone River*. I found it absolutely riveting. And please compare it with Steinbeck's *The Wayward Bus*. It shows what a pitiful juggler of words Steinbeck has become – how vulgar and how far removed from real people. Paul has chosen almost the same types and also uses coarse language, but what a different impact he has. How he loves people and understands them.

Rare but very cheerful letters from Micha. In his university exams he was fifth out of 120 students. His new life is absorbing him completely.

Micha had won a scholarship to the University of Aberdeen and was studying Philosophy. He was highly gifted but he couldn't be bothered with practical matters and was quite unreliable about them.

In the autumn of 1949, Len had a motorbike accident. When the factory heard how long it would take before he could return to work, they sacked him.

To Jürgen:

17th October, 1949

. . . Len is in hospital in Banbury. One arm with two breaks and one leg with two serious breaks. The doctor reckons that the leg will have to be in plaster for eight months . . .

28th January, 1950

. . . For Peter it is of course wonderful to have Len at home all day. They amuse themselves with the Meccano set and in the evenings Peter gets half an hour of 'The World'. This includes answering all the questions Peter can think of and looking at picture books on animals, inventions, geography and machines. Len has the great gift of explaining things simply. He makes it so interesting that Nina and I often listen too. As you see, even a broken leg has its advantages.

As soon as Len could get up and move around in his plaster, I enquired again about a visa for Germany. Things had become a little easier by now. Should I try for one without waiting for approval from Centre? They had not answered my letter via the Embassy in Czechoslovakia. I refused to carry on living in this state of inactivity, and we hardly had any financial resources left.

Once again I cycled to the railway underpass and at last I found a note under our tree. My journey was approved. I was happy that they had contacted me and even happier about the content of their message.

My preparations started. I buried my party card and the transmitter. We bought four US Army waterproof canvas kitbags with zip fasteners, the sort the G.I.s used. Now they had to transport all our belongings. They were practical, durable and lightweight. We still use them on holidays.

I tried to persuade Len to move in with one of my sisters. They were all willing to put him up. But he didn't want to leave Great Rollright until he was well again.

With things the way they were, Len could not really make any decisions about his future. As soon as he was capable of working again, he wanted to move to an industrial city where he could be useful to the party. He would then wait until he heard from me and from Centre. Micha, now eighteen years old, had to stay behind too. Nina and Peter, as minors, could travel on my passport and come with me. They loved Great Rollright. At thirteen Nina did not like leaving her school, the County Grammar School in Chipping Norton, and six-year-old Peter was attached to Mrs Thomas, the vicar's wife who ran his little school in Chipping Norton, as well as his teacher Miss Willets. (Hard to believe, when visiting England in 1990, he found their address and paid them a visit, Mrs Thomas being now ninety years old, and Peter forty-seven. She and Miss Willets remembered him as a little boy who helped to clean the school windows – at home I never noticed that golden quality of his!)

Our plans had progressed to this point, when something happened which made my leaving the country an urgent necessity. In February 1950 we read in the papers that Klaus Fuchs had been arrested. The press presented the news as sensational. My first reaction was shock and sorrow – quite apart from the loss this meant to Centre and, far beyond that, to the Soviet Union. My second thought was to wonder how far the discovery of his activities concerned me. There was no evidence of our contact. I had never spent the night in Birmingham where he worked, so that no hotel registration could be found. As already mentioned, I had never been in his home nor he in mine. As far as I knew, he did not know my name or my address. There were two possible dangers: a betrayal, but I did not consider him capable of this, or a conjecture on the part of MI5, given all the information they might have on Klaus and myself: he was a German communist, and I the same. Klaus was known to the London party group; my brother had been prominent there. Klaus had sent his valuable material to the Soviet Union through an intermediary; they knew through Jim's (Allan Foote's) betrayal that I had worked for Centre in Switzerland. My husband had fought in Spain.

When the press mentioned that Klaus had been meeting a foreign woman with black hair in Banbury I expected my arrest any day. In that case I would refuse to make a statement. Nothing else was possible.

Klaus's trial was announced for the end of February. I prepared for my departure in great haste and left England. I believe it was on the 27th, a day before the trial.

Either it was complete stupidity on the part of MI5 never to have connected me with Klaus, or they may have let me get away with it, since every further discovery would have increased their disgrace.

The American FBI were furious about the indolent attitude and naïvety of MI5. The US had put their development in Klaus's field of work at England's disposal, and he had passed all of this on to the Soviet Union. The British were not anxious to reveal their ignorance any further.

I recently read an assessment of the Philby case by a former MI5 employee who explained that the English left Philby unmolested, after they as good as knew of his work on behalf of the Soviet Union. 'Our nation's reputation has suffered enough; we cannot cope with another George Blake scandal. That's why the Philby case never became a scandal.' (Blake, for years a Soviet spy, had escaped from prison after his conviction.)

It was mere guesswork on our part, whether my being able to leave the country, my being left alone by MI5, was due to inefficiency or due to the desire not to add to the uproar – a sort of 'let sleeping dogs lie'. Or was it possible that there was someone at MI5 who was, at the same time, working for the Soviet Union and had protected us? We had no clue, let alone facts, to go by.

I repeat: these were merely our thoughts. In view of the rubbish some journalists have since published about me, I want to make it crystal clear that it is pure nonsense to proclaim that 'the masterspy still hides her biggest secret' – this secret doesn't exist. I was never asked by Centre to contact anyone from MI5, and I had no contacts there. I do not know if anybody protected me, or, if so, who it might have been. I know no Fifth Man, and I must also spoil the speculation or, as some writers state, 'the fact', that I ever had anything to do with the one-time director of MI5, Roger Hollis. I resent the way journalists try to turn me into a sensation, simply to make money.

Having got that off my chest, I shall return to my last day in England. The farewell or goodbye – we did not know which it would be – was sad for Len and me. The two children and I flew from London via Hamburg to West Berlin. From there we went to Friedrichstrasse station. I telephoned Jürgen, who lived in Schlachtensee. It was ten o'clock in the evening and the children sat in the freezing cold on our US kit bags. Marguerite came to

Friedrichstrasse and told me that they had just moved and that Jürgen was staying with friends. This was not such good news for us. Where would we spend the night? We went from one hotel to another with Marguerite, but in vain. Around midnight a porter in what is now the Hotel Sofia told us about an old couple who let rooms to travellers in the Elsenstrasse (now the Wilhelm Pieck Strasse) near the Rosenthaler Platz.

We kept ringing the bell until we woke the landlady. The children slept together in one cold, damp bed, I in the other.

It was early March. The room was only heated one day in three, with three or four pieces of coal. The ravages of war were still very evident in that part of town. Lots of pubs, lots of drunks and many bombed-out houses. Peter was the only one who found the room wonderful because he could spit from the fourth-floor window on to the street.

Jürgen informed someone at the Embassy or in the Soviet Union of my arrival. Without Centre's agreement I could not rejoin the party as I wanted to do. For the time being I lived in isolation. Jürgen arranged for us to have lunch at the German League of Culture and supported us financially for many weeks. We did not have ration cards and so we made our meagre breakfast in the café on the Rosenthaler Platz last as long as possible. Since we couldn't endure our cold room we left the house again well before lunch and would stop on the bridge near Friedrichstrasse Station to watch the gulls; then we would walk to the League of Culture in what is now the Otto Nuschke Strasse. All the guests there were strangers. The only one to show any friendliness towards us when he heard the children speak English was Bodo Uhse. After lunch we usually went to the House of German-Soviet Friendship to be in the warm; often we would see a film there.

I had to send the children to school as soon as possible so that they would learn German, but I still had no idea what the future held in store. I had no German papers, so once again I decided to send Nina and Peter away until things had been sorted out.

In Finkenkrug there was still a semi-private boarding school – the one where Ollo had tried to denounce the headmistress, who now welcomed both children with open arms. It was from her that I heard about Ollo's dangerous behaviour. Nina joined in the lessons and learnt German much more quickly than the shy, dreamy Peter. I went on living in our room.

Only at the end of April did I hear from Centre. The comrade responsible had come from Moscow to meet me and invited me to a festive supper in somebody's flat.

I told him about my last years in England. He showed sympathetic understanding for all I said. He explained to me that Centre had reason to interrupt contact for a prolonged period, but they had put money and news for me under the fourth tree after the railway underpass and not after the crossroads beyond the underpass. Only when I wrote from Czechoslovakia did they correct the hiding place. Either they or I had made a mistake.

He asked me how I envisaged the future; they could offer me several choices of work. I was surprised. After the business with Foote and the long break, I had no longer even considered the possibility of working for Centre again. I wanted to live as a citizen and a party member in my own country. The comrade was equally surprised. He had firmly expected me to work for Centre again and tried to win me over in a fraternal manner. I told him that nothing had altered in my commitment to the Soviet Union and the work I had done, but that my nerves and powers of concentration were no longer as good as they had been. I felt that twenty years were enough and that now I would like to be in the GDR. He must understand that after such a long absence I would want to stay at home and return to my party. The party would find work for me.

We discussed the matter for a long time. The comrade asked me to think it over again. I stood by my decision. Only then did he ask me what I thought of the conduct of Fuchs. I told him what I thought. The chain of proof had been collected partly through betrayal by others in the US, partly by reforms in the previously sloppy MI5. Klaus considered denial senseless. He did not reveal anything that was not already known. He was, incidentally, examined by William Skardon, the most psychologically astute interrogator of the British secret service. Klaus, a scientist, inexperienced in such matters, no doubt behaved naïvely when faced by such people.

After his trial in 1950, the world's press produced 'explanations' which suggested Fuchs was schizophrenic; it was also alleged that he had been on the point of ending his connection with the Soviet Union.

This seemed implausible to me. Like other communists, wherever Klaus had found himself, he had fought against German fascism. This had been his aim when he took part in the US and British military projects during those years. He wanted to make it impossible for the Nazis to anticipate what was being achieved there. He worked honestly on the project, had friends among English scientists in his field and was certainly liked for his modesty and his achievements. As a communist, he was concerned about the delays in opening the Second Front. For him it was a clear and unambiguous decision to put the results of the project at the disposal of the only socialist country which seemed to be carrying the major burden of the war against fascism, and whose philosophy of life was his own.

My superior seemed satisfied. I still consider my evaluation valid.

Various publications in various countries, even East Germany, have maintained that Klaus Fuchs admitted to his activities because of a repugnance of the Stalinist reprisals. No doubt, like all of us, he did go through this difficult period, but not *before* the Twentieth Party Congress of the Soviet Union in 1956, when Khrushchev made his revelations about Stalin. It cannot have been before that. As far as I know, Klaus was never in the Soviet Union during the time that he was transmitting his material. And even a visit then would hardly have made it possible for him to see and understand those terrible happenings which, before 1956, were not regarded as Stalin's crimes even by the Soviet citizens themselves.

I am convinced that Klaus Fuchs never became estranged from the Soviet Union. It was out of political conviction that he put his scientific information at the disposal of the Soviet Union for nine years. He was imprisoned for this in England for the following nine years. It is gratifying that through the GDR DEFA-film *Fathers of a Thousand Suns*, finished in 1988, this unusual personality was at last publicly honoured.

I only heard more about Klaus's father after my return to the

GDR in 1950. I was touched by the way this progressive theologian supported his son. I saw the film *Einer trage des anderen Last* (One should carry another's burden) which the director Lothar Warnecke dedicated to Prof. Emil Fuchs, who had been his own teacher. I thought the relationship – the atheist son and the Christian father – would also be worth making a film about. If it is true that the father's choice to make his home in East Germany (where he did so much for the younger generation), became a political burden to his son in England, that is particularly tragic.

I myself visited Klaus more than thirty years after my work for him, just before *Sonya's Report* was published in the GDR. I went to Dresden where he lived. I took a large bunch of dahlias, so it must have been autumn. He and his wife welcomed me. I handed him the flowers, and Grete understood the gesture. We embraced.

Despite my unsettled situation, I had been happy at home from the very first day. Someone addressed me as 'comrade' and I was moved. A man in the street spoke to me in Berlin slang and I beamed.

From a letter to my sisters:

> Spring 1950
> My daily life here is of course quite different from the beautiful but insulated little world of Great Rollright. I am drinking it all in – theatres, cinemas, problems, progress, the negative and the positive people. I read three newspapers a day from the first page to the last, listen to everyone I can find and squeeze them like lemons. I go to meetings and am slowly getting the feel of things, so that now I am ready to start work. It hasn't been decided what yet. I should like a serious professional job with political activities in the evenings. But that is where the family becomes a problem again. The children! Jürgen, the brute, suggests that I leave them in the boarding school permanently. But I refuse. It is bad enough that the family may remain separated for years – at least I want to have the two little ones with me . . .

The Soviet comrades found me a flat in Karlshorst, their district

Reconstruction, 1952

of Berlin. Three weeks later, in the latter part of May, I was allocated another one, outside their area. It was gloomy and had a great heap of rubble in front of it. I did not like it. Next door was a pub. I used to sit and read all day in the nearby park, which is now the East Berlin Zoo.

Around the middle of May my wish was granted. Centre put me in touch with the German party. Comrade Willi Kling of the Central Committee's cadre department received me. From the first day on, we were bound by a quite special friendship until he died in 1973. I wish that one of his many friends who have known him longer than I would commit the story of this fearless, obstinate and unshakeable German Bolshevik to paper.

In the summer of 1950, after a consultation with Willi Kling, I started work in the 'Office of Information' as section head in the Press Department. I had no experience whatsoever in this field, but once again I was lucky. Gerhart Eisler was director and Comrade Albert Norden was my superior. Deba Wieland was in charge of the Soviet Section and later took over as director. About half an hour after work began, the section heads used to meet in Gerhart's room. He and Norden, still known by his illegal cover-name of Konni, would already have scanned the British, French and American press. They sized up the situation and often gave their views with amazing speed, until a clear picture of the international class struggle unfolded before us. Deba Wieland had read through the Soviet press and delivered her considered views with quiet confidence.

Gerhart Eisler was an extremely disciplined worker. He was never late. If he had returned from a working visit to the provinces at five that morning, he would still arrive at the office as usual, punctually at eight. At some point during a discussion he would unearth a battered aluminium tin from his brief case, take out two sandwiches, and perhaps an apple if one was available, and without interrupting the work would begin his meal.

As Konni Norden was my direct superior, we were in daily contact. He spiced his guidance and criticism with wit and irony. The mixture was a familiar one thanks to Jürgen, so I thrived on this mode of working together and learning. Deba taught me how to tackle my new job methodically and thoroughly. Her comradely help meant a great deal to me. Soon I was responsible for the fortnightly *Bulletin against American Imperialism* and later for the daily government press releases which went to all newspapers.

We were given a better flat and I was able to bring the children back. Peter started school and in the afternoons he went to the rather overcrowded after-school centre. To begin with he did not learn German so much as Berlin Cockney. He had a hard time adjusting and was happy whenever I arrived home punctually in the evenings. I will never forget how on one occasion he embraced me and – beaming with pride in his newly-learnt phrase – greeted me with, 'Hallo, you old sow.'

Nina, at fourteen, felt at home much more quickly and soon forgot her collection of photographs of the English Royal family. She became a keen member of the Free German Youth.

Nina at 14

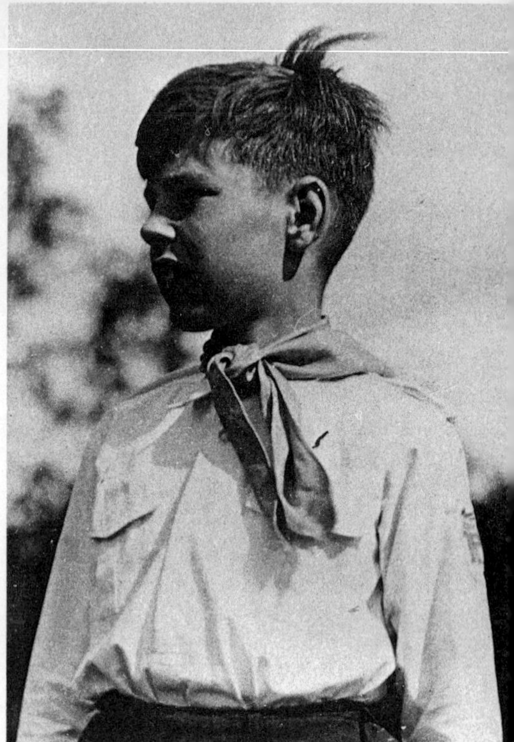

Peter at 10

Centre had agreed to Len's emigration to the GDR. The Socialist Unity Party of Germany would find him work to match his abilities and show him all the solidarity that was due to him as a comrade and resistance fighter. I informed Len of the offer and he came.

With Willi Kling's support, Len started work for ADN (the GDR news service) where he stayed for twenty years. The leading people there – Georg Hansen and Max Kahane and, after 1953, Deba Wieland – appreciated his work and showed understanding for his problems. Len's integrity as a comrade, his firm principles, his competent devotion to his work and his political analyses of the English and American press were valued by all his colleagues. They accepted it, if at times he was given to difficult moods.

A year after Len's arrival, Micha decided to come to the GDR too, and I was happy to have all the family together again.

My association with Centre was ended, I heard nothing more from the Soviet Union; nor did I expect to. I regarded the past as closed and was doing a job in the GDR which taxed my abilities. Only Willi Kling knew a little about my former life. Our friends in the Soviet Union had mentioned my decoration, and he felt I ought to have it back. To my great surprise I received it. But I have already recounted that elsewhere.

In 1953 my Office changed its name, purpose and leading personnel. My relations with the new leadership were not as good. On one occasion, when I forgot to lock the safe, which in fact contained no confidential papers, I was given a party punishment for 'insufficient vigilance' and it was suggested that I should resign. I was discharged with a bad personal report. Among other things I was accused of 'petty-bourgeois tendencies'. I was unable to dismiss this as an 'irony of fate'. In fact, I could not come to terms with the situation. Willi Kling helped me to transfer to the Chamber of Foreign Trade.

At the Office of Information I had seized every available opportunity to write anything from press articles to literary material. Gerhart Eisler and Konni Norden had encouraged me after my first newspaper publication. In the Chamber of Foreign Trade I became head of the press section. Apart from my other duties, I began to write topical pamphlets for our export enterprises. The response from my readers and a positive review by F. C. Weiskopf, a well-known and respected German writer, strengthened my self-confidence. I needed it, now I was approaching fifty, to change my profession yet again and realise an old dream.

In 1956 I gave up full-time work in order to write my first book. Since then I have been working uninterruptedly as a writer – apart from the time spent on these memoirs, which I regard as a personal, not a literary work.

It is a marvellous thing still to have such a demanding profession at my age. Perhaps this fulfilment has something to do with the fact that I am so intensively absorbed in the present rather than living in the past. Yet you can never escape from your history altogether.

If a nightmare haunts my sleep, the enemy is at my heels and I have no time to destroy the information.

If I find myself in new surroundings, I am forever discovering hiding places for illegal material.

I cannot bear to see parents saying goodbye to their children on railway stations.

The past! In 1970, at a reception for veterans in Moscow, I met an elderly Soviet comrade. After talking for a little while we fell joyfully into each other's arms. It was Natasha, the woman who worked with us when Andrei had been my superior.

Perhaps only old people can understand how deeply this meeting moved us. I invited Natasha to Berlin. She asked me whether by chance I knew the author of the book *Olga Benario*, published in the GDR. She would so much like to meet her when she came to stay with me. When I told her that the author stood before her she embraced me again. Natasha was 76 years old. She had been on active service during the war, and was now a retired colonel. We often visited each other. Sometimes our eyes met and it seems a miracle that we both survived. Now she is eighty-nine and I am eighty-three, so we have had to break the habit of travelling between Moscow and Berlin. We just write letters, and about once a month I hear her lively voice on the telephone.

The past was reawakened when I was asked to write a record of those twenty years of my life, which was published in 1977. Although I felt inhibited and needed confirmation before I broke the long-accustomed code of silence, I was glad that the party was asking old comrades – I wasn't the only one – to write down their memories.

In 1977 I heard from a relative of Ernst that he was gravely ill and living in poverty. Being myself confined to a hospital bed for several weeks, I did not write. But he sent a letter from South America – two short sentences: could I tell him what was wrong, and was it serious? The tissue paper which lined the envelope concealed a five-dollar note. It pained me and I felt guilty. Soon after, the news reached me that my friend had died.

In August 1988 I was part of a delegation of old 'China veterans' invited by the then Premier to revisit his country. It was madness to go in my state of health and at my age. But I took

Meeting Chen Han-sheng again, 1989

the risk and I never regretted it. In Beijing, I turned to Israel Epstein, editor-in-chief of the foreign language paper *China Reconstructs*, and the unbelievable came true – he told me that my old friend Chen Han-sheng was still alive and much honoured. I had brought with me that photograph, showing him, me, and a bit of Agnes Smedley's skirt, taken sixty years before. It was just an amateurish snapshot. Israel Epstein told me that Han-sheng was not able to see it. During the cultural revolution he had to work in the fields and, not having the medicine he needed for his eyes, had become almost blind.

I visited him and found his alertness and memory astounding. He asked me if I remembered how I helped him and his wife – she was no longer alive – to board a Russian boat to escape to the Soviet Union. I had forgotten.

In Shanghai, our GDR general consul had another wonderful surprise for me. He had found the house in which we used to live. Now, there is no longer a British settlement. The Chinese family invited us in. I went into the living room and looked out of the window into the garden. Here I stood in 1932 when Richard Sorge said farewell to me. Here Rolf lived with me – and my first baby son was born, now sixty years old. Here Egon Erwin Kisch, Agnes Smedley, Chen Han-sheng had been visitors – and of course Grisha and Richard.

Silently I bade a second farewell to all those who had been close to me so long ago, who worked for the better world in which we all believed.

At home

Afterword

This book was first published in German in 1977. I have had to answer many questions since then and would like readers to know of them, and how I would answer.

Was it right to have three children under such dangerous conditions, and what has become of them?
I began this kind of work when I was twenty-three years old and stopped doing it twenty years later. This is the age to have children, and though I was a Red Army officer, I was a woman and wanted children badly. I took the risk and feared for them almost constantly. But to imagine life then without them, and now without my six grandchildren and three great-grandchildren is unthinkable.

Micha, my eldest son, is a Shakespeare specialist. His translations of some of Shakespeare's plays have been published and he works with the theatres during their production. My daughter Janina is a teacher. Provoked by a letter to me, complaining of my lack of responsibility in having the three children, she wrote a book for ten-year-olds about her memories as the daughter of an illegal political worker. Peter, the youngest, became a biologist-philosopher at the Academy of Sciences in East Berlin.

The children feel strong ties to England. They revisited our former home in Great Rollright in the Cotswolds and were received warmly by the present occupant and her son. Len, to whom I have now been married for over fifty years, was as close

With the family, 1972

to my two children as to his own son, and that goes for the next two generations as well.

Readers in Germany don't ask about my brother Jürgen because he is well-known as an economic historian and statistician and as the author of many popular as well as academic books. My sisters are all still alive, have families, and all seem to have the habit of working professionally until they are seventy years or older.

Would you live your life again the way you did, now that Stalin's crimes are known?

During Stalin's time, with so many people being imprisoned or murdered on his orders, I never met one person who believed him to be responsible for those crimes. A woman who had spent ten years in labour camps told me how the inmates cried when they heard of his death. I talked with innocent prisoners who had written to Stalin many times; when no answer came, they were sure the letters had not reached him. During my short stays in the Soviet Union I looked in vain for old friends. All I found were padlocked doors and I believed the explanations which I mention

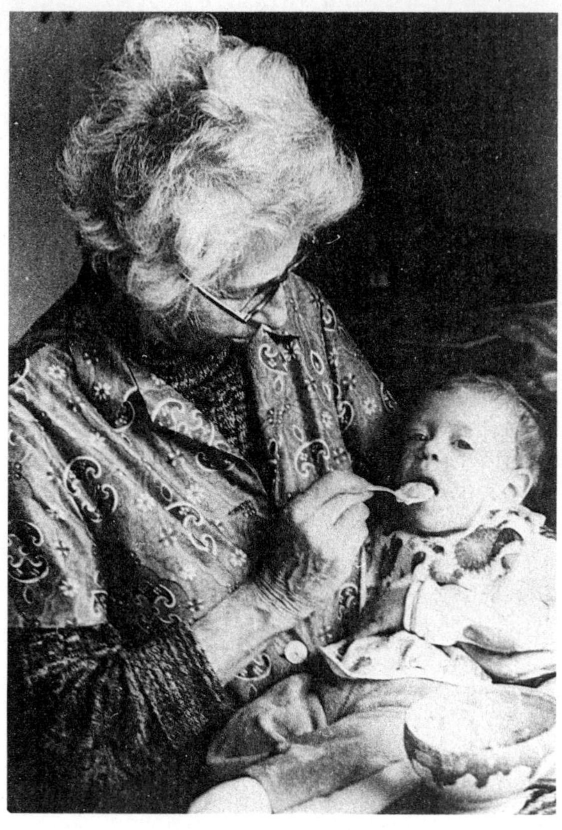

Max, 1975

in my book, that imperialism in its last desperate struggle tried everything to undermine the Soviet Union by infiltrating saboteurs and agents. It would stop at nothing in its efforts to destroy that country from within. And it seemed logical that it should be so, after the capitalist countries had tried to destroy the Russian Revolution by military intervention after 1918.

When Stalin died in 1953 I was in East Germany, and every communist I met considered it as I did – a great loss.

This might seem inexplicable today. But I would like to quote the reaction of a man regarded as one of the most intelligent and highly respected citizens of the Soviet Union, the famous physicist Andrei Sakharov, whom Stalin's successors later sent into exile in Gorki. At the time of Stalin's death he wrote to a friend: 'I am under the influence of a great man's death, I'm thinking of his humanity.' But, as he comments in his memoirs:

Ruth and Len in the countryside (Photo: Barbara Köppe)

> very soon I would be blushing every time I recall these sentences. I can't fully explain it – after all, I knew quite enough about the horrible crimes that have been committed . . . but there was still a lot I did not know. Somewhere in the back of my mind, the idea existed . . . that suffering is inevitable during great historic upheavals . . . and above all, I felt myself committed to the goal which I assumed was Stalin's as well: after a devastating war to make the country strong enough to ensure peace.

When Khrushchev revealed Stalin's guilt at the Twentieth Party Congress in 1956, the Russian people and communists all over the world were stunned. Many would not believe it. And I must mention, personally, the particular pain and shock I felt when I heard, much later still, that Kolzov, Borodin, Manfred Stern, Karl

Rimm – all honest and brave communists – had been destroyed by Stalin.

But I must also add that I had not worked those twenty years with Stalin in mind. We wanted to help the people of the Soviet Union in their efforts to prevent war, and when war broke out against German fascism, to win it. For that reason I hold my head up high.

What are your views, what is your reaction to the breakdown of socialism in your country?
The realisation that what we thought was socialism was fatally flawed came late – too late. In the German Democratic Republic I had been active for forty years, be it cleaning bricks from the rubble of war for building new houses, be it writing articles or books (eleven in number) or giving lectures on ideological questions in courses of 'Party Education'. All this time I accepted our government and party leaders with only minor criticisms.

It must not be forgotten that I had returned to the poorest part of Germany, which possessed no raw materials except soft coal; Eastern Germany lay in ruins and was obliged to pay heavy reparations to the Soviet Union. At the same time, the United States supported or initiated the West German cold war policy against the German Democratic Republic. The Soviet Union's proposal for unification, made in our name in 1952, got a hefty 'no' for an answer. Chancellor Adenauer of West Germany said in 1954: 'The best way to regain the German East is rearmament.' And secretly, rearm he did, with the United States' help. These were our problems. Against all odds, we had built up our economy. The people worked, a modest living standard was achieved, nobody had overmuch, good social measures were introduced gradually. Our children grew up as anti-fascists. As my work was connected with the press, I experienced the strong antipathy of capitalist countries towards us, and read the lies they were spreading in their newspapers (and also the truths I mistook for lies).

What I did not like in our country was the dogmatism within the party which increased with the years, nor the exaggeration of our achievements and the covering up of faults. And these grew worse when our economic growth came to a stop. I felt more and

In the 1980s (Photo: Frank Splanemann)

more sensitive to dishonesty in the reports and speeches from above, showing the isolation of the politbureau from the people. It pained me and it angered me to see how we made ourselves look ridiculous in the eyes of the workers who knew the facts from their own factories.

In 1985, when it needed courage to praise Gorbachev in front of party functionaries, it became unbearable. But I still believed that a better socialism could be achieved if the old men were forced into their long-overdue retirement, and younger, able ones, took over who might cure our almost chronic ailments. I was relieved, and so, I would say, were most of our party members, when the first ones left and others from the politbureau followed. We hoped that with glasnost and perestroika, with more democracy instead of dictatorship and absolute power, with realistic economic measures we could win back the disillusioned masses. As we did not know of the scale of immorality and corruption among the leaders, we did not recognise either how deeply in trouble we were economically, and we did not foresee how quickly the larger, richer, capitalist part of Germany would utilise its advantage and annexe us.

Seen historically, unification was a necessity. You cannot divide a nation forever by a wall, but much is now being destroyed in culture, science, industry and social institutions that would have been worth keeping.

You might ask what I, personally, have done against the growing dogmatism and deformation of socialism, of whose existence I was, after all, not unaware. And do I feel that my life was wasted? Do I feel guilty that I knuckled under to what I knew was wrong?

I fought the ills that were known to me, but only to the extent that would permit me to keep my party membership and to write further books.

When I attended our regular meetings at the Writers' Union after the first major changes in the GDR, some of my colleagues said to me, 'you need not have a bad conscience, you were always honest'. I was, but I followed the advice of a Russian woman writer (I am not certain of her name) in *My Hundred Lives*: 'give me the calmness to accept things which I cannot change, give me the courage to change things where I can achieve a change, and give me the wisdom to differentiate between the two.'

I worked within the possibilities open to me. Today that may seem opportunistic, and I have to ask myself how often was I dogmatic? How often did I believe in things which now I know were wrong? How often did I think of comrades as traitors, who proved to be victims of our form of German Stalinism? The memory of that makes me blush, and the thinking about forty years of the GDR and arriving at my own understanding of it, is not yet complete.

I have to come to terms with my bitterness against the party leaders who could manipulate me and mislead me to the extent they did. Many good men and women now live in deep disappointment and have turned away from all they believed. I cannot do that. Maybe I am now living through the most difficult time of my life, but I believe that Marx, Rosa Luxemburg, and Lenin were great revolutionary figures. And for future generations I still want social justice, access for everyone to a good education, and most of all I want no one to starve, and peace in the whole world. As much as ever I hate the arrogance of the rich, the power of money. I hate racism and fascism.

Am I without hope?

I agree with a youngster who, finding me depressed, said: 'You don't for one moment believe that capitalism is the solution. Wait thirty years, and by then we will be building a socialism without the gross mistakes we made at our first attempt.'

Well, that's a bit long for me to wait. But as long as I still live, I can work towards that aim. Can't I?

June, 1991

Notes

1 Germany, 1918–30

1 Georg Theodor Ledebour (1850–1947). Co-founder of the USPD (Independent Social Democratic Party of Germany) and in the leadership of the International Workers Aid Organisation from 1924.
Ernst Thälmann (1886–1944). Working class leader. Headed the Communist Party of Germany from 1925. Arrested by the Nazis in March 1933, he endured prison and concentration camp until he died at Buchenwald in August 1944.
Wilhelm Pieck (1876–1960). A carpenter, prominent trade unionist, he joined the rebel Spartakus group and helped found the Communist Party of Germany. Became the first President of the German Democratic Republic in 1949. Like Thälmann, was a Reichstag (Parliamentary) deputy at the time of this letter (1926).

2 These agreements, to return to the 'princes' lands confiscated in 1918 or to pay them a high rate of compensation, had been made by the Hindenburg government in 1925. In this, one of the most successful united progressive campaigns of the Weimar period, the requisite number of signatures to force a referendum were collected in a matter of hours. In the referendum itself, 14.5 million (36 per cent of the electorate) voted against the government's decision.

3 The Anniversary of the 'Glorious German Revolution', November 1918. Inspired by Russian example; betrayed by the right-wing leadership of the Social Democratic Party, the revolution was short-lived.

4 *Rote Hilfe* (Red Aid), left-wing solidarity organisation to support imprisoned revolutionaries.

5 *Rote Fahne* (The Red Flag). Daily paper of the Communist Party of Germany, 1918–33, after which it appeared illegally, at intervals.

6 Arthur Hollitscher. Radical left-wing writer, friend of the Soviet Union; frequently visited my father in Schlachtensee. Died in 1941.

7 *Die Schmiede* (The Anvil Press). Anarchist publishing house.

8 Larissa Reissner (1895–1926). Russian journalist and writer, Commissar of the Red Army. Works include *The Front*, sketches and articles on the

Civil War in Soviet Russia and *Hamburg on the Barricades* and *In Hindenburg's Country*, observations from her travels in the Weimar Republic.

9 *Neue Rundschau*, literary magazine produced by the progressive publishers S. Fischer and featuring their authors.

10 Johannes R. Becher (1891–1958). Leading poet and writer. In 1954 became first Minister of Culture in the German Democratic Republic.

11 Käthe Kollwitz (1867–1945). A painter, and graphic artist, she married a doctor who lived and practised out of social conscience in Berlin's poor quarters. Käthe Kollwitz fought with her art against hunger and exploitation. After her son Peter was killed in the First World War, she became a bitter opponent of the war. Her art was of high standing. She was the first woman member accepted by the Prussian Academy of Art in 1919 and became a Professor in 1928. At the same time, she was loved and respected by the people. In 1933 when Hitler came to power, she was turned out of the Academy, and forbidden to exhibit. Her pictures were removed from museums. She also produced political posters like *Vienna is Dying, Save the Children!*, and passionate woodcuts in two scenes of the 1920s: *War and Proletariat*, (1920) and *Never Again War* (1924). Her tribute to Peter, a sculpture entitled *Father and Mother*, was completed in 1933.

2 *China, 1930–33*

1 Seebohm belonged to the well-known German family connected with the powerful chemical concern, I. G. Farben.

2 He was the brother of the White Guard Baltic baron who was mixed up in reactionary espionage affairs.

3 Carl Zuckmayer, writer, b. 1896. His most popular play was the comedy *Hauptmann von Köpenick* (1931), in which an unemployed Berlin shoemaker obtains a captain's uniform, and finds that blind Prussian obedience to militarism opens all doors to him, and makes him a rich man. When discovered, he ends up in prison, a poor man again. (Based on a true story.)

4 Agnes Smedley (1890–1950). Born into an agricultural labouring family and brought up in Colorado, she became an active socialist in New York, and in 1918 was imprisoned for her activities against British rule in India. In 1928 she went to China as special correspondent for the *Frankfurter Allgemeine Zeitung*. Her books include *Daughter of Earth* (1928), *Chinese Destinies* (1933), *China's Red Army Marches* (1933) and *China Fights Back* (1938). In 1940 she returned to the USA, where she wrote *Battle Hymn of China* (1943) and *The Great Road: The Life and Times of Chu Teh* (1956). After persecution as a 'Russian spy' in 1949 she decided to return to China, but stayed in London on the way and died there.

5 Richard Sorge (1895–1944). Born in Baku, Russia. His mother was Russian, father German. He studied political science in Germany and joined the Communist Party in 1919. He was a journalist, editor of communist newspapers and wrote several pamphlets on economics. After going to Moscow, he took Russian nationality, joined the Russian Communist Party and

worked from 1929 to 1941 as an intelligence officer of the Red Army General Staff in China and Japan. In Tokyo he formed his own group, 'Ramsay'. His information was of outstanding value. He managed to gain the full confidence of the German Nazi Embassy in Tokyo, and this enabled him to transmit top secret information, such as the exact date of the German Army's planned attack on the Soviet Union. Unfortunately, Stalin mistrusted the information. Of great import was his news that war-hungry Japan would not attack the Far East of the Soviet Union. His frequent wish to return to the Soviet Union, since, after nine years service, he and his group were in a dangerous situation, was not fulfilled. He and fifteen of his co-workers were arrested: Sorge and Ozaki were executed; the others got long prison terms. The whole 'Ramsay' group consisted of thirty-two Japanese, four Germans, two Yugoslavs and one Englishman from fourteen different professions.

6 Gerhart Eisler (1897–1968). Austrian. His father was a Professor of Philosophy. During the First World War he distributed anti-militarist leaflets. Member of the Red Guards during the Austrian Revolution in 1918. Member of the Communist Party, Austria, 1918–20. From 1921 Berlin Communist Party, Germany. Editor in central organ of C. P., *Red Flag*. Representative of Communist International (Comintern) in China, 1929–31. The same in the USA, 1933–5. Arrested in Paris, 1939. Up to 1941 was kept in Camp le Vernet. Was brought from the camp to the USA, was refused permission to leave for East Germany, but succeeded in escaping in May 1949 on board the steamer *Batory*. Was detained briefly in England before returning to East Germany. 1949–52, head of GDR office of information. Sacked, because under Stalin's influence, no 'Western emigrants' were permitted to hold State positions. For some time worked as freelance journalist. From 1956, Deputy Head and later Head of the GDR Radio Committee. Later became member of the Central Committee of SED up to the time of his death.

7 Max Christiansen-Clausen, b. 1899 in Schleswig Holstein, where his father was a bricklayer. Max became a sailor, joined the Communist Party, and went to the radio-operator school in Moscow. Worked with Richard Sorge in China and Japan, became an excellent transmitter, very skilful in finding legal cover as a businessman. Was arrested with Richard Sorge's 'Ramsay' group in Tokyo in 1941, and sentenced to life imprisonment. Freed after the Japanese defeat, he made his way to East Germany.

8 Hozumi Ozaki (1901–44). A member of Richard Sorge's group in China and Japan. Talented journalist and specialist on Eastern Asia, co-opted into Prince Konoe's cabinet as specialist for Chinese problems. A highly valuable contact for Sorge, and a close friend. Arrested with other members of the group and executed on the same day as Sorge, 7th November, 1944.

9 Olga Benario (1908–42). The daughter of a lawyer in Munich, she joined the Communist Youth League. In a sensational way helped to free political prisoners from Berlin-Moabit, fled to Moscow, and took part in the international congress of Communist Youth in 1928. Met Louis Carlos Prestes,

revolutionary leader in Brazil, in 1935. Went with Prestes to Brazil, worked under cover for the illegal Communist Party. Married Prestes and they were arrested, together with Arthur Ewert and his wife Sabo. Olga was deported to Nazi Germany, in the seventh month of pregnancy. Her daughter, Anita Leocadia, born in the women's prison, Barnimstrasse, Berlin, was taken away from Olga, and grew up with Prestes' mother. Olga was transferred to Ravensbrück concentration camp, and was block leader of the Jewish block. Proud, unbroken, and a help to many women. In 1942 she was brought to Bernburg and killed there, together with other women, by poison gas delivered by I. G. Farben. See Ruth Werner, *Olga Benario*, Neues Leben, Berlin, 1961. Fernando Morais, *Olga*, Peter Halban, London, 1990.

3 *Moscow and Manchuria, 1933–35*

1 Mikhail Borodin (1884–1951). Russian political adviser to Sun Yat Sen in China in the 1920s, who forged the loose-knit Guomingtang into a centralised organisation. After Sun Yat Sen died in 1925, his successor Chiang Kai-shek broke with the communists and Borodin returned to Moscow in 1927. He served as deputy Commissar for labour and from 1932 edited the English language *Daily News*. He disappeared in Stalinist arrests, 1949, and died in Siberia.
2 *Dr Sorge funkt aus Tokio*, Julius Mader, Militärverlag der DDR Berlin, 1966.

4 *Poland, Danzig and the Soviet Union, 1936–38*

1 Simon and Helena Syrkus were a major force in Polish and international avant-garde architectural design from the late 1920s. They worked for the Underground Polish Government during the Second World War and afterwards led the team for the reconstruction of Warsaw.
2 Ivan Vinarov, *Kämpfer der lautlosen Front*, Militärverlag der DDR, Berlin, 1976.

5 *Switzerland, 1939–41*

1 See Marietta Shaginjan, *Weihnachten in Sorrent*, Verlag Volk und Welt, Berlin, 1974.
2 Sándor Radó, *Code-name Dora*, Abelard-Schumann, London, 1977.

6 *England, 1941–50*

1 Hans Kahle (1899–1947). Trained at a military college, served as First World War lieutenant 1914–18. From 1918 to 1920 he was a prisoner of war in France before returning to Germany. From 1921 to 1927 he was a businessman in Mexico. In 1928 he joined the German Communist Party

and was involved in journalism and cultural work. In 1933 he emigrated to Switzerland, then France and England. In 1936 he went to Spain, organising the International Brigades and was Commissar of a Division and Lt-Colonel. He returned to England in 1938, as a journalist, and after the war went back to East Germany where he helped to develop the police force.

2 *Seven, Magazine of People's Writing*, No. 4, 1942.

3 Hanson W. Baldwin, *The Crucial Years, 1939–41*, Weidenfeld and Nicolson, London, 1976, p. 444.

4 Edited by Tom Hopkinson and published by Penguin Books, 1979, p. 152.

5 *Ein ungewöhnliches Mädchen*, Neues Leben, Berlin, 1958.

7 *Return to Berlin*

1 Dealing with the harmful nature of the bourgeois 'theory' of the Managerial Revolution, this had just been published (1949) as No. 2 in the Wille und Erkenntnis series of *Einheit*, the theoretical journal of the Socialist Unity Party of Germany.

Index

Chinese names have not been inverted. Page references to illustrations are in italics.